Praise for *Running Uphill*

Sally's memoir is a truly engaging story that speaks of a time when passion alone could—and often had to—create a life in theater. Her unbounded commitment to finding the music in theatrical storytelling, challenging herself artistically, and providing artists and audiences with provocative works of substance, all while managing the administrative challenges of founding and running a small theater company, is a powerful reminder of why we do what we do.

—Ben Krywosz, Artistic Director, Nautilus Music-Theater

Sally Childs is a force of nature. A major contributor to the great, male-dominated Minnesota theater community, she triumphed by talent and tenacity. If you want to learn about how a small theater works, read Running Uphill. If you want to know more about Minnesota's literary world, read Running Uphill. And if you want to know how a woman can thrive in a historically male-dominated field, read Running Uphill.

—David Unowsky, Bookseller and Publisher (Hungry Mind)

Running Uphill is a stunning memoir of Sally's life in theater. Her rich memories of the Lyric and Jon Hassler Theaters spin out a treasured list of artists that reads like a "Who's who of Minnesota theater."

—Ron Peluso, History Theatre's Artistic Director, 1995–2022

Running Uphill is filled with raw emotion and good storytelling that illuminates the uphill climb for a woman in a once male-dominated profession. It is a personal story of a difficult journey but one that resonates with so many in the theater. Running Uphill is a cautionary, informative sourcebook but, more importantly, a thought-provoking story of success. Bravo!

—Erica Zaffarano, Theatre Professional

Too often, Theater can be a man's world. There have always been many more roles for men than women and far fewer men than women for said roles. Female directors are even more rare, especially in the time when Sally was running uphill in this world. She gives us a glimpse into that journey with this book. Things are starting to slowly change, and women like Sally are part of that change. As a woman, I thank her for fighting upward and sharing her experience. As an actor, I thank her for taking a chance on me at a time when my health didn't want to let me have that chance. We women stick together. Onwards and Upwards!

—Jen Maren, Actress, Singer, Voiceover Artist

I'm so proud of my dear friend Sally. She's written a great book! She's lived an amazing life! She's made a ton of delightful theater over the years! All with that warm twinkle in her eyes and her signature quiet strength and determination. Sally has devoted her life to the theater, and so many of us have benefitted from that devotion. What a woman! A leader, an artist, and a true-blue friend. With a rich and fascinating story to tell. I love you, Sal!

—Tod Petersen, Actor

Running Uphill

Running Uphill

A Minnesota Theater Memoir

Sally Bronski Childs

AFTON PRESS

Minneapolis

Afton Press
Ian Graham Leask, Publisher
6800 France Avenue South, Suite 370
Edina, MN 55435
www.aftonpress.com

First Edition June 2023
Running Uphill: A Minnesota Theater Memoir
Copyright © 2023 by Sally Childs
All rights reserved.

10 9 8 7 6 5 4 3 2 1

ISBN: 978-1-736102-14-5
LC record available at https://lccn.loc.gov/2022033659
LC ebook record available at https://lccn.loc.gov/2022033660

Cover and book design by Gary Lindberg
Beaded Necklace by Beth Bronski
Cover photo by Erik Saulitis

Excerpt from *Boxelder Bug Variations* by Bill Holm (Minneapolis:
Milkweed Editions, 1985) re-printed with permission from Milkweed
Editions, milkweed.org.

Excerpt from "The Death of the Old Plymouth Rock Hen" by Eugene
McCarthy from *Selected Poems* published in 1997 by Lone Oak Press in
1997 (now defunct).

All other quotes are from scripts produced by the Lyric Theater or Jon
Hassler Theater in collaboration with the originating poet or novelist.

The publication of *Running Uphill: A Minnesota Theater Memoir* has been made possible by our generous donors:

Pauline Anderson
James Bassett
Kathleen Born
Beth Bronski
Donald and Dorothy Ann Caba
Dorian Chalmers
Alva Crom
Rebecca Erickson
Gusztav Fogarassy
Mary Gearen
Delta Giordano
Vicki Goetz
Laurel Gregorian
Benjamin Hain
Pam Hardiman-Jackson
Cyd Haynes
Virginia Hazboun
Brian Johnson
Shawn Korby
Mark Krmpotich
Joneene Lobe
Norah Long
Carol Marcoux
Jen Maren
Kristen Mathisen
Barbara McCormick
Leon McCormick
Kenneth McCullough
Meghan Michels
Peter Moore
Lynda Nelson
Rita and Ben Olk
Carol Orban
Michael O'Rourke
Jennifer Paulson
RBC Wealth Management
Denee Riley
Mary Schultz
Sara Skelton
Bick Smith
Michaelle Sparrow
Sandra Stanley
Tasma Swanson
Kaye Thibault
Linda Twiss
Eric Wood
Thomas Woldt
Barb Zabel

To my smart, savvy and supportive daughters
Beth, Barbara and Carol

To my Mentors
With special thanks to Donald Bronski
And teachers at The Loft, Angela Foster and Nicole Helget

Sandra Stanley, Deborah Locke, and Erica Zaffarano

For the ongoing friendship and support of all the
Friends of the theater celebrated in this book.

Table of Contents

Prologue 1
Introduction 3

PART ONE: CLIMBING A MOUNTAIN

Chapter 1: Sheltering Among Tall Pines 9
   1979: Nearly Forty, Restless and Spent 9

Chapter 2: A Change in Sea Level 20
   My Sabbatical 20
   A Man with a Horn 22

Chapter 3: Changing Landscapes 25
   New Sneakers 25
   1982–84: Running in Place 38

PART TWO: LYRIC THEATER

Chapter 4: Warm-Ups and Stretches 43
   1984: Chance Encounter 43
   1942: Mother Learned to Drive 45
   The Belle of Amherst Opens the Lyric Theater 48
   Road to Rouen 50

Chapter 5: Rough Roads 55
   Back to 1985: The Prairie Beckons 55
   On My Own 60
   Limping into Year Two 62
   Concessions 67

Chapter 6: Gaining Traction 71
   Boxelder Bug Variations 71
   Minneota (not Minnesota) 78
   A Second Venue 80
   The Prairie Garden 83
   Onstage 87

Critical Response 90
Hunting Cockroaches 97
1989–90: Bridges to Cross 100

Chapter 7: Curves in the Road **102**
A New Partner - Cyd 102
Leah 103
1990: Wordplay Antics 105
Prisoners of Conscience Strut the Boards 107
The Critic's Role 110
A Trip to St. Cloud - Jon Hassler 111

Chapter 8: Steady On **115**
Simon's Night 115
The Demands of Success 123
Vicarious Romance 124
Catsplay - The Union Comes on Board 127
A Lesson in Lighting 129
Sales and Marketing 131
Play Practice vs. Rehearsal 132
Dear Liar 134
Small Disappointments 137
The Ravages of *Troy* 139

Chapter 9: Rainbow on the Horizon **141**
Enter Erica Zaffarano 141
To Whom It May Concern 142
A Change in Fortune 148
Payments Due 150
Strategic Planning 159
Herbert Hoover in the Flesh 162
"Chief" 164

Chapter 10: Cramps and Recovery **168**
1993: An Implosion 168
The Curate Shakespeare 169
The Doldrums 173

The Octette Bridge Club and Its Sister 174
On Being an Actor Again 178
Starting Here, Starting Now 180
Bit Parts 185

Chapter 11: On a Wintry Hill **187**
The Murphy Initiative 187
Too Big for our Britches? 190
Soldier Boy 191
Hoover Crosses the Prairie 193
Beyond Performance 195
The Decorator and *The Golden Age* 197

Chapter 12: Jogging South, Down River **203**
Rural Roots and Small-Town Values 203
The Play, *Grand Opening* 205
"Hello... Lyric Theater" 210
Finding Plainview 212

Chapter 13: A New Patch of Road **219**
Learning to Adapt 219
Dear James, the Play 224
Legwork 230
Scouting the Territory 231
Regrouping 239

Chapter 14: Many More Miles to Run **243**
Finding *Old Man Brunner Country* 243
Good News, Fear and Loss 252
Back to Work 253
Agatha Joins the Marketing Committee 259
The Hustlings 261
Callaway Directs 264
The Staggerford Murders 265
Over Hill and Dale 271

PART THREE: JON HASSLER THEATER

Chapter 15: Pushing the Pace **279**
 Hindsight 279
 Moving Along 280
 Dad Carries On 281
 Grand Opening Revised 282
 Where Would I Sleep? 284
 Success Breeds Success: *To Whom It May Concern*
  and *On Golden Pond* 289
 Waving Good-Bye 295
 The Gifts of the Magi 299
 A Foray to the Commonweal 305

Chapter 16: Feet Planted Firmly on Rural Roads **311**
 The Second Year 311
 Poet Eugene McCarthy 319
 Summer Season: *Simon's Night* and *The Fantasticks* 321
 Streets and By-Ways 324
 Grace and Glorie 326

Chapter 17: Cracks in the Road **330**
 Change in Staffing 330
 A Widening Fissure 332
 Talley's Folly 333
 Playing Together 336

Chapter 18: Solid Gains **338**
 A New Agatha Takes Charge 338
 HONK! 341
 "There's No Place Like Home" 343
 Morning's at Seven 346
 A Bug Story of a different Stripe 349

Chapter 19: Two Roads Diverged... . . . . **351**
 The Spitfire Grille 351
 Funding 351
 High School Drama 352
 Rewriting *The Staggerford Murders* 354

Words 357
How to Talk Minnesotan 360
Honk! 2 362
Driving Miss Daisy 363
Winds of Change 365
My Way 366

Chapter 20: Covering Ground **368**
All But the Art 368
The Rememberer 371
Night Vision 375
Dueling Divas and a Grand Piano 376
The First-Ever-15-Minute Lobby Gala 377
Proof 378
My Side of the Ledger 380
Clark's Side of the Ledger 382
Third Wednesdays 383

Chapter 21: Rough Patches **388**
The West Side Waltz 388
Winter Camping 392
Charlie Brown 393

Chapter 22: Hitting My Stride **396**
2006: My Busiest Year in Theater 396
A Dark Play 404
A New Hill to Climb 405

Epilogue 410
Postscript 411
Glossary of Theater Terms 412
Acknowledgments 415
About the Author 418
Endnotes 420

Prologue

Honestly, I don't look like a theater person, I am quietly ordinary. As a child, I was shy and lacked self-confidence. But many theater people are shy and drawn to theater because onstage, we can be someone else. So, how do we find each other?

My friend, Deborah Locke, is an editor who believes she isn't a "theater person" because she finds "The Theater" to be magical and wonders how a group of people can come together and make this magic. She asks, "How do actors put themselves aside and dissolve into a role, a transformation that brings them sheer joy?"

My friend *is* a theater person because she is a thoughtful audience and demands that I answer her questions. She is trained as a journalist and has a fine, analytical mind. She shared an observation—that people who make theater appear to be possessed by it and to have incredible fortitude:

> Whether praised or damned by the critics, you
> still go ahead. It's a difficult process, like making
> sausage. A lot goes on that you don't see—but it is
> done by people who feed on Theater, who <u>eat</u> The-
> ater. And they do this in a continual state of high
> anxiety. They don't know what comes next—will
> they get into an audition, will they get a role?

And how about the rest of the players—directors, designers, writers?

I can't answer these questions, but I can tell my own story and let my friend extrapolate what is meaningful. As I write, I continually go back to what playwright, Anne Welsbacher, said in her program notes for *Road to Rouen.* She was writing about music:

1

It teaches what "failure" and "possibility" can mean—and how intertwined the two inevitably are, living in the past, present, and future tense simultaneously.... This applies as well to how a play unfolds for an audience when a character on-stage reveals "who she is not, and who she might become."

I would argue that theater-makers, unlike secretaries, accountants, ushers, or box office clerks, must use everything they've ever learned. They must be 100 percent invested and understand how their part fits into the whole. Theater work is never just a job—like the priesthood, it is a vocation.

Theaters use music in various ways, from setting moods and covering scene changes to interpolating songs and dance numbers. When I helped start Lyric Theater, I knew that Broadway musicals would be beyond our financial means, but I felt compelled to work with musical concepts to try to make music integral to the play itself. Therefore, the mission statement would have to include a musical concept.

Lyric Theater's story begins with its first production, *The Belle of Amherst*, where I interpolated a musical concept into a play that had been intended to be produced without live music. Then the story will jump to Lyric's last production, *Road to Rouen*, where the actors are also musicians, and the music score is integral to telling the story. In both cases, original music had to be written for the production. You, the reader, will know where the Lyric started and how far we developed. And then the intervening years of plays will reveal what we were not, but also what was possible.

The last section of the book will show the changing—or clashing—of gears as we became the Jon Hassler Theater (JHT) in rural Minnesota.

Introduction

The most revealing epiphany I discovered during the six years I've given to researching and writing this memoir occurred in 1972 at a bridge game at a neighbor's house just outside of Ely, Minnesota. My husband Don and I were paired off against Bob and Jane in order to feel each other out, Don and I as novices—Bob and Jane as seasoned players. The men were drinking the hard stuff while Jane and I nursed Diet Cokes.

As the evening progressed, Don's bidding became reckless, finally rocketing up to the Blackwood convention that could lead to a slam. We followed the convention. He now knew we were missing an ace, but he still went to a grand slam, seven no trump. Jane "doubled," which would penalize our failure. I had to play the hand, and when Don laid down his cards, I flushed with embarrassment and asked, "What were you thinking?" He rose, drink in hand, smiling broadly, and said, "You know, I bid 'em, you make 'em." He swaggered away to the kitchen to refresh his drink. I lost the contract by one trick. "How could he?" played over and over in my head. Don had just described our marriage in one succinct sentence.

I was nineteen to Don's twenty-three when we married after a two-year courtship in Richfield, Minnesota, where, following deployment to Korea and Japan, he served out his last year in the Air Force in a desk job at Fort Snelling, and I finished high school. Many of our early dates were spent foraging for props for the Junior and Senior class plays at Richfield High as we fed our creative spirits and fell in love.

When we married, I put my education on hold while he used the GI bill to get a teaching degree at the University of Minnesota. I worked as much as possible and gave birth to two daughters. A third was on the way when we moved north to Babbitt, where Don joined the high school faculty in 1961 to teach a core curriculum of English and Social Studies.

Neither of us had forgotten our love for theater, and Don got busy, first directing several children's plays, and then coming home to announce that he had borrowed $1,000 at the local bank, and we were going to produce *The King and I* with the help of a talented speech teacher who had agreed to play the king. I cared for three little girls and squeezed in a part-time job. But he told me he needed someone who could handle the music side and was relying on me. We made it work. The show was successful, and we paid back the loan with about ten cents left over. This led to a second production, *Finian's Rainbow*, and a decision to leave Babbitt after five years to return to Minneapolis, where I would finish a degree in English education and Don would teach Special Ed for the St. Paul public schools.

A year later, Don was offered a job teaching Sociology, Psychology, and Theater at Vermilion Community College in Ely, fulfilling his biggest dream. (He had taken Psychology, Theater, and Sociology courses every summer which led to his qualification to take the job at Vermilion.) So off he went while the girls and I stayed in Minneapolis so I could finish my B.S. degree.

In 1968 I applied for teaching jobs in Ely and Babbitt but was denied by Ely because I was a married woman. A court case was in progress which removed that requirement but not before I was hired as an English teacher in Babbitt. We resettled, first in Babbitt for a year and then in Ely, where Don was developing a theater program that included a spring musical co-sponsored by the college and the Ely Music and Drama Club (of which I became a member). I took part in twelve spring musicals in the ensuing years.

Of course, all of this didn't happen without a struggle and living most of the time near the poverty level, sometimes teetering on the edge of bankruptcy.

As Don and I weathered the years in Ely, he appointed himself The Director, spending his creative energy teaching and directing plays—and even coaching football—essentially supplanting marriage and family with what he loved best. I picked up all the other pieces, traveling to Babbitt to teach and, eventually, direct plays, keeping the home fires lit and trying to keep track of where the kids were most of the time. Don and I didn't go to bed or get up at the same time. Notes were left on the kitchen counter when necessary. I shared Don's life primarily by participating in his plays. We were no longer partners in bridge. His bridge now led to the theater.

Six years ago, I set out to write a memoir. Then I attempted to focus on the history of the Lyric and Jon Hassler Theaters. But the borders kept bleeding together, merging into a theater memoir where even the history has become a memoir for having lived so long inside my head.

Writing this book has led me to understand that The Jon Hassler Theater, vis-a-vis the Lyric Theater, resulted from my longing for a marriage, for acceptance, and a place to fulfill my own creative spirit. I wasn't so much passionate about theater per se, but passionate about creating a place where I could partner fully with other people, a place where no one (no man) would point out, based on my gender, that I lacked the authority to take charge, to make choices, to think outside of the box. The Women's Movement was sweeping the country, and Helen Reddy was singing "I Am Woman, Hear me Roar."

Imagine that this story is told from behind a scrim, from the point of view now filled with shadows. But this story comes from my heart as well as my head. Theater was in my blood. Words filled my brain.

> Tell all the truth but tell it slant,
> Success in circuit lies.
> —Emily Dickinson

5

Part One
Climbing a Mountain

Chapter 1: Sheltering Among Tall Pines

1979: Nearly Forty, Restless and Spent

One winter day in 1979, after eleven years as an English teacher in Babbitt, exhausted from a full day of classes, I ignored the piles of papers on my desk. I was required to remain in my classroom for another half hour before heading home to Ely. Absentmindedly, I paged through a publication from the Minnesota Department of Education. On page 4, "Bread Loaf School of English" begged for attention. General Mills was offering two $650 scholarships to teachers from Minnesota to participate in a workshop for rural teachers of writing during the following summer at the Bread Loaf School of English, a part of Middlebury College in Vermont. I fit the profile for candidates. Was such a thing possible? Two of my daughters were away at college, and the third was a junior in high school.

The idea germinated on my drive home. As soon as I entered the kitchen, I laid the newspaper on the countertop and circled the article about Bread Loaf. Sure enough, when Don walked in, he picked it up and started reading.

"Bread Loaf?" he asked. "As in the one talked about in the *Saturday Review*?"

"Same place," I answered. "In the summer, it sponsors a grad school program. The real writers gather in the fall."

"And you circled it because…"

The air between us felt heavier as I chose words to downplay my desire.

"Because I'd like to apply. General Mills will cover the full tuition. I probably won't get it, but on the off chance that I did…" I turned back to the burgers spitting pearls of grease all over the stovetop.

Don laughed uncertainly and thought out loud, "Barb and Beth are at school in Mankato. Carol is the only one who will be home, and she has a summer job. I guess the two of us could batch it together."

And so I applied. The final item in the application form was to write a one-page essay describing my hometown/rural setting. I wrote it in what felt like a single breath, and when I proofed it, I found I had made good use of the element of surprise. It was fun to juxtapose Babbitt's Lutherans and Democrats with its token Socialist. I dropped the application into the mail and tried not to get my hopes up.

The acceptance letter arrived, on March 13, 1979, a letter from the program director, Paul Cubeta, typed by a secretary on college stationery, a letter that ended with a personal P.S.:

> Your description of Babbitt was so moving I could
> laugh and cry. You're more like Vermont than
> Vermont. You may think you've never left home.
> But welcome!

I was elated, but I had no idea how I would pay for my flight or room and board. Don and I both had teaching jobs, but we had been in debt since he started classes at the University of Minnesota under the G.I. Bill and I delivered our first daughter, Beth, all in the same week in 1958. When I married at age nineteen, my parents strongly disapproved and told me not to come begging to them when it didn't work out. In the twenty years since then, they had offered financial help twice, but it was still difficult to ask them for a loan. But before I could ask, they jumped in with an offer to pay for my flight. I applied for financial aid to cover some of the room ($160) and board ($315). I paid very little out-of-pocket.

The Bread Loaf School of English was located in a mountain bowl 19 miles above Middlebury in old buildings that had once been a summer playground for the wealthy and later donated to Middlebury College.

A mile away, Robert Frost's cabin was maintained by the college. Frost taught at the Bread Loaf campus when he was in residence, and students and staff traditionally celebrated the Fourth of July with a picnic at the cabin. From his front porch was a great view of what I thought must be the Bread Loaf Mountain (I was wrong). The summer school brochure said students came to experience "the liveliness of literature, writing, and dialogue." According to a faculty member, students could expect "to probe the limits of what Frost calls 'literary belief.'" The summer promised to be sink or swim.

On June 26, 1979, I flew to Boston, stayed overnight, and took a bus to Middlebury in order to see some of the countryside. Three of us who boarded that bus had tickets to the last stop in Middlebury, Vermont. That bus stopped at every quaint Main Street and arrived too late for the dinner bell. After a phone call from the bus depot to the Bread Loaf campus and a half-hour wait, a battered station wagon screeched to a stop beneath the streetlight. A young man appeared to fly out of a half-opened door, his cap sprouting wings like Hermes. He practically threw us in the wagon along with our luggage and took off at top speed up the mountain. Darkness pressed down on the old vehicle, relieved only by an occasional sign announcing a hairpin turn or a "hidden drive." I never saw any driveways and wondered about the psychological state of Vermont natives.

Upon arrival, Hermes shoved us into the dining room. Supper was already in progress, so we three innocents were relegated to the kid's table. The kids were all faculty offspring and much more sophisticated than any of us. Every accent known to the USA was evident in the loud conversations taking place around us. The East Coast accents suggested a level of upper-class sophistication and money that set my stomach acid boiling. The faculty was from the Ivy League Colleges or down South. I tried unsuccessfully to identify the other "rural teachers of writing" among all these strangers, most of whom were studying for a Masters or an M.Litt. degree (Masters of Letters). I felt lucky to be late, granting my entree to supper with the kids.

11

**The Inn/Dining Hall, Bread Loaf School of English, Middlebury College.
Photos courtesy of Bread Loaf School of English.**

After eating, we gathered in the theater for the opening speech given by Paul Cubeta, the Director of the Bread Loaf School of English. He announced the new program for the Rural Teachers of Writing workshop and read from some of the successful applications. He quoted from mine at least four times. Perhaps I would swim after all.

Dr. Cubeta also announced that auditions would be held Monday evening for the two plays to be produced that summer. An undercurrent charged the air, rippling the hair on my arms, as he introduced the stage directors. A second-year student with an East Coast accent explained his idea for staging Tom Stoppard's long one act, a surprisingly playful criticism of totalitarianism titled *Every Good Boy Deserves Favour*. It featured a cast of five and a small orchestra representing the regime. Andre Previn had written the musical score. Through a special arrangement, the orchestra would be represented by empty chairs and music stands with lights that came on while orchestra music came through the speakers. A maestro in a white tuxedo would conduct, and the music would be selected from the public domain. I marveled that such an arrangement could be made, but then I considered the reputation of the Bread Loaf School of English—this was the stuff of dreams.

The second night of theater was traditionally a classic play. Alan Mokler, who taught in the Theatre Program at Princeton University, would direct Ibsen's *The Seagull*. His large dog nestled lovingly in his arms as he spoke enthusiastically about his staging concepts and mentioned a guest artist who would play a major role. He encouraged everyone to audition. I was torn. Both directors were men. Should I risk another failed audition? If I didn't, would I dine on regret for the ensuing weeks?

Later, I settled into a private room in my "dorm"—a lovely white two-story mansion resembling Mount Vernon. Designed to house faculty, it stood atop a knoll on the far side of a large recreational field. The faculty hadn't liked being so far from the action and chose to remain in their old-fashioned three-story house with a mansard roof, which sat next to the inn, replete with a dining hall and rooms for young women. Mount Vernon was re-allocated to the older women—like me. I later discovered that the younger crowd referred to it as Menopause Manor. I didn't care. There was no lord of the manor. We had a kitchen and common room that the younger women lacked. We also had mice. The rest of the campus included a barn that housed classrooms and a large recreational room with a snack bar and grand piano, an infirmary, and outlying cottages devoted to housing the men. A library and a small theater completed the campus.

On Monday morning at 8:30 a.m., I gathered with the other students in the hallway outside our classroom in the barn. Our teacher came strolling to class, smiling broadly at the lot of us, a rag-tag nervous bunch from places like rural Iowa, Minnesota, and Maine. She had dressed her ample, middle-aged figure in an Indian print tunic. A few wisps of white escaped from her dark hair, and she spoke with a touch of Southern drawl. She exuded comfort as she invited us in and wrote her name on the board: Dixie Goswami (a writing specialist from the University of Tennessee). She told us she was married to an Indian, and the spelling of her name was easy— "Just remember, Go Swami!"

My second class followed at 9:30, "Introduction to Theatrical Production," taught by Doug Maddox, Associate Professor and Production Coordinator from Penn State University. He told us that most of our class work would occur during tech week for the two on-campus productions that were part of the Bread Loaf summer program. So, I was assured of a backstage assignment. I could settle for backstage invisibility and skip the evening audition. My classes were over at 10:30, and I had the rest of the day to read, write, sunbathe, walk or eat ice cream. My evenings were free for rehearsals. I chewed on indecision.

On Monday night, I left the manor, still debating the pros and cons of auditioning. Then, entering the artificially bright theater, I muttered, "What the heck." I was already suffering from overcharged nerves, so why not? I took a place at the end of the line, the last hopeful who would read from the script. Afterward, I thought my reading was no better or worse than the others, but my age might give me an edge.

The next afternoon, I approached the call board where the cast lists were posted. Several young men buzzed around, close to the board.

The chubby one asked, "Does anyone know this Bronski babe? Was she the one in the brown sweater?"

The cute one said, "You remember the color of her sweater?"

My face was in flames, and one of the men connected me to the unknown name. He congratulated me heartily: "Wow, you usually have to be in your second summer before you get cast."

"Well, I've been in quite a few plays back home," I said.

"But you're in that new program for rural teachers, right?"

"Yes. Does that matter?"

He shook his head as if to say, "Wonders never cease."

Another man chimed in, "I'm afraid some of the second-year students have made some stuffy remarks about our country bumpkins."

I felt like some kind of special ed orphan.

"Keep the faith," he said as he walked away.

I had been cast as the Teacher in *Every Good Boy Deserves Favour.* I could feel acid entering my esophagus. I looked at the cast list again. The son of Martin Meisel, Professor of English at Columbia, would play The Student. At least I had met the kid at supper the previous night.

Teacher and student in *Every Good Boy Deserves Favour*.

Not only did we have rehearsal every night, but the young director also met with each actor privately. I tried to follow his direction, but I'm sure it was a technique he had learned in an acting class, and I didn't really understand what he was looking for. I no longer remember what he asked me to do. I do remember that I tried over and over without success. "I thought I could, I thought I could," rang in my head, followed by "Think again, think again." Did the director cast me by mistake?

During every spare minute, I holed up in my room with my portable manual typewriter. All meals were in the dining room, where I often said little but slurped up conversations that were unlike anything I had experienced in the teacher's lunchroom in Babbitt—or anywhere else. But one day, I was drawn into the conversation by a lovely young woman with a Georgia accent so thick that I had to read her lips to get her meaning. As I answered her questions, she leaned over and rested her delicate hand on my arm. "You know," she drawled, "you just have the cuuutest accent I evah heard!" The men at the table burst into laughter, to her great puzzlement. "Well, what ah you'all laughin' at? Don't you think she's cute?" The male laughter felt friendly, inclusive.

As part of my theater production class, I had to learn to draw a three-dimensional facsimile of a building, so one morning I met the teacher outside of the library to get started. I followed his directions (which I no longer remember), and when he was satisfied that I understood, he left me to it. As the library emerged on my drawing pad, a slim, young, Asian woman with huge brown eyes sat down cross-legged on the lawn. "Is this your first summer at Bread Loaf?" she asked. I recognized her from the bus ride to Middlebury.

"Yes," I said. "How about you?"

"I was here several years ago. Every few years, I have to come back and give myself a Bread Loaf summer. This is such a special place, restorative."

"This will probably be my only chance to come here. It feels like a pilgrimage for a small-town English teacher from Minnesota."

She pulled a book from her tote bag. "I wouldn't have guessed that." She smiled and settled into her book, ending the conversation.

I loved every minute and everybody I met, especially Dixie Goswami. She required students to meet with her for one-on-one discussions of our papers in the Barn and treated us to hot fudge sundaes on her nickel. Hot fudge sundaes cushioned criticism, were held out as bait, and rewarded good work. A week before the end of the session, she threw out a challenge to our class to write a roast and present it on the porch of the infirmary. She would pop for ice cream and hot fudge for everyone who came. I took her up on it. I was the only person who had completed the coursework early.

Dixie Goswami with a mint julep on the porch of "Menopause Manor" (a Bread Loaf tradition).

Three well-known gurus in the teaching-of-writing field had visited our class, so I decided to base a parody on a cutting from MacBeth replete with witches, gurus, and ghosts. I cast it with students, and we had one rehearsal. The performance resulted in hilarity, but I no longer remember why. The day was very hot, and we polished off huge hot fudge sundaes. At his insistence, I gave my only copy of the script to Paul Cubeta. It was a great ending to a summer that changed not only my perception of myself but also my perception of how others saw me. Dr. Cubeta had speculated I would feel like I had never left home. Instead, I felt as if I had found home.

I wondered what awaited me in Babbitt. For years the only time Don and I said "I love you" was at anniversary dinners at a local restaurant. To say these words at home might have implied expectations that Don avoided, a situation I now took for granted as part of his mental state. I had written to Don several times that summer, but the only letters I received were from my mother.

The next day I boarded the bus in Middlebury for the slow descent to Boston. As I watched the trees, bridges, and small towns appear alongside the bus, it was hard to believe they were still right where I had left them six weeks ago. I thought back to an earlier summer school session I had attended at the University of Minnesota Duluth, where at the opening session, I was introduced as Don Bronski's surrogate. It no longer bothered me. I was still breathing the rarefied mountain air. I had found my people, my tribe, and they had treated me as an equal.

Back in Boston, I went directly to Logan Airport and flew to Minnesota, where my father picked me up at the airport. Where was my husband? I found him at my parent's house, sitting passively on the loveseat. He barely looked up when I entered the room.

We were soon back in Ely and resumed our teaching jobs and the roles we had been playing for many years. Don was married to his work, and I was married to Don. He was willing to add the technical side of the high school productions that I directed twice a year to his busy schedule, and I jumped back into teaching semester classes of writing, drama, and multi-media, the latter a team-teaching effort with a friend and colleague. The last of our three daughters would graduate from high school in May and move to the Twin Cities. I thought about living out the rest of my teaching years in a mythical marriage whereby I was but a surrogate of my husband. A friend had recently told me that the word on the street was that I was just a figurehead as a play director—that Don was the actual director.

I wanted to fight back. Don had enough grad credits for an "equivalency," whereby he was qualified for his job at the community college level but paid accordingly. He had tried to complete a graduate degree through Mankato State University by transferring his earned credits but returned home before the end of a required on-site semester, ready to end any formal pursuit of a master's degree. He was a much-beloved director in Ely, and I didn't understand why he ran away from many things that he well-deserved.

It was my turn now. I applied for a sabbatical leave for the 1980–81 school year, whereby I would be paid two-thirds of my $25,000 salary up front and the other one-third after two more years of teaching in the Babbitt District. I took the deal. Don was delighted, making all kinds of plans of how he—oops—we would spend the final payment. I was also delighted and made no plans beyond getting through the next year at Mankato State. I would be nobody's surrogate.

Chapter 2: A Change in Sea Level

My Sabbatical

The dictionary defines a sabbatical as "a period of paid leave granted to a university teacher or other worker for study or travel, traditionally one year for every seven years worked."

For me, it was a year to find out who I might become in the Ivory Tower if I dropped all my other titles—wife, mother, teacher. In Mankato, I was a grad student with a part-time job as the theater department publicist and a directing slot in the student union coffeehouse called "The Pit Theater" when used by the theater department.

The classroom work was familiar and held few worries. But choosing a play to direct in The Pit made me long to be back among sheltering pines. One year, one chance to direct, to make my mark. No spare time to research, to think.

Edward Albee's plays had fascinated Don, and I remembered how twenty years ago, the promise of a weekend away from the kids gifted to us by a wonderful babysitter and her family sent us driving from Babbitt to Minneapolis to see Albee's *Who's Afraid of Virginia Wolfe?* at the Orpheum Theater, followed by a night at a downtown hotel. We started our romantic evening at a Japanese restaurant, then jammed swollen feet back into shoes and stumped through the slush for several blocks, taking our seats right at curtain. On stage, the manipulations of the older couple and their impact on the younger couple became more and more familiar as the undercurrents of marriage were revealed. We were both disturbed and silent on our walk back to the hotel, and Don went to the bar for one last drink while I went to bed. Later I felt Don get into bed and turn away, so I curled on my side and drifted off. Around 3:00 a.m. I woke, a little cold and alone. After an hour, I dressed and went to the parking garage, wondering if the car would be there. It was.

Don entered our room at about 8:00 a.m., and we left for the five-hour drive home. Along the way, Don pulled off on a side road, stopping for no apparent reason other than to deliver a tongue lashing that put me on notice that we were in big trouble emotionally. I don't remember the words, only my feelings and the darkly looming pines beyond my side window.

We returned to Babbitt and continued with our lives for the next twenty years, but I still had some unfinished business with both Don and Edward Albee. I studied the play catalog and chose two of Albee's one-act plays for my pit production, *The Sandbox* and *Counting the Ways*. The first was a satire on the false values and lack of love and empathy in the American family. The second explored the downward spiral of two people long married but no longer sure of each other's love. The structure was sheer vaudeville, with twenty black-out scenes, brief sketches with or without punch lines, and a few with ice-cold combats reminiscent of *Who's Afraid of Virginia Wolfe?*

***The Sandbox* by Edward Albee, Seated Musician, Darwin Williams; Standing Young Man, Brian Crow; Background Grandma, Anita Herdina.**

Counting the Ways by Edward Albee, Singer He, (Tod Petersen),
Actor He, (Duane Sanford), Actor She, (Donna Laabs).

I used my memory of that long-ago weekend to direct *Counting the Ways* and added romantic musical olios between scenes—songs from the 30s and 40s—to underscore the long distance the married couple had traveled from their youthful, romantic days.

The singers, Tod Petersen and Dorian Schaller, tempered the bitterness and gave the audience time to breathe before the next onslaught. They added to the absurdity, the incongruity within the marital partnership. I was gaining insight into the impact of the musical productions that had provided the foundation for my own marital partnership. I was also building friendships that would carry into the formation of the Lyric Theater in 1985.

And then I met…

A Man with a Horn

When spring arrived, the prairie heat arrived, too. The Student Union was cool, and I often headed to the cafeteria. One day I was eating a skinny hamburger when a lanky guy plopped down across the table and asked, "So when are you going to need a horn player?"

I searched my brain quickly. Had I ever met this guy? Nope. "Why are you asking?"

"You had a piano player and two singers in your last show. Why not a horn player?"

He leaned forward and rested his chin on his hands, smiling. He was definitely flirting.

"Do you have a name?" I asked.

"The name's Jack."

"A grad student?" I asked, trying to get a handle on this conversation.

"Not quite. How's your burger?"

"Not so hot."

Jack enjoyed keeping me off balance. This kind of banter went on a little longer. I finally learned that Jack had been a professional musician for many years. He played in several bands and had met his girlfriend in an elevator after playing a gig in Duluth. She was a college professor at Mankato State University, and now that he lived with her in Mankato, he had enrolled as a music student. He was a bit of a hybrid, taking classes but also leading a jazz group and playing alongside faculty for musicals in the theater department. I reluctantly told him I had no plans for a horn player. My year at MSU was almost over. I would complete the writing for my master's degree from home in Ely.

Jack walked me back to the Performing Arts Center (PAC), and we stopped at his locker, conveniently located along the hallway leading to my tiny office. He said his trumpet wouldn't fit very well, but he pulled out a smaller version, a Flugelhorn, and warmed up. The corridor was totally deserted at that hour of the afternoon.

"This is called *Yesterday's Romance*." He lifted the horn to his lips. A luscious, warm melody echoed off the row of lockers. I was astonished. He was serenading me, watching me from the corner of his eye.

"Wow," I said. "I don't recognize the tune."

"Why would you?" he asked. "I wrote it a while back."

He put the horn away and walked with me to my office. I don't remember how long we talked, but we continued the conversation whenever we bumped into each other for the rest of the spring quarter. This was fun. I tried not to think about the Babbitt classroom that awaited me.

I was beginning to understand the word faith outside of a religious context. Years later, in 2008, I received a card from my former teaching colleague Jill Pollar that defined faith as "believing that one of two things will happen—that there will be something solid for you to stand on—or that you will be taught to fly." I could not have articulated that in 1981, but I sensed the need to fly.

Jack Carter's magic started to work on me, and I started to think about next year—maybe a master's degree (MA) wasn't going to be enough. A second year and a Master of Fine Arts (MFA) degree was a pipe dream at the time, but the seed was planted. I didn't know how I might use a horn player but adding in Jack as a composer sure had possibilities.

Chapter 3: Changing Landscapes

New Sneakers

I returned to Ely in May, where Don had been awarded a grant for his first summer theater program at the college. He asked me to direct Neil Simon's *The Prisoner of Second Avenue*, which freed up his time for administration and directing a musical. I saw very little of him. After rehearsals, I headed to bed alone.

I thought Don's mental illness was controlled with medication, so I came up with another theory to explain why we no longer had a face to face relationship: his unstable childhood had shaped him into a large, empty vessel, and no matter how hard I tried to fill his cup, it wasn't possible. We were always in debt. For years he regularly saw his psychiatrist in Duluth. His arrival home got later and later, and he confessed to driving across the bridge to Superior, Wisconsin, where bars filled with seamen stayed open very late. He was on Valium. He shouldn't drink, especially if he had to drive.

I had been to the mountain (Bread Loaf). I had been in Mankato for a year. I had started listening to Helen Reddy and reading *Ms.* magazine. (Click) I was unhappy.[1]

When I wasn't busy working on plays, I lay on the couch and thought about the fifteen-mile drive to my classroom in Babbitt, the piles of papers created by my writing classes, the endless Babbitt-Ely winters, the ever-widening rift between Don and me. If I pulled out the $3,000 that had accumulated in my Teacher's Retirement Account, I could return to Mankato. So, I forfeited the remainder of my sabbatical pay and squelched my guilt.

When Don found me on the couch one afternoon, I told him what I wanted to do. He whistled and said something to the effect that I must want this pretty bad to suggest such a plan.

I prattled on with my idea for incorporating music into a production of *The Belle of Amherst,* based on the life and poetry of Emily Dickinson, working with some people I had met at MSU. He looked at me quizzically and said, "You can't do that… that play…" He fizzled like a punctured balloon, groping for words, but left it there. Had I implied criticism of his earlier direction of the play at Vermilion College? None was intended. He shrugged and told me to go ahead. So I did. Was I sneaking away from home? I still wonder what Don thought I was doing.

I returned to Mankato for another year, entering the newly formed Master of Fine Arts (MFA) program in theater. I was assigned a Pit directing spot in the fall, fell into another directing position facilitated by my adviser in the winter, and completed an internship in the spring. Each event brought more people into the circle of friends who would make Lyric Theater a reality five years down the road.

Fall Quarter: I had been chewing on *The Belle of Amherst* by William Gibson ever since my couch time in Ely. The script called for Emily to be middle-aged and reclusively shy. The play was a three-hour monologue for one voice. The role had been a tour de force for Julie Harris, who starred in a film made for PBS, but even her voice and cadence wore thin and, ultimately, sleep-inducing. I was ready to risk my short-lived Mankato reputation and incorporate another musical concept. I cast another grad student (my roommate), Chris Samuelson, as Emily and added a second Emily to sing some of the poetry. Jack Carter set the poems musically for a small wind ensemble and guitar. I was working from intuition, from a second sight inside my head that I could not yet articulate.

The set developed into a partial Victorian interior with a bedroom furnished with a writing desk and chair facing front and a trunk filled with Emily's letters at her feet. Behind the desk, her canopied bed was draped with deep maroon opaque panels. When lit from inside, the bed transformed into a nested miniature of Emily's bedroom with a tiny writing desk and chair, and trunk. Fortunately, our singer, Patti Munson, was a tiny soprano with a big voice.

Christine Samuelson captures the essence of Emily.

**Foreground, Emily (Chris Samuelson) listens to her younger self
(Patti Munson) singing behind a scrim.**

The woodwind quintet led by Jack was seated to the side, behind a low picket fence, and once the show started, the music became a living part of the set. Despite being only twenty-eight, Chris was a fabulous Emily—ethereal, vulnerable, enchanting. When she sat on the garden bench and turned upstage to stare into her bedroom, Patti became an extension of the magic that Chris wove from the script. When Patti sang the last lines of "I dwell in possibility," Chris slowly raised her arms "to gather paradise." At last I was able to articulate what my gut had been telling me—that the Emily behind the scrim was the young person still alive inside the older Emily's head, singing some of the poetry. This discovery lofted my confidence. I was learning to fly.

Winter Quarter – Where the Prairie Meets the Plains: At my adviser's urging, I applied to Southwest State University in Marshall to direct a winter production of *Oklahoma!* He offered to cover the acting class that I was to teach in Mankato until I could return to complete the winter quarter. He suggested I return to Mankato on weekends and visit my Monday classes to stay current with my classroom assignments. And so, I initiated a pattern of state-wide commuting, changing elevations like other people change shoes—from Mankato at 781 feet above sea level to Marshall at 1,161—then home to Ely at 1,427, climbing north or coasting south.

When I arrived for that first interview in Marshall in October 1981, the weather was beautiful but cool enough for my tweed blazer and felt fedora, perfect for my first entrance. The theater faculty gathered in the lobby. All men. I would have to up my game. Dr. Hezlep (Bill), a staff director, looked the role—middle-aged and dapper in a tweed blazer, lively eyes engaging mine as he shook my hand. He introduced Charles Autry, the costume designer and thinnest man on campus, and Ray Oster, the set and light designer and tallest man on campus. Charles' bony but handsome face was topped by a gorgeous mop of gray hair—he could have been sent by Central Casting. Ray's youngish oval face was elevated to nearly seven feet, a presence demanding attention. Two members of the music department nearly completed the roster. The choreographer, Dr. Gusztav Varga, showed up just before the end of the interview and sat slumped on the small sofa with his eyes on the floor. Although I had never directed a full-scale musical, I had been in at least twelve, including *Oklahoma!* and had no qualms about directing it. They wanted a traditional staging and invited me to ask questions. We wrapped up the interview, and I had the job.

Dr. Varga lingered for a few minutes to chat with Dr. Hezlep. I stepped back to observe him. He was a few years older than me, about five feet, eight inches and slender with silky dark hair feathered around his face and longer in back. A mutual friend had described him as a real character, full of fun and creativity.

Gusztav had fled Hungary right after the 1956 Revolution, finished his dance education at Arthur Murray's studios and San Francisco State College, and landed a job at SSU in 1971. He had an interesting accent, a deep voice, and a long-nosed Hungarian profile. Well, I had heard that Hungary was known for its cowboys on the Great Hungarian Plain (now a tourist attraction). So, I hoped his knowledge of cowboys extended to *Oklahoma!*

**Gusztav Varga (who later took back his family name, Fogarassy).
Photo by Sally Childs.**

The irony of that day wasn't lost on me. I knew that an MFA could be my ticket out of Ely. I also knew I would have to keep pushing the stone in the pit of my stomach up a steep hill paved with the success of men who dominated the world of theater. And now, I would direct the musical that had sent me spiraling into a treacherous path that had threatened my participation in future musicals with my husband.

My first year of teaching in Babbitt and Don's second spring musical production for the college in Ely coincided. Don had cast a lovely young teacher to star as Laurie in *Oklahoma!* I sang in the chorus and observed firsthand Don's infatuation with her. A week or two after the show was over, he came home for supper one day and announced that he was in love with his star. To make it worse, he said, "I'm in love, really really in love, for the first time in my life." I was standing at the top of the basement stairs. I looked down into the darkness and wondered how it would feel to let go and tumble. Instead, I suggested he ask her to dinner and find out if she returned his feelings.

Don followed my suggestion. When he returned home, he looked several inches shorter as he studied his shoes. We started to figure out how to move forward as a family. I cut Don's valium in half and used it to finish out the school year.

Summer came. We moved to Ely, I commuted to Babbitt in the fall, and we played out our marriage through another ten musicals.

Now, directing *Oklahoma!* in Marshall, I would need to rise above some difficult memories. After rehearsals, I always dropped into the costume shop to check in with Charles. He was usually at a machine, a cigarette hanging from his mouth, with students busily putting things away. As soon as Charles saw me, he was on his feet, his spine curved from curling over a sewing machine, a lock of white hair falling forward.

One evening Gusztav followed me to the costume shop. Charles wanted to show him costumes he had pulled for the dream ballet. Gusztav aimed for comedy and wanted a corset with very long laces so the bridesmaids could reel in one of the heavier girls to prepare for a wedding dance. His choreography was more mime than dance in order to accommodate the limited experience of the students.

31

Gusztav approached the garment with relish, "Yes, yes, that will do very well!"

I teased him. "So, you know what to do with this thing, eh?"

I was flirting a little, and as we left the costume shop, he took my elbow and walked me to my car. Snowflakes fell abundantly, glimmering in the overhead lights. I was caught in a snow globe, miles from reality.

The weather gods saved the blizzards for the weekends when I drove back to Mankato to drop in on Monday classes and then back again to Marshall in time for a 6:00 p.m. rehearsal. The last weekend I did this, I awoke to snow and wind on Monday morning. The professors asked, "Are you crazy or what?" They almost pushed me out the door for an early start back to Marshall.

I pointed my powder-blue Ford Fiesta westward into the prairie wind as fingers of snow crept across the highways. As daylight faded, I turned onto the last five-mile stretch and straight into a huge curve with snow piling up into a fist. I pushed the accelerator hard and plowed through. Finally, I could see the campus ahead, rising from the prairie like a giant UFO with lights from the curved roof of the student center barely cresting the snow drifts.

The last weekend of rehearsals, I stayed in Marshall. The blizzard conditions prevented the off-campus actors from leaving for home. They worked in the scene shop all day Saturday and slept that night in the green room or doubled up in a friend's dorm room accessed by underground tunnels.

I spent Saturday in my rented room. Gusztav arrived at 5:00 in his very old yellow Volkswagen bug. We headed to Club 59, a roadhouse on the confluence of highways circling Marshall. I wondered if this little car could handle the snow building up in every direction. "Don't worry," he said. "The car knows it is carrying precious cargo."

At Club 59, Gusztav helped me remove my coat and then peeled out of two layers of heavy coats, stamped the snow off his feet, and reached into his cardigan. He slowly withdrew a fat white candle and a box of matches.

"I didn't know if there would be a candle on the table, so I brought my own. "

The waiter looked sidewise at these two middle-aged people, grabbed the candle, and showed us to a booth, where he lit the candle with a great flourish.

"Order anything you want," said Gusztav. "There are no limits tonight."

I pondered that statement—and ordered a steak followed by a Chocolate Bunny, ice cream smothered in amaretto.

We drove away in the yellow bug; snow piled high except for a cavern that housed two windshield wipers swiping a-rhythmically, hitting ice at the edge and bouncing into the backward swipe. Gusztav didn't miss a beat. "May I offer you an espresso coffee? I will make it personally in my little Hungarian espresso pot."

How could a woman resist? We entered his bachelor's pad, and after sipping espresso laced with heavy cream and raw sugar in tiny cups, he put a 45 r.p.m. on his record player. "Let's Get Physical" filled the room, and Gusztav pulled me into a dance. He was easy to follow, and follow I did, all the way down the hall. That night we both satiated our skin hunger, a hunger built over many years.

On Sunday, I couldn't see my way into the Performing Arts Center from the parking lot and was rescued by Gusztav, who literally led me through the drifts until we found an unlocked door. We were the only ones who hadn't spent the night in the theater, and no one thought to unlock a door to the Performing Arts Center.

**On Stage, Jeanette Goblirsch (corseted) and Girls Ensemble.
Photos by Gusztav Fogarassy.**

Everything's up to date in Kansas City, featuring Brian Johnson as Will Parker with Boys Ensemble and Laura Andres as Aunt Eller.

Jon Gottskalken as Ali Hakkim, demonstrates kissing techniques with Susan Schafer as Ado Annie, while Will Parker pays close attention.

The performances were unforgettable—the costumes perfection, the acting and singing well done, the dancing both fun and funny, the set and lighting dynamite, the audience enthusiastic, and the orchestra out-of-tune. I had heard stories from other directors of this happening, but this

34

was my first experience. When I discussed it with the orchestra director, he had a string of excuses. Nothing improved during our tech week, so I took the orchestra out of all numbers except the Overture, the Entr'acte to Act II, and big production numbers, including our foreshortened ballet sequence, but the solos and chorus work were covered by our excellent pianist. It was an unhappy compromise, but no one questioned me. The seats were filled to capacity at every performance.

After the show closed, I continued to explore a romantic relationship with Gusztav, driving mostly after dark, grateful for the stunning white moon lighting the snowy rural landscape—the same moon that lit the towns at each end of my drive. And yes, the same moon that lit the snow-covered landscapes of Northern Minnesota where a nearly empty house awaited my return. I added Marshall to my state-wide circuit of places to work as an independent contractor.

Spring Quarter: I spent the entire quarter as an intern under the direction of Brian Rehr, stage manager for the Cricket Theater located on the eighth floor of the old Masonic Temple, reincarnated as the Hennepin Center for the Arts at 6th and Hennepin in Minneapolis and later annexed by the Cowles Center. Brian was a gentle giant, age thirtyish, and his biggest concern was whether I could take direction from someone so much younger. I assured him I could. We shook hands and left the details to the administrators. I moved to my parent's home in Minneapolis into a tiny bedroom tucked under sloped ceilings.

The Cricket's mission was to produce new American plays by emerging playwrights and hired primarily union actors. I was viewed as a member of the staff and given hands-on assignments that gave me lots to think about. I went from show to show, sometimes entering blocking notes into the stage manager's "Bible," working backstage with props and costumes, and during Sam Shepard's play, *True West,* standing behind a curtain, clutching a fire extinguisher, as the actors onstage worked with a dozen toasters and then started a small fire in a waste basket.

Bob Moss came in from New York to direct *Dear Ruth,* a bit of a departure for the Cricket. Although certainly American, it was written in the 1940s. Its author, Norman Krasna, pushed people to laugh during the world's bloodiest war to date.

The Cricket's production was as successful in 1982 as the play had been in 1944, a predecessor of the TV family-based sitcoms popular throughout the 80s. When a teenage daughter writes letters to an Army Air Corps Lieutenant serving in Italy (letters filled with passionate poetry, undying love, and the prospect of much more) and signs her sister Ruth's name, the family is upended when the Lieutenant pays a call. Young and attractive, he is madly in love with Ruth, who has never heard of him before. The fun comes as all of this gets sorted out. The scenes were framed by the maid who danced with her feather duster in hand to wonderful 1940s music emanating from the onstage radio. "Drinkin' rum and co-ca co-la…" Using a minor character as a musical source gave me new ideas to chew on.

I learned a great deal from Bob Moss. He began the early rehearsals by asking the actors to sit on stage and read the scene to be blocked that day. He told them that at such-and-such a line, he knew he wanted them to be in such-and-such, a specific spot on the set, but he didn't know how they got there. As they read, he invited them to get up and move around as the urge took hold of them. Then they would talk about what felt appropriate. They would sort the movement a bit and then do the same thing again. As they repeated the process, Mr. Moss began fine-tuning the movement patterns. He insisted that every movement be motivated, either by feelings or the handling of props. He was a master at keeping everything in focus.

My previous experience with blocking rehearsals was from academia, where a director came to rehearsal with copious blocking notes and dictated every move to the actors. High school students needed this structure, or so the academics believed. When I had taken part as an actor in a Vermilion Community College production directed by my husband, I resented so much control. I wanted to find my character through experiments with movement, but that was not allowed. As a director at MSU, I had followed my intuition and invited actors to experiment, but I always had worried that I was doing it wrong. The Bob Moss style of directing was a revelation, perhaps an epiphany, and I took away from it lots that I could incorporate into my own directing.

On opening night, I crossed paths with Mr. Moss in the lobby. He had never spoken to me other than to give an order. We nodded in recognition, and then he surprised me by turning back. "I don't know much about you," he said. "What kind of theater work do you want to do?"

I answered honestly. "I want to direct plays. I would love to direct in a theater similar to The Cricket."

He reared back slightly and looked at me appraisingly. "What makes you think you can control professional actors?"

As I fumbled, reaching for an answer, he turned abruptly and exited to the hall leading backstage. I was stunned. Other men had questioned me with those words, "what makes you think that you can…" Tears threatened to cloud my vision. I have no other memory of that opening night. That encounter dogged me for a long time as I practiced the Bob Moss style of directing.

My internship at the Cricket was really a practicum and a course in overall theater production and management. Fortunately, it didn't stop there. But first, I had to direct *Private Lives* in Mankato and graduate. I also had to adjust to the end of my short-lived romantic relationship. That summer, I received a letter from Budapest. Gusztav described family obligations that changed his circumstances. He assured me that we would remain friends and share a coffee date now and then. I felt myself growing smaller, leaving Wonderland for good. Indeed, what had made me think that I could…

Following graduation, I told Don that I would not return to live in Ely. I would look for work in the Twin Cities. I sent a letter of resignation to the high school in Babbitt and moved to Minneapolis. I was back in my tiny attic bedroom, and my parents cleared a wall in the living room for my spinet piano, which they had handed off to me twenty-five years earlier following my wedding day. I took a daytime office job with the Cricket Theatre and worked evenings part-time backstage, all for $5 an hour. Chris Samuelson (*The Belle of Amherst*) and I looked at several apartments, but neither of us could afford the rent. After three months, I moved to an attic bedroom at my brother's house, and Chris moved in with a cousin. In the meantime, Gusztav and I continued in a state of limbo. I put off any discussion with Don about dissolving our marriage. He still needed the marriage even if he no longer needed a wife.

1982–84: Running in Place

For two years, I explored the Minnesota theater scene—interning at the Guthrie, working backstage and in the office for the Cricket, running sound for The Women's Theatre Project, performing in a community production in Burnsville, and directing community shows in Luverne, White Bear Lake, and Eden Prairie. During the summers, I returned to MSU to direct *South Pacific* (1982), *Six Rooms Riv Vu* (1983), and *Some Enchanted Evening* (1984). I continued to rent a bedroom in my brother's house and worked as a temp at Ehlers and Associates in downtown Minneapolis, where, on a Wang computer, I typed entries for inclusion in offering statements for municipal bond sales. Gusztav visited on weekends from time to time, never lying to me but holding back information. I had an M.F.A.—a terminal degree for those who wanted to practice the craft rather than teach. I wanted a turn at the wheel.

On Friday, May 4, 1984, I picked up the newspaper from the front steps and turned to the Weekend Variety section. Half of the first page was filled with a picture of a former student of Don's at Vermilion Community College. I had shared the Ely stage with her in Don's productions of *No, No Nanette* and *Man of La Mancha.* The headline read, "Director Cherne Strives for Greater Stage Recognition."

The article portrayed Beth Cherne as a comer in the small theater scene in the Twin Cities. In the course of the interview, Beth told Theater Critic Peter Vaughan that her interest in theater was sparked by a teacher in Ely named Don Bronski:

> He was very good, and if he had not been there, I
> probably would not be involved now. I think it is
> often true that the first person you encounter in
> theater determines the direction you will take.

A caricature of Donald Bronski drawn by Bob Cary, aka Jackpine Bob, well-known woodsman, writer, and wit in Ely.

Beth had completed her theater degree at UW in Superior and had been in the Twin Cities for seven years. She helped form the Rose and Thorn Puppet Theater, which performed at fairs, parks, and libraries on weekends, and worked a full-time day job. In 1980 she left the puppets behind and began directing for small theaters such as Up and About,

Unabridged Theatre, and Harmon Place Players. Her goal was to direct at better-known community theaters like Theatre in the Round, Park Square, and Centre Stage, and then break into the larger professional theaters.

Betsy Husting, an old friend from my Cricket Theater days, once pointed out that most theaters are started by directors who can't find work in the bigger theaters, and they last on average seven years. Betsy and two of her colleagues had started Theater Three, with a focus on women in theater. It, too, lasted about seven years. I asked Betsy what happened to the theater founders when they closed. She replied that most became teachers. Beth Cherne eventually followed that path. If I were to start a theater company, apparently, it would not be a failure if it only lasted seven years. I could return to teaching.

Part Two
Lyric Theater

Chapter 4: Warm-Ups and Stretches

1984: Chance Encounter

Six months later, after a long day of typing, I walked through the Minneapolis Skyway to the food court in City Center, where I nearly collided with a colleague from Mankato State University. He grabbed my arm. "Steady there." I was nose to nose with Tom Woldt's familiar square-jawed face framed by beautifully styled, wavy, dark blonde hair. I hadn't seen him for over a year when we both served as interns at the Guthrie.

"Sally! Good to see you. So, how are you doing? Any theater work?"

"Not much. Some volunteering. I'm working temp jobs in order to eat."

Tom rocked back on his heels. "Speaking of eating, do you want to grab a slice of pizza and talk for a minute?"

"Sure… Gotta eat."

Between cheesy bites, I learned that Tom was performing singing telegrams and looking for work. We chewed in silence for several minutes. I thought, *I wonder if Tom would be interested in starting a theater…* when Tom broke the silence.

"I've been thinking of starting a theater. Have you ever considered anything like that?"

"Yes… but I'm scared. I don't know where to start."

"I think the first step is to build a board of directors. Neither of us have any money to invest."

"You're right. To incorporate as a non-profit, we have to start with a board."

"Do you want to do this together?"

"Well, I wouldn't think of doing it alone. Do you have a mission statement in mind?"

"No. Do you?"

I fumbled for words. "I don't have a statement, but I want to work with music—make it an integral part of each production."

"That would be fine with me." Tom smiled like an idiot.

I smiled back at him.

And so we began.

The next week, we gathered possible board members in my brother's living room and came up with a mission statement: "The Lyric Theater is dedicated to fostering partnerships between music and theater professionals to produce finely crafted plays." At the suggestion of Chris Samuelson, we sold Freddie's Fudge made in Duluth to friends and family to raise our $45 incorporation fee. Our Articles of Incorporation listed our first board: Sally Childs, Tom Woldt, Carol Bronski (my youngest daughter) and Christine Samuelson.

I attended a class taught by Barbara Davis, who headed an agency called Resources and Counseling (which later became Springboard for the Arts) in St. Paul. I had never driven in downtown St. Paul, and despite specific directions, I missed the entrance to the recommended parking ramp and decided to "circle the block," a concept that worked in Minneapolis. The block turned out to be a triangle. By the time I figured it out, I was late to the meeting, which was held in a gorgeous wood-paneled conference room on the second floor of the Landmark Center. I walked in, feeling exposed, a country mouse in this old world setting. Barbara smiled warmly. "Welcome. We just got started."

I said, "I'm sorry. I circled a triangle and lost my way."

A male voice quipped, "You must be in the arts."

I slipped into a chair and out of my coat. I had found my people.

I gathered lots of information about starting an arts organization and learned a new term, "working board." The Lyric formed just such a board: in addition to Tom Woldt and me as the Artistic Directors, Chris Samuelson (professional name of Noalen Stampe when acting) as Secretary, Carol Bronski as Treasurer, and Marge Stanton (a work colleague from Ehlers & Associates) as Publicist and Fundraising Director. I invited Jack Carter to serve but he said no. Woldt, Samuelson, and I qualified as show directors. Shortly thereafter, I went to Barbara Davis' tiny office and created by-laws from a template on her computer. We were official.

The first year of Lyric Theater production grew out of our student days in Mankato. We planned to stage three shows with each director free to select a play and direct and produce it. Chris and I were old pals, introverted and analytical, and we were comfortable sharing the artistic responsibility with Tom, who was outgoing and quick to articulate ideas. Since Tom and his wife had a house that was centrally located, we decided to hold meetings there and named Tom as Chair.

The Carlton Dinner Theater, a former bowling alley on Killebrew Drive in Bloomington (now the Mall of America), wanted to explore using its small comedy club as a theater space, and so we arranged to use it rent free on off nights, Wednesday and Sunday. This entailed setting up the stage and tearing it down for each performance with help from faithful volunteers.

We wanted to be a professional theater right from the start—designers, crew, and performers would be paid. We were very democratic—for the first production everyone (including me as director) received the same stipend: $75 for the total project. To raise money to cover these expenses, we sold advance tickets to performances by Ray Charles in the dinner theater, from which we extracted a small percentage of the sales.

We lined up our season, starting with something familiar—*The Belle of Amherst* by William Luce, which played from August 25 to September 18, 1985. I was proud of my grad school production at MSU, and it seemed the least risky of our ideas for our first production. I wanted to share the musical concept with a larger audience. But I forgot a very important concept learned from my mother at age four, a story my brother and I talked about all our lives.

1942: Mother Learned to Drive

Mom settled David and me at the kitchen window to watch as she disappeared into the dark garage. She carefully backed the car down the driveway. Gray fumes poured from the tail pipe. She stopped level with the back door, set the emergency brake, and hurried into the kitchen to herd us outside. I was four and David was five.

The car was a coupe with only two doors. She opened the door on the driver's side and pulled the back of the driver's seat toward the steering wheel, creating a path to the back seat. "Shush and get into the car."

We climbed in, excited and a little afraid.

"Now get down on the floor and don't move or say a word until I give you permission."

We crouched conspiratorially, facing each other, knees bent to chins. David's eyes lit up with expectation. Mom started the car, ground the gears a bit, and drove up and down the driveway three times. Then she ordered us to sit up on the seat, one of us in each window as she backed out and circled the block once, twice, and a third time before turning back into the driveway. David wanted to go farther, but mom said through gritted teeth, "Later. We'll do it later." She pulled into the garage, stopped, and quickly helped us out of the car.

Supper in the formal dining room that night was "mighty good," in Dad's opinion. On that note, Mom folded her napkin and said, "Orville, I have something to tell you." He folded his napkin, too, and waited for the announcement, bemusement and affection written on his face. Mom took a big breath. "I know how to drive." She searched his face for a response, and finding only astonishment, said, "Ask them," looking at David and me.

We nodded. Even David held his tongue. Dad stood, picked up his plate to carry to the kitchen, and said, "Well, come on, kids. Let's go for a drive." He sat my dirty plate on top of his and turned to wink at us. "Laura, I guess you can find the car keys."

The rest of us grabbed more dishes and marched to the kitchen. Once we cleared the back door, David talked a mile a minute, reporting on our afternoon as he and I ran to the garage for our first family outing with Mom at the wheel.

Seen from the back seat, I didn't think Mom appeared nervous, but as she let out the clutch, the car lurched into reverse. We were off, backing into the street.

"Hang on, kids," Dad shouted, grinning ear-to-ear. He was having fun.

"I can do this," Mom hissed quietly. She shifted into first gear and smoothly let up on the clutch. Then second gear, and Mom stuck out her arm, bent at the elbow for a right-hand turn. David chanted, "I think I can, I think I can, I think I can, I think I can," in a perfect imitation of Dad reading to us while Mother made supper. We looped the block twice and then she pulled into the driveway and stopped. Dad got out and stood by the garage door, a gentleman waiting for his lady to pass.

Dad's Scandinavian pedigree declared him ethical to a fault, a stoic and a natural leader, classically handsome. He had an eye for good work as well as the ability to recognize and enjoy it when others (especially my mother) found ways around his stringent rules. Dad's back stayed straight as a ramrod 59 percent of the time. Mom was cut from a different cloth, growing up among four brothers, always flexible, always fighting for space. After the outing, Dad shooed Dave and me off to bed, skipping the bedtime hug. Maybe Mom would get a real one later.

David and I were too little to understand the dynamics built into this event. When Mom's driver's license had arrived in the mail, she had asked Dad to teach her to drive, but gas was rationed and tires were scarce. Available rubber was diverted to the war effort, so Dad took the trolley downtown to work at the War Production Board, and he expected the car to stay in the garage. But Dad at age 36 had been scheduled for a physical at Fort Snelling to test his fitness for military service. Mom was imagining a world where she would have to cope on her own with two small children and aging parents who lived in an old house without inside plumbing in Mantorville, sixty miles to the south. She became feisty, willing to risk Dad's anger and a fender bender or worse to prepare for her own battles.

The day had been filled with adventure and supper of my favorite "pasghetti" and cherry jello with whipped cream for dessert. What I learned from this day was a means to an end: Don't always ask for permission— but count on forgiveness later. Forty years later, I sublimated this lesson and erred on the better side of caution.

The Belle of Amherst Opens the Lyric Theater

College students are encouraged to explore, and if royalties are paid, no questions are asked. But now I was entering the profession in the Twin Cities, a mecca for the arts in the Midwest, and I worried about the legal ramifications of setting some of Emily Dickinson's poems to music. I sent a tape of the Mankato production to the playwright William Luce in California, and he turned us down. He didn't care how many Emily's or how much underscore we used, but he would not allow poems to be sung.

Luce had built his play out of a limited selection of Emily's poems and letters. The play read as an open invitation to innovation. I thought, *I should have used my Mother's M.O. After all, the Midwest was nothing but flyover country to people on the West or East Coasts. Where did ethics begin and etiquette leave off? Was singing some poems really a legal issue?* I was in a trap of my own making. Jack Carter rescored the music as underscore for an offstage piano, and the second Emily spoke the words, some of the ethereal magic of the college production was lost.

When Chris Samuelson begged off from playing Dickinson in this production, I cast Rita Olk, who was closer to Dickinson's real age. Rita's maturity lent her competence, which overrode her vulnerability, but she gave a fine performance, and the show was solid enough to earn us a good review from the *Pioneer Press*. We presented additional performances—first under the aegis of the Eden Prairie Community Theater where Rita served on their board, and later in the black box at SSU in Marshall.

I still wonder what would have happened had I used the concept developed at Mankato State University. Years later, I was told that the Belle production lived on in departmental memory for quite some time. In Mankato I worked from a position of faith—that the play would land on its feet—or it would fly. In a modest Pit Production, I had accessed a kind of freedom that comes with faith experienced outside of the religious framework.

As founders of Lyric Theater, we often struggled to hold onto our mission as a partnership between music and theater. To operate on a shoestring budget that could not cover the expense of a Broadway musical,

Rita Olk played Emily for Lyric with Carol Allesee as her non-singing alter ego.

we attempted to retain the musical element by stretching our definition to extend to the lyrics (lyricism). Over our fifteen-year duration, we worked with several well-known Minnesota writers, a concept which also became part of our mission. But before I revisit all the bumps in the road on my journey as the leader of Lyric Theater, I will jump to our last Lyric Theater production, which fully realized our original mission to produce newly evolved musical plays.

Road to Rouen

Road to Rouen by Anne Welsbacher ran from September 11 through October 10, 1999, just three months prior to our transition to rural Minnesota. The play was the culmination of everything I envisioned for Lyric Theater—a spirited script, original music integral to the story, a Minnesota playwright and composer, and a high level of professionalism exhibited by many long resumes that added up to hundreds of years of experience.

Rehearsals began on August 9. The play had undergone a process of six readings, including the Playwrights' Center in Minneapolis, the annual New Play Competition at the Center for the Performing Arts in Minneapolis, and an honorarium staged reading with the Women Writers series at Wichita State University, at which time music was incorporated into the staging. Miriam Gerberg, a local composer, wrote the music for the Lyric production, and Richard (aka Dick) Welsbacher, Anne's father, picked up the reins as director.

In the play, a musical battle zone develops when Meg and Stuart, respectively the daughter and former husband of world-famous composer

Director Richard Welsbacher discusses musical ideas with Playwright Anne Welsbacher. Photos by Nancy Campbell.

Suki Schulman, are called to Suki's Paris apartment for the reading of her will by her attorney and longtime companion, Solange. A surprise clause in the will stipulates that Meg (a pianist) and her father (a violist) must perform together a new, never-before-heard concerto written by Suki—or forfeit any proceeds from Suki's estate. So, Meg feels forced to return to the music she abandoned as a child prodigy. She must face her estranged father, her surrogate mother Solange, and memories of her mother and of her bitter Chicago childhood.

Stuart (Ron Duffy) and Meg (Jennifer Connelly) listen to Solange (Edith Elliott), Suki's partner.

Meg has a career as a businesswoman and a new life in France, but the piano and her mother's relentless control still haunt her nightmares. From beyond the grave, Suki forces Meg to come to terms with the ghosts of her past—and of her future.

As Meg begins exploring the new composition, she makes a number of discoveries about her family's past—love notes from her mother hidden within the music, secrets about the relationship between her mother and Solange, and the previously unrecognized depths of her father's difficult but real love for her. From the dissonant chords of her mother's music, Meg ultimately finds new possibilities for a family.

Anne's play was a deeply personal statement. Previously, when her own mother, a musician and teacher, told Anne she had cancer, Anne turned to Mozart as the old friend who would help her deal with this news. That memory provided inspiration when a friend urged Anne to take this play beyond words—*let the audience watch Meg rediscover her mother, her childhood, her family from inside her music.* Anne's pithy program notes encapsulate the potential offered by music.

> The second half of the play becomes a music lesson
> of sorts. Not as tedious as the real ones can be—
> but a lesson in several ways. It teaches Meg who
> she is. It teaches others who she is not, and who
> she might become. It teaches what "failure" and
> "possibility" can mean—and how intertwined the
> two inevitably are, living in the past, present, and
> future tense simultaneously—as does music itself.

The Lyric not only had to hire three actors, but also two musicians. Both the father on viola and the daughter on piano required musical shadows, actors who performed the actual music.

Stuart with his musical shadow played by Violist Milton Wright.

Meg with her musical shadow, Aurora Marin.

Audience response to the use of shadow musicians ranged from intrigued to confused. Anne admitted that, in retrospect, she "could have done more work to clarify for the audience who these people were—that they were metaphorical and not literal characters in the story." Anne does not apologize but points out that this "is one of the elements in the first production of any new script—you see what you need to revise afterward."

Anne said the music by Miriam Gerberg was "completely unexpected—and perfect." She had expected music more "traditionally Classical Romantic, something with echoes of Rachmaninoff or Chopin, or at most, Bartok-like. The bars that Miriam wrote eschewed such easy choices; they expanded beyond borders with unusual modes and chords that pushed two seasoned musicians to be 'brilliant.'"

Anne watched her two-dimensional script grow into a "living creature that breathed through three actors and Miriam's music under her father's direction. She loved working with her father. Originally, she had envisioned him playing the role of Stuart, but he had retired from acting in favor of directing. One of his students told Anne that "the safest place in the world was on stage with Dick Welsbacher." Dick said that when directing a new play:

> The words have never been made flesh in a theatre;
> the artists are truly on a voyage of discovery. Hav-
> ing the playwright on board during the gestation
> period does provide something of a literary hand
> on the tiller; if, however, as very rarely occurs,
> the director happens to be the father of the play-
> wright, familial deconstruction may occur. In that
> case, we can only trust our good players to keep
> the ship afloat. May I say, in all honesty, I am very
> proud of Anne's creation. I only hope I have not
> damaged it beyond repair.

The *Road to Rouen* fulfilled Lyric's mission as no other had in our fifteen-year history. It was too risky to take a new play to Plainview, but fifteen years later, I was happy to learn from the playwright that it received a second staging at the Wichita Center for the Performing Arts.

Stage manager, Alva Crom, discusses a cue with the director.

Chapter 5: Rough Roads

Back to 1985: The Prairie Beckons

As soon as *Belle of Amherst* was open, I left it in the capable hands of my stage manager, my youngest daughter, Carol. From September 1985 through May 1986, I replaced Professor and Costume Designer Charles Autry at Southwest State in Marshall. I knew Charles was hoping to find interesting work in California that could lead to a permanent move for him. I hoped to be first in line for a full-time job, which meant the Lyric Theater might be short-lived.

While I was out of town, the rest of 1985 included two more shows for the Lyric: Tom Woldt's minimalist production of *Mother Courage and Her Children* by Bertoldt Brecht, also staged at The Carlton Comedy Club. Shortly thereafter, the Lyric left the Comedy Club because it was located beneath the tiers of seating for the big dinner theater, where large audiences often expressed their appreciation and enthusiasm by pounding their feet on the floor to flood the building with a metallic deluge. In the Comedy Club, giant ice machines regularly ejected mounds of cubes at noisy intervals to accommodate the dinner theater crowd. Chris Samuelson moved her Valentine production of Edward Albee's *Counting the Ways* to the Women's Club near Loring Park in Minneapolis. The space was old and tired, a cavernous, pillared space better suited to Lyceum shows of a hundred years ago. But it had no ice machines.

When I left for Southwest State, I retained the bedroom in my brother's house and found a small apartment above a vacuum cleaner shop in Marshall. Gustav's private dance studio was above the movie theater at the other end of the hall. On weekends, I commuted to Minneapolis for Lyric meetings and performances.

Part of my teaching load included speech and theater classes, costuming the fall show, directing and costuming the winter musical, and costuming the spring show. I attended Gusztav's dance classes when possible, and we ate together often. Without the exhaustion of maintaining a home, raising kids, and teaching full time, I achieved the level of exhilaration that I had observed in Don but minus his valium-induced manic highs.

I chose *Pajama Game* for the winter show, in part because it would be a good dance opportunity for Gusztav. He was delighted to choreograph the show and appear as a dancer in the "Steam Heat" number. I was nurturing a working partnership, one that might work better than marriage. Either one held risks.

"Steam Heat" featuring Ramona Welsand Larson, Dwight E. Patillo, Gusztav Varga, and Lisa Welsand. Photo by Sally Childs.

Gusztav spent the Christmas holiday in New York, and after a quick trip to Ely, I spent much of it in the costume shop, preparing for the hectic weeks to follow. Fortunately, I had a wonderful costume assistant in Margaret Hohenstein, an older student who kept the shop going while

I was in rehearsal. I still have a beautiful blown glass angel that Margaret gave me in 1986.

I truly needed that angel. On the Sunday before classes resumed, I waited for Gusztav to knock on my door. When the 10:00 TV news finished, I tried to reach him by phone. When he did not respond, I walked down the hall and tried his door. It opened to his studio, unlit and empty except for a pile of dust and debris that sparkled from streetlight pouring through a row of windows. The sparkle bounced off a Christmas bauble bearing a mime dressed as Harlequin on a shiny red background, reminiscent of the mime movements he taught as part of his dance fusion work. I had given it to him to hang on the small faux tree that had traveled with him from apartment to apartment, his only piece of greenery. Intact, though carelessly tossed aside, it spoke volumes as I plucked it from the dust and carried it back to my place. I assumed Gusztav had moved out over the weekend under cover of darkness. I expected to see him at rehearsal on Monday night. I also expected another rejection. I wondered how he would orchestrate it.

On Monday, I spent the supper hour in the costume shop and met with Margaret to set up the work schedule for her costume crew. When we were ready to begin in the theater, Gusztav walked in with a beautiful young woman whom he introduced as a visiting doctor from Hungary who would be his guest for the rest of the school year and would attend rehearsals. She spoke little English but communicated with nods and smiles and then sat down to watch. Her presence pressed against the nape of my neck. Gusztav took dancers to the black box to rehearse, and I stayed in the theater with the leads. That sick feeling of loss leeched from my shoulders to my gut.

After the rehearsal, I crossed through the black box theater and the green room and into the costume shop to check on the evening's progress. A few students followed me as far as the green room and settled on sofas and chairs with soft drinks, ready to talk and laugh a bit. Gusztav followed with his visitor and introduced her to each student amidst smiles and a much bombastic description of meeting her in New York and his plans to take her on tours of the University of Minnesota Hospital and Mayo Clinic in the coming months. I listened, trapped in the safety of the costume shop, putting things away, waiting to escape without further contact. The cold pain in my chest flowed up to my nose, turning to drips that I caught on my sleeve. No tears—yet. An actor came into the costume shop, offering to help put things away, extending what comfort he could. He had played a leading role in *Oklahoma!* and knew that Gusztav and I were an item, although he didn't know of Gusztav's prior rejections. I said I was fine and turned away in case tears had risen to my eyes. He turned to leave. If he noticed my wet sleeves, he had more sense than to ask if I was "all right."

Gusztav entered the costume shop alone and told me briefly that he had attended a Hungarian event in New York and believed someone had tried to poison him. (Could this be paranoia?) The doctor had accompanied him to furnish protection, and in turn, he would house her and take her to medical facilities to visit. He asked me to understand. What I understood was that this might be an opportunity for him to connect with a woman of child-bearing age so he could realize his goal of carrying on his family's name. A manufactured excuse for infidelity. The truth would have been acceptable. Anything less only tarnished our friendship.

Of course, the show must go on. A strong cast that included both students and faculty told the story of labor conditions in a pajama factory in the 1950s where the union workers wanted more than a raise of "seven-and-a-half cents." Throw in a love story and some big production numbers, plus a tug-of-war between pajama-clad characters and some Fosse-style dancing in the "Steam Heat" number, and you have a crowd-pleaser. Going forward, I returned alone to the costume shop after rehearsals to see how Margaret and her students were coming along and then took my hollow chest to my lonely apartment above the vacuum cleaner shop. The show landed solidly with audiences, and I found myself able to land on my feet, pondering my future.

The last five months of my contract left me in a socially awkward position. I spent some time with a younger female teacher who was from Iran and, like me, on a one-year contract. Otherwise, I worked hard and prepared for classes.

Throughout that year, I heard story after story about Bill Holm but never encountered him on campus, where he taught in the English department. Holm was a legend in his own time, the red-haired Paul Bunyan of the mid-western prairie. He was born in 1943, the only child of Icelandic parents who farmed on the outskirts of Minneota, Minnesota, a small town in the southwestern corner of the state. Holm's mother protected her long-legged son from farm chores. His world flowed with books and music and chess games with old men.

Bill now lived alone in a little old house in Minneota. Another teacher mentioned it had been moved from an outlying farm and resettled in town. He lacked both a basement and television set but filled his house with books and visitors. The front door was never locked. Everything he did or said was at full throttle. He smoked two packs of Camels a day and carried a radar detector in his car, an older sedan. He was totally engaged in his world, a world of ideas. Bill's profession was thinking. Had I sought him out, I would have been tongue-tied.

The weather turned hot in May and Gusztav called. The doctor was gone. Could we have supper together before he left for a summer in Hungary and I returned to Minneapolis? My curiosity overcame common sense. It turned into a night in his ghastly hot apartment with very little conversation.

During my last week in Marshall, I attended Bill Holm's on-campus reading from *Boxelder Bug Variations,* an eclectic collection of poems, music, essays, and other speculations. This Icelandic giant towered above the lectern and mesmerized us, his shoulders hunched, blue eyes glinting with dry wit, red-blonde hair and beard circling his large head. I searched the stage in vain for a piano, hoping to hear "The Boxelder Bug Gavotte" or "Boxelders on Parade"—musical compositions which appeared in the book. Perhaps to compensate for the missing piano, Bill read poems that were not in his book—"The Boxelder Bug Waltz," "The Boxelder Bug Polka," "The Boxelder Bug Gavotte," and "Boxelders on Parade." My head took off, riffing on the many movements and dance possibilities.

Bill's writing ranged from funny to witty, was often whimsical, sometimes elegant, always surprising, and at times, stageable. By the time Bill finished reading, my adrenalin had reached dizzying heights. Was a staging possible? I needed to study the book, think it through.

After the reading, I plunged into a crowd of admirers and reached out for a handshake.

"Bill, I'm Sally Childs. I have an idea I'd like to share with you. Would you be willing to talk to me?"

He held onto my hand and said, "Yes, if we can find time. I leave for China in a few weeks. Call me."

When I got my hand back, I shook it hard to restore circulation. Shortly thereafter, I left for Minneapolis with visions of boxelder bugs dancing in my head. And fool that I was, I hoped that Gusztav might join in the fun.

At the end of May, I returned to an unfamiliar bedroom in my brother's new suburban home in Bloomington, jobless. I went straight to Manpower and was placed as a temp at Briggs & Morgan, a well-known legal firm. By day I floated from desk to desk on the twenty-fourth floor of the IDS tower and spent evenings afloat on theater ideas.

On My Own

In August, after settling into my first apartment on Diamond Lake Road in Minneapolis, I phoned Bill Holm for permission to create a theater/dance piece based on his book.

"You caught me just in time. I've started packing for my trip to China to teach for a year," he boomed. "I'll be in Minneapolis tomorrow, and I can drop off some poems. I should get to your place around 3:00."

Upon arrival, he carried a box down the short flight to my apartment. He professed no curiosity about my ideas for the project but asked where he could smoke. I led the way back to the courtyard, and we sat on the steps. I felt tiny in the shadow Bill created. The roar of incoming jets swallowed our voices. Bill raised his arm and said, "By god, you can almost touch them from here." It was 4:00 p.m. in South Minneapolis. Rush hour at the airport. Bill finished his cigarette and said good-bye. I wrote to Bill on August 13, 1986, just before he left for China:

> I cut apart the poems/fables and spread them out
> on the living room floor. After reading aloud over
> the past several weeks, I discovered three general

categories—Part I is simply "Consider the Box-elder Bug"—an introduction to the bug. Part II is based on the line, "I, too, dislike them," or violence and killing on the prairie. Part III is based on "A man, a woman and a boxelder bug are one." Thus, Part I is light, whimsical, delightful, like the bug. Part II is focused more on man's (and woman's) reaction to the bug and that nasty part that encourages us to kill that which is unfamiliar or not understood. Part III is positive—a real celebration of the bug (and at the same time, man/womankind).

I pitched many staging ideas in the letter, most of them impractical and never implemented, but it gave us lots to talk about. On August 26, Bill sent a handwritten two-page letter from Port Townsend, Washington, answering some of my questions and giving me his address in China.

And then he was gone for a year. I talked to myself constantly. Restless. Reckless.

In the fall, I signed on as a full-time legal secretary at Briggs and Morgan and settled down in my apartment, only a mile from my aging parent's home. The Lyric Theater's filing cabinet took up residence in my front hall closet, and the spinet relocated to the longest wall. During the course of the next year, Gusztav became a regular visitor. At Christmas, he brought a second Hungarian visitor, his mother Iluska (pronounced Il-loosh-ka). On Christmas Day, I chauffeured them on a tour of Christmas lights, ending with the mansions on Summit Avenue and Cathedral Hill in St. Paul.

If I compared the evening when Gusztav introduced me to the doctor he brought back from New York to the day that Don arrived home to tell me he had fallen in love with his leading lady, I discovered similar pain levels. Was this becoming a pattern? Was there something lacking in me? I valued loyalty in friendships. Did that make me vulnerable to being used? I had learned from Don's announcement that it was possible to carry on for a long time if I accepted an altered role in the relationship. Would the same hold true in my new relationship?

Iluska, Gusztav and Sally. Note the Hungarian profiles.

Limping into Year Two

With three stage directors as part of Lyric's working board, we ran the theater by committee. Absurd. We selected plays for widely divergent reasons. Tom tended toward modern experiments with the classics. Chris embraced plays that could be felt deeply. I wanted to work with living Minnesotans who were open to using live music endemic to the plot. I believe we all paid lip service to The Lyric Theater, but if I had to place a bet, I would not have put money on survival. We were still thinking like grad students, still breathing that rarified air of academia, where taking risks didn't spell financial doom. We were underfunded and understaffed. Our theater education continued in the harsh reality of the commercial world. We were all dependent on our day jobs.

Chris was deeply interested in psychology and invited Lyric founders and friends to explore the Myers-Briggs system as a means to a deeper understanding of each other. My type, the INFJ, was found in only 1 percent of the population. INFJs possess an unusually strong drive to contribute to the welfare of others. They are not martyrs. They genuinely enjoy helping their fellow men/women. This aspect of an INFJ explained my penchant to cast people despite a red flag in the audition process. When I cast a woman who did a great reading but had a reputation for instability, a colleague told me brusquely that "theater is not a rehab program." My belief that participation in theater could help and heal continued to dog me far into the future, sometimes placing me at cross-purposes with other people. I became critical of the placement of loyalties, not only in personal relationships but in theater and academia—and in corporations. I hadn't yet learned that "there is no loyalty in the workplace."

Lyric Theater used volunteers as much as possible and tried many fundraising projects, but the struggle to meet the bills overwhelmed us. We pumped friends for ideas, and many gave us moral support and small donations. We held a rummage sale in my daughter Carol's garage with good results, thanks to donations of furniture, some of which I bought and used for twenty-two years. We looked for more board members and had to replace some. Growing pains almost stalled our engine.

We moved performances to the Howard Conn Theatre (more a concert hall than a theater), which was attached to the Plymouth Congregational Church on the southern edge of downtown Minneapolis. Chris Samuelson was up first with *The Grass Harp* by Truman Capote. The story and dialogue had a lyrical quality, but it had not been successful in New York when it was first produced. Chris thought she could overcome the minimal budget with imagination, but the script wasn't strong enough. Reviews were mediocre at best, and audiences were small.

In the nonprofit world, survival means successful grant proposals. I took what I had learned when I typed proposals at the Cricket, added Tom's research into requirements for submission to the Metropolitan Regional Arts Council, MRAC (pronounced M-rack), and milked Chris' brain for ideas. After we finished our first proposal, Tom, Chris, and I went to the panel review and sat with other grant seekers around the periphery of the room in mandatory silence while the panel exposed every weakness in our proposal. Afterward, we sat in the car and rehashed the information. We planned to go back with a new proposal in a year or two. Meanwhile, I was slotted to be the next director.

Before I left Southwest State in Marshall, I had talked to Professor Bill Hezlep about adapting one of his plays into a small cast musical. He suggested *Nessie,* part of a series of published children's plays. The main theme was the art—or science—of seeing and believing. The two main characters, Dirk and Erin, were based on Bill's children. The story revolved around their adventures exploring Scotland and the myth of the Loch Ness Monster. I was charmed by the material. Now I needed a composer, one who would not demand a large commission. Jack Carter wasn't available.

I had met Bob Hindel through Gusztav's association with the Andahazy Ballet, where Bob accompanied classes. Bob was both a gifted and highly trained musician and composer who carried paper and pencil at all times, jotting down melodies almost between breaths. He agreed to write a score for *Nessie* for whatever amount of money I could pay him. He wanted to play for the show as well.

Bill Hezlep wrote the song lyrics at his home in Marshall, unwilling to drive one hundred and fifty miles from Marshall. I was flattered that he trusted me with his script and set aside my vision of collaborators gathered at the table in rehearsals. An INFJ doesn't cajole, push, insist, demand—or flatter. I didn't know how to ask for help. I never considered the use of charm. I had so much to learn—or unlearn.

I used every free resource available, even a huge puppet borrowed from Mankato State who represented St. Columba, an Irish missionary reputed to have saved a swimmer from the Loch Ness Monster. It rose from behind a castle wall for a brief scene, but a large puppet couldn't overcome the holes in my thinking.

As a kid, I never saw live theater. I went to Saturday movie matinees as a tween. I hated cartoons. The noise and physical aggression didn't match my picture of the world. Even as a kid, I wasn't like that other 99 percent. But children's shows draw from cartoons to make the action BIG. Kids need to be actively engaged, calling out answers to questions, helping the actors solve the problems, resolving the conflict. The imaginary fourth wall separating actors from audience doesn't exist in theater for children. Although my direction was playful and incorporated physical humor, it just wasn't big enough, loud enough, or direct enough. The rental theater was more of a concert hall, wide and curved, so the back wall was a long way from the front of the stage. Kids like to be upfront and close to the action, but even the front row was quite a ways from the lip of the stage. I didn't see this or consider it until long after our opening.

I took a huge risk by casting a blind actor, Eric Peterson, expecting to create some interesting tension in such songs as "Seeing is Believing." I was forced to replace him when he landed in the hospital for cancer surgery. I found myself in a state of turmoil and confusion, angry because Eric had not leveled with me about his physical situation when I cast him—wretched that I was angry at a sweet young man enthralled with theater, despite a physical disability. During tech week, he came back to rehearsals to listen and sat cross-legged at the lip of the stage with his arms around his seeing-eye dog. It nearly ripped out my INFJ heart.

I replaced Eric Petersen with Dale Pfeilsticker, a natural physical comedian. Dale created comic moments, and I could have pushed him farther. He would have loved to help me learn to do this. Bill Hezlep might have allowed us to make script changes to accommodate interaction between actor and audience. None of this occurred to me then.

The review was not sympathetic; we were clearly being held to Children's Theatre Company standards, and the playwright took it particularly hard. I thought of our production as a family show. I had little experience with children's plays and directed as if the show were styled for families—adults accompanied by their children rather than the other way around.

Gusztav supported *Nessie* with great enthusiasm. He wrote a lovely article for the *Marshall Independent*, which was published with a picture featuring the former SSU students who built and painted our set. Ironically, our greatest support was in Southwestern Minnesota, but our venue was in the Twin Cities.

The cost of choosing something that was not in my wheel box was a formula for failure resulting in financial hardship. But we proceeded, thanks to a fundraising idea that brought in over $10,000 in 1987.

Eric Petersen poses for a picture with the cast with his dog stealing the show when he appears to be whispering in Eric's ear. Dale Pfeilsticker is behind Eric. The rest of the cast is seated in a semicircle with Sarah Carter and Cathy Shapiro laughing on the left, Michael Sward and Jay Ramos at the top, and Robert Durley to the right.

Concessions

Lyric took over running a concession booth at the Metrodome for a small share of the profits. Upon arrival, our small band of eight volunteers counted the inventory (every hot dog and bun, every drink container). We cleared the beer taps with bleach, set up the popcorn, and memorized the prices, taping a cheat sheet by our workstations. We added the cost in our heads as we filled orders, took money, gave change, and moved on to the next customer. We were allowed a very slim margin of error. If we exceeded it, the difference came out of our profits. There were no chairs or stools. The only time we sat down was on a ten-minute break when we could squat on a toilet. I was the oldest in our group and, during the eight-hour shift, sometimes folded my aching body into the bottom shelf of the supply area, fearing my body—or the shelf— would break.

We staffed the booth with board members and friends (and my daughters), who were still willing to give us hours, especially on Saturday or Sunday afternoons. The Mankato connections were still strong; Jack Carter and his partner Joy Joyner drove up from Mankato over and over, and I often picked up Becky Adams, who lived nearby. She had been the theater secretary at MSU and married a former Mankato actor, Brian Crow, who had hired onto the backstage crew at the Guthrie. (They were married on the Guthrie stage, and I was the maid of honor.)

We kept working through the 1987 World Series and the Vikings football season. It was long and grueling, but we became so good at it that two of our newest board members, Rebecca Bringgold and my oldest daughter, Beth Bronski, were entrusted with managing the booth. I first met Rebecca at the Cricket Theatre where she was framed by the box office window, her bush of curly blonde hair catching reddish highlights, glossy lips smiling. She immediately dubbed me "Sally-bo-bally." Beth and Rebecca were about the same age, but Beth had been a late bloomer and was still studying Occupational Therapy at the University of Minnesota. Bless them, they made selling beer and hot dogs as much fun as possible. We even held a "Dome-A-Thon," collecting pledges to match a portion of what was earned at a particular game. A year later, we were burning out our volunteers, so Beth recruited her fellow university students to keep us fully staffed and to share in the profits for a second year

**Brian and Becky's wedding. The maid of honor is
wearing red shoes and a belt.**

We kept working through the 1987 World Series and the Vikings
football season. It was long and grueling, but we became so good at it
that two of our newest board members, Rebecca Bringgold and my oldest
daughter, Beth Bronski, were entrusted with managing the booth. I first
met Rebecca at the Cricket Theatre where she was framed by the box
office window, her bush of curly blonde hair catching reddish highlights,
glossy lips smiling. She immediately dubbed me "Sally-bo-bally." Beth and
Rebecca were about the same age, but Beth had been a late bloomer and
was still studying Occupational Therapy at the University of Minnesota.
Bless them, they made selling beer and hot dogs as much fun as possible.
We even held a "Dome-A-Thon," collecting pledges to match a portion
of what was earned at a particular game. A year later, we were burning out
our volunteers, so Beth recruited her fellow university students to keep us
fully staffed and to share in the profits for a second year.

Rebecca's box office experience at the Cricket Theatre prompted her
to draw up a box office report which we used for sixteen years. After

Sunday shows, I routinely went home to reconcile the money received with the number of tickets sold and put together the weekly deposit. When it was dark outside, I closed every blind and curtain so no one could look in casually and see what I was doing. Staying on top of every chore helped me organize my priorities for nighttime worrying as I got ready for bed. We couldn't afford a separate phone number, so we used mine. Lyric Theater became my bed partner.

Next, Tom Woldt adapted *Lysistrata* by Aristophanes and moved the story to Appalachia with a feud modeled after the Hatfields and McCoys—Lil' Abner gone Greek. Herb Dick, another MSU grad, created the musical score. We performed in the basement of the Hennepin Center for the Arts. It had been vacated by a restaurant, and rent was very cheap.

We simplified and generalized our mission statement: "The Lyric Theater is dedicated to fostering partnerships between music and theater artists." We lacked the money to work with people with big reputations. We were gaining ground with the acting community but not with the reviewers.

Tom and I met with the staff of the Metropolitan Regional Arts Council (MRAC) for coaching, attended workshops, and gathered material from other foundations. I wrote grant proposals with editing help from Tom and Chris. Many rejections and several years later, Lyric finally received grant money. In the meantime, we used every resource available.

We continued to build our board of directors. This became critical when Tom announced his intention to return to graduate school. Our working board of mostly theater practitioners had little business acumen. I was forced into the role of Board President. I quickly looked for help from the Management Assistance Project (MAP), a clearing house for matching nonprofits with corporate volunteers. They sent us Everett Janssen, an independent entrepreneur, who soon applied his business background to the role of Board President, freeing me to pursue the creative work. I met with Sally Anderson at Dain Bosworth, and although she didn't see how she could be of help, she became a long-standing and valuable board member. Going forward, most new board members came from the corporate world, which often led us to corporate giving programs.

The corporate culture also demanded volunteerism from employees who wanted to advance.

In 1987 both Tom and Chris left to pursue additional university theater training. After only two years of Lyric productions, I felt orphaned and overwhelmed. Choosing the next production was totally my responsibility. No more playing second fiddle. No more trio. Just a small train of volunteers on a track that ran back across the prairie. Year three lay ahead.

I was dumbfounded when the humble boxelder bug that lived in a symbiotic relationship with the box elder tree (a form of maple that proliferated the prairie) pushed me into innovation and impassioned creativity based on bug behavior.

Chapter 6: Gaining Traction

Boxelder Bug Variations

But why not? My favorite line of Emily Dickinson's was "I dwell in possibility," an attribute of my 1 percent of the population. We also exhibited "an unostentatious creativity, over-perfectionism, and putting more into a task than perhaps is justified by the nature of the task," according to David Keirsey and Marilyn Bates.[2]

In 1986 I had no computer. On Saturdays—like Eudora Welty in days gone by—I continued to read, sort, and pin the poems onto yellow legal pads. True to type, I "exercised my imagination both as memory and intuition." I was creating for "masters of the metaphor, wallowing in language which contained an unusual degree of imagery, language both elegant and complex." I still have that first script, the pins still intact.

Nine months later, I had a script comprised of the three parts described in my letter to Bill before he left for China.

Bill believed we must look for metaphors in our own backyard. Boxelder bugs crawling around his classroom and living in a tree in his front yard in Minneota had become an extended metaphor. I envisioned actors costumed in basic black with red stripes. The show opened with Bill (or his counterpart) saying:

The piano string trembles

and boxelder bugs

start dancing.

Followed by "The Boxelder Bug Polka," sung and danced:

When the polka starts up playing in the boxelder tree,

71

Then the bugs go find themselves another bug,

And they leap, and they twirl, and they circle round a leaf,

While the clarinet, the cornet and the big bug drum,

Keep time to the tune with a one, two, three,

Four-five-six-seven-trouble-now—(dance and song fizzle out)

Not so easy on six legs as on two.

Hang them by the antennae for tangled dancing?

No! Brave Bug! Carry on as if that branch were Poland!

So (dance resumes) -- the polka starts again with a flapping of the wings,

And the red striped company is dancing up a fling,

With a one and a two and three four five—

Six—(dance falls apart)

(The actors talk to each other—lines assigned by director.)

So, this year your house is full of the little buggers, too.

Would it be a better America without boxelder bugs?

Cleaner.

No, I don't think so.

More to eat, maybe?

They eat nothing of yours. You're too fat, anyway.

They're ugly, too.

Well, you think that because they don't look like you.

It's my house, not theirs!

The deed says so, doesn't it?

The deed must be God.

God speaks truth!

They have no money,

So, they're poor!

They sure don't carry credit cards.

Yes.

They're not Americans!

There's not a passport among them, but they've lived here for 75 million years.

Ignore them and they'll die.

(The actors continue to speculate about how to get rid of the bugs and finally declare that nothing can be done. This is edited to shorten length of excerpt.)

Nothing?

Nothing… so make works of art, make beauty, dance.

But they are only little things.

So, sing… a little.

So… consider the boxelder bug!

The bug's Latin name is several times as large as itself: Leptocoris trivittatus.

Bill:

The bug slides

out from behind

the radio dial

where all winter

he lived

eating music.

Bill (begins singing Gregorian chant and others join in.)

LEP-TO-COR-IS TRI-VIT-TA-TUS.

The script continues with Bill singing "Auch Kleine Dinge," a song composed in 1890 in Vienna by Hugo Wolf, "who never saw a bug, but understood small things, and made a small song to praise those kleine dinge, which delight us if our eyes are open, our bodies are alive—pearls, olives, roses, bugs." This segues into the actors singing a translation of the German song, which then segues into a transcription, and finally a comparison of the bug to the Shakers—

who danced! bending and bowing, turning,

until the physical air inside their own bodies

lifted them up into the valley of love and delight.

which segues into the bugs (actors) doing a Shaker Dance to a musical interpretation of "Tis a Gift to be Simple" played on the harpsichord.

The script continues in this vein, with boxelder bug parodies of famous poems, the Dickinson parody sung to the tune of "Amazing Grace."

When the bugs (actors) pray, Bill joins them, and they sing,

I want so little

for so little time,

A south window,

and a wall to climb,

The smell of coffee

and a radio knob

Nothing to eat

Nothing to rob

Not power, not love

Not even a penny

Forgive me only

For being so many.

The full ensemble, Minneota Opera House, Hector Cruz, Novik Inge Stubbs, E. E. Balcos, Laura Taswell, Elizabeth Wiley, and Joey Babay. Photo Nancy Campbell.

The show alternated between song, dance, and spoken word. Many of the dance numbers were built around pieces found in the box of extra poems rather than the published book. More of Bill's work still needed to be set to music—The Boxelder Bug Polka, The Boxelder Bug Blues— "I'm just a bug in a window, Lord, don't nobody want to love…" Bill did not want to compose these numbers, so they were turned over to Bob Hindel, who could improv on any musical style.

But I'm getting ahead of my story. In 1987 when Bill returned from China, I used a lunch break from my job in the IDS Center at 8th and Nicollet to meet him—jogging in inch-and-a-half heels, a photocopy of the script in hand. I pushed through the heavy double doors, panting, to wait in the lobby of the Hennepin Center for the Arts at 6th and Hennepin. Bill came in the side door, glowing from the early summer sunshine.

"My god, I never thought you would really do it!" His blue eyes danced above his Viking beard. He was buoyant, like a man in love (he

75

was, but I didn't know it yet)—and he had lost sixty pounds in China. His summer shorts exposed at least forty inches of leg. "I'm on my way up to Milkweed to talk to Emily Buchwald about my China book." He took the script with his usual exuberance. "I'll get back to you tomorrow—oh, and I'll tell Emily about this."

I legged it back to the IDS. My mind raced. What have I done now? Will they like it? Can I really do this without Tom and Chris? How long will it take to get this show on stage? What will it cost? Developing a new piece of work outside of an academic setting was going to take a lot of running uphill. I could hear my husband Don's voice, "You can't do that,"—and Bob Moss, the New York director brought in by the Cricket during my internship, "What makes you think you can…" I sorely needed to replace those voices.

In just a few days, Bill phoned.

"Emilie Buchwald loved the idea of the boxelder poems onstage."

"Okaaayyyy," I nearly sang. "Now I have to figure out funding."

"Emilie will have some ideas for funding. I think Milkweed Editions might take on some financial responsibility."

"Would a non-profit press do that?" (I thought, *Dream on, Bill.*)

"I don't know. Can you meet Emilie and me at the New French Cafe in the Warehouse District at 5:00 tomorrow?"

"I can be there at 5:15 if I put on my track shoes."

"Take your time. We'll see you then."

When Bill hung up, I felt lighter, as if riding on breath like a dancer, ready to levitate.

At five the next afternoon, I headed to the cafe at 4th and First Avenue North, a part of the old Warehouse District comprised of brick and mortar grayed by soot from coal-burning furnaces. The New French Cafe was co-founded in 1977 by Pam Sherman, an extraordinary chef, and Lynn Alpert, whom she met in Paris in the 70s. Together they introduced the concept of the French Bistro to this fast-developing artsy part of Minneapolis.

I arrived out of breath as usual and took a moment in the entry to take in the stark white walls and fresh flowers on each table. Bill and Emilie were seated near a window with coffee in hand. Emilie was as tiny as Bill was large, a sparrow perched next to a giant parrot.

Emilie readily granted the rights to produce the piece and asked nothing in return. As she talked, it became clear that the Lyric Theater was on its own for funding. She offered grant writing ideas, including the obvious MRAC and McKnight Foundation grants. She also suggested applying for a grant from the Jerome Foundation, which funded emerging artists. The volume of grant writing work she suggested nearly stripped me of hope. I eventually pursued all of her ideas but without results. We just hadn't been in business long enough.

Hope returned when the phone rang: "Hi. You don't know me, but Bill Holm gave me your name. He said you were going to do a play based on his *Boxelder Bug Variations*."

I didn't recognize the high, girlish voice.

"Yes," I said. "We're in the planning stages."

"Well, I'd like to tell you a little bit about myself. My name is Nancy Campbell. I went to a concert a few weeks ago that featured Bill Holm reading his poetry accompanied by a harpsichord player. Afterward, I waited until almost everyone else had gone and then got up the courage to tell him how much I enjoyed the concert. I even told him I played recorder and had my own harpsichord..."

I interrupted, "You own a harpsichord? Do you play it yourself?"

"Yes but wait. I want to tell you my idea. Bill said you needed to raise money for the play. I have a large house in Plymouth, and I think it might be a really good place to have a private party—like a gala or something... if you're interested." Nancy sounded shy, a kindred spirit.

Nancy was as girlish as she sounded on the phone, although she was forty-ish. Her slim figure was topped by naturally curly dark hair cut short around a sweet, young face. Her clothing often draped artistically over snug under-layers, usually black.

Before long, Nancy and I scheduled the Lyric's first gala fundraiser. With the help of the Lyric board, we rounded up a group of people who shared a lovely afternoon at Nancy's house, her walls filled with black and white photographs of her children. Bill played ragtime on Nancy's grand piano and Bach on her harpsichord, and the guests expressed appreciation with modest donations. Nancy asked Bill if she could photograph him—she was not only a musician but a professional photographer as well. What kind of rabbit hole had I fallen into? Breathe, I told myself, breathe.

Rita Olk, who played Emily Dickinson in the Lyric's inaugural production, stepped up to the plate for another private gala held at the Decathalon Athletic Club in Bloomington. Once again, Bill performed, and again, the word spread and more money came into the coffers. A third gala transpired at the posh Tangletown home of Rita's friend, Mary Anderson, near Minnehaha Creek in Southwest Minneapolis. Again, Bill worked his magic, and the numbers continued to build slowly. Meanwhile, the Lyric Theater Board of Directors held steady with six to seven members, albeit with two to three people shifting in and out every year.

Minneota (not Minnesota)

Without a successful grant proposal, a full staging seemed impossible until Linda Canton, a community activist in Bill's hometown of Minneota, and Rob Ross of the Southwest Minnesota Arts and Humanities Council (SMAHC) became interested. I visited Minneota on a wintry weekend to see the space called "The Big Store" by locals, which had once housed an emporium on the first floor and an old-fashioned opera house on the second. The opera house had gone through many transformations, including a dance floor and a community basketball court.

As I pulled up to Bill's little house in Minneota, he stepped out on the open porch, pulling on a jacket. "Just park right there. I'll drive." I rolled under the curbside boxelder tree and transferred to his large sedan. He pointed out the city park and bandshell as we crossed the railroad tracks and the highway to drive two more blocks to The Big Store. He parked by a side door, and we mounted the dusty stairs. At the top, he opened an old elevator door and assured me the manually operated ropes were all in good order. "The plumbing works, too," he said, grinning. We walked into the large room, currently filled with secondhand furniture and old organs salvaged from small rural churches that had been forced to close their doors. A tiny stage framed the end of the room. Bill pointed out the wooden traps along the stage apron, now empty of footlights.

Suddenly Bill raised a warning hand. In the silence, a deeply threatening sound rumbled across the prairie floor as if the voice of a train had moved underground. Bill flew to the window. A wall of snow was closing in. Bill grabbed my hand, and we rushed down the stairs and into his car. We barely closed the car door when the pelletized wind hit. Bill drove at walking speed with his head out the window, looking for shadows that could be people, another car, or even a real train.

Bill negotiated the highway and the railroad tracks and parked in front of my car. My little Honda cowered, whipped by the boxelder branches. We were blown across the sidewalk, and Bill pushed hard on his unlocked door, shoving me under his arm to safety. As we hung up our coats, Bill laughed and said, "You won't be going anywhere until tomorrow. Let me show you the guest suite upstairs."

Bill led us into a large, finished room under the eaves lined with bookshelves floor to ceiling. A bathroom nestled next to the chimney in the center, and behind it, a door led into a small bedroom with a sloped ceiling. I was to learn later that Bill's home was a Friday night oasis for local writers and had sheltered many others trapped by circumstance in Minneota. Bill spoke with great affection.

"This was my mother's bed. You should be comfortable for the night. Now come on downstairs, and I'll start some coffee."

Comfortable? This was an unimaginable situation for a kid from Richfield. I had stumbled into a book but didn't recognize the author.

The rooms downstairs were also lined with books. They may have been the only insulation. The windows were stuffed with rags and dead boxelder bugs, harmless dead or alive. We sat in the central room where a space heater worked hard. I was in awe of this Icelandic giant and struggled to loosen my tongue. How in god's name would I keep talking all afternoon? Bill solved the problem. When he experienced discomfort, he drifted into his music room to play his grand piano, and I heard some of the boxelder music for the first time. It was more abstract (my parents would have said "artsy") than I had anticipated and would require a choreographer who could bridge many dance styles. Not Gusztav. His lifestyle was incompatible with the Lyric's development—he would be in Hungary during the upcoming summer of rehearsals.

That evening as the wall of white turned into a mere blizzard, Bill called a friend named "Rez." He told Rez we would be over for supper and promised to rent a movie. Bill handed me my coat, and we were off into the snow to the local video store where we rented *The Producers*. When we arrived at the home of John and Lorna Rezmerski, I was flabbergasted. John (Rez) had conducted a poetry residency in my classroom in Babbitt several years earlier, and Lorna was Bill's cousin.

Before I left the next day in brilliant sunshine to follow the plow back to Marshall where Gusztav waited and worried, Bill and I laid out a plan to perform the show at The Big Store in Minneota. I had been snowed into a working relationship with Bill Holm.

Back in Minneapolis, I wrote proposals asking for support from the Minneota School District Community Education Program and from SMAHC. By Spring, both proposals were funded. I booked a fall performance weekend in The Big Store, followed by two weekends in Minneapolis. The voices in my head had quieted into boxelder bugs "breathing in the dark grove." There was room for music now. The Boxelder Bug Polka stuck in my brain for days at a time.

A Second Venue

When I first entered the Minneapolis Theatre Garage at Lyndale and Franklin in Minneapolis, Hosmer Brown, a young actor/entrepreneur, peeked up at me through dark, sweat-soaked curls from his position on hands and knees. He was laying hardwood flooring that was suitable for dancers. The building originally had been a garage for repairing trucks. Hosmer promised to have it ready by fall. I signed up for the first rental slot in September, 1988.

Next, I hired Lewis Whitlock, a well-known choreographer and dancer at the Chanhassen Dinner Theatre and Penumbra Theatre in St. Paul. He had trained locally and later danced in *The Wiz* (an all-black staging of *The Wizard of Oz*) on Broadway and then in its first national tour, followed by the role of "Zooter" in the Broadway production and subsequent film of *Zoot Suit*. Lewis later directed and choreographed *The Color Purple* at Park Square Theater in St. Paul in 2015.

Lewis Whitlock. Photo by Nancy Campbell.

The highly strenuous dance auditions at the Theater Garage left some of the dancers limping with bloodied feet. Of the six actor/dancers that we cast, two were proficient actors and the others were primarily dancers willing to take a risk. Their ethnicities added visual interest— Pacific Islander, Caucasian, Puerto Rican and African American.

LEP-TO-COR-IS TRI-VIT-TA-TUS. E. E. Balcos, Laura Taswell, Elizabeth Wiley, Hector Cruz, Joey Babay, Novick Inge Stubbs.

Bill Holm offered his services pro bono, and Bob Hindel composed additional music. Since working with Bob on *Nessie*, I not only knew him as a brilliant musician, but as a free spirit who had left a well-paid job in the computer industry to pursue an itinerant life in music—teaching, directing church music programs, accompanying ballet classes, writing a musical based on the abortion issue, and sustaining friendships within the arts community.

Bob paired up with Bill for performances, and they alternated between the piano and the harpsichord. In Minneota, Bill moved his harpsichord from home to the opera house, where an old upright piano had been tuned for the show. Later at the Theater Garage in Minneapolis, Nancy Campbell provided the harpsichord, and I moved my own piano from home. It's always good to have a friend with a harpsichord, right?

I was working full time during the day and at rehearsals every evening and weekends. My colleagues were my closest friends. With help from board members, I whirled in time with the Boxelder Bug Polka, covering clerical and production chores:

1. printing mailing labels, delivering bulk mail to the post office,
2. scheduling board meetings,
3. preparing financial reports,
4. interviewing and hiring designers and crew members,
5. signing contracts with actors and staff,
6. paying bills,
7. managing the production schedule,
8. and keeping up with phone calls.

Marge Stanton whirled in her own fashion—designing and writing the Lyric newsletter featuring Nancy Campbell's photograph of Lewis Whitlock, writing press releases, and producing invitations to the fundraisers.

The Prairie Garden

The set design had been developed from abstract drawings by Randy Scholes in the Milkweed edition of *Boxelder Bug Variations*. I loved the images, but I needed to spend time in the natural world that had bred Bill's relationship with planet Earth. Whereby I loved trees, shade, and dappled light and felt less vulnerable cocooned in shadow. Bill loved the big sky of the wind-swept prairie, the sun-drenched spaces where everything was visible all the way to the horizon. Nancy Campbell wanted to capture Bill's world with her 35 mm camera.

Nancy and I pulled up to Bill's house and found him waiting on the porch.

In July, Nancy and I spent a weekend roving the rural by-ways around Minneota, including a trip led by Bill to Daren Gislason's unique garden. Daren was Bill's older cousin. His garden had been memorialized in Bill's first book, *The Music of Failure*, and was beloved by Bill's fans. The garden was in Westerheim Township (western township) in Lyon County, organized in 1876. The north end was an Icelandic settlement where Daren's folks lived. Bill's folks lived further on in Yellow Medicine County. The rest of the township was Belgian.

The garden was an unused piece of farmland owned by a Belgian family named Buysse, located at a bend in the Yellow Medicine River which came from the west and curved to go south and east, where backwaters flooded a tree-filled ravine every spring and then receded to leave the soil well-watered and fertilized. A bird feeder and beaver dam endured this seasonal change.

Our car approached the garden through a narrow passage framed by corn nearly six feet tall, and then we drove onto dry prairie grass. An old sofa faced west, badly faded and suffering from mildew. As we got out of the car, a slim man with rumpled hair emerged from a wooded area. He carried a large pail of river water in each hand, pulling attention to his arms. He wore denim cut-offs, a sleeveless shirt, and running shoes. Nancy murmured, "Look at those biceps. Those pails must weigh a ton."

Bill called out, "Daren, I've brought you some charming guests."

Daren set down one pail and poured water from the other on some giant cactus plants, Opuntias native to Minnesota, that he had dug up and transferred from the Minnesota River Valley just east of Granite Falls. He smiled shyly, "Make yourselves at home. You know your way." His face was weathered from the sun, his hair bleached nearly white.

We set off on a worn footpath cut through prairie grass by Daren's mower along a fence line, which sported empty bird houses claimed by squirrels and guarded carefully from any sparrows or martins that would have fit through their holes. So far, Bill was the tallest structure in view. Daren had thrown some wildflower mix across the fence line. The pink of wild roses and purple of spiderwort and sweet clover blinked under the long grass. The path took us downhill, along the perimeter of a small woods filling a ravine, and ended at the river, where an old recliner faced the water. Towering, fast-growing cottonwoods fluttered lustrous green leaves, stubbier box elders rustled their maple shapes, and weeping willows draped the riverbank, a favorite habitat for all three.

We entered the woods along a deeply shaded path that broadened into a circle open to the prairie on one side. The rest of the circle was framed by white rocks from the nearby river, nearly uniform in size, reminiscent of the Icelandic gardens on the windswept island in the North Atlantic that were pictured in a coffee-table book newly arrived at Bill's house. The rocks were backed by round clusters of hostas planted by Daren, which gave way to the greenery of the ravine below. A row of immature tomato plants marched in single file from east to west. Nancy started photographing, the only sound the click of her camera—and birdsong. Bill led us to a small one-room cabin built by Daren and a friend from 4 x 8 pieces of plywood with tin for the roof. It measured about 8 x 10 inches and was set on stilts for protection from flooding. We climbed several steps and found a table with a guest book, which Bill invited us to sign. I studied the other names but found none that I recognized.

I had learned from reading *The Music of Failure* that the greatest mistake a visitor could make was to ask who owned the garden. The idea of private ownership dissolved in the sacred space beneath the box elder trees. Nancy clicked again and again, trying to capture the magic of that circular space. The treetops were eye level with the hill that would return us to the cacti and our cars. We climbed slowly, passing flowers spared by the local rabbits and deer—four o'clocks, marigolds, gladioli, and chrysanthemums. We walked in silence to the car, shimmering in the prairie heat.

Nancy Campbell rests before getting back into the car.

Onstage

Thanks to a gracious offer from Loyce Houlton, then retired from the Minnesota Dance Theatre, we rehearsed in her private dance studio at the Hennepin Center for the Arts (now part of the Cowles Center). But when Bill and Bob found two pianos side by side in another part of the building, they squeezed together on the skimpy piano bench and improvised on themes from "The Boxelder Bug Polka," turning it into a wild and fast duet. To find them, I followed the sound and shooed them back to rehearsal. The duet became the finale in the show, a wildly spinning dance that ended with the music dropping out as dancers lost their footing one by one until they were all sprawled on the floor. "The piano string stops trembling, but boxelder bugs keep dancing…"

On Labor Day in 1988, we moved everyone to Minneota. Volunteers led by Linda Canton had put in long hours preparing the second-floor performance space of The Big Store in temperatures ranging from 90° to 103°F.

The real thing, dancing on the screen door. Photo by Nancy Campbell.

I arrived first with Rebecca Bringgold, my stage manager, and climbed the now dustless steps to find Linda polishing old organs that still rimmed the room. Tall windows filled the street-side wall, thrown open in hopes of cross ventilation. Near the high ceiling, several huge power cords snaked directly from the transformer outside, passing through the open window closest to the stage, feeding power to the stage lights. Rows of old furniture had been removed, revealing a solid wood floor. The first fifteen feet in front of the stage formed the actor's dance space, and the rest of the room soon would be filled with rows of folding chairs. We were on the prairie with no air conditioning and lots of dust.

Kevin Egeland and Pat Danz (Mankato grads) pulled up to the side door in a rented truck, toting the set they had designed and built. I had met them as students at Mankato State. Kevin was blonde and stocky, his body already gaining a mature shape, contrasting with Pat, slender, boyish, tall, and dark-haired. Bruce Schultz, the lighting designer, arrived next, with lighting instruments, dimmers, and a lighting board in his small truck. Taller than the other two, he was well muscled, blonde, and handsome. He was also a Lyric Theater board member.

Kevin and Pat gloved up, loaded the primitive elevator, and hauled on the ropes. Schultz bounded up the long flight of steps carrying an eight-foot metal pipe balanced on one shoulder. He then crawled out above the ceiling to drop and install the pole which would hold lighting instruments. Kevin and Pat installed a curved step unit resembling piano keys to convey the actors from the tiny stage to the dance floor and to create an elevated stage area when they weren't dancing. The piano and harpsichord already sat at opposing ends of the small stage. Kevin unrolled a canvas drop sporting a huge bug stylized in shades of deep blue and tomato red to be hung upstage, masking the back wall. A large, elliptical bug gave shape to free-standing wing pieces, one at each side of the set. Floor-bound lighting trees threw side light to add dimension but also added to the prairie heat.

In the meantime, the actors arrived and were housed in empty units at the senior living complex. The staff stayed at Bill's house. Dozens of hands helped with every step. People from the regional arts council, from Southwest State in Marshall, and from the towns of Minneota and nearby

Canby appeared as if by magic, including Bill's teaching colleague, Perry Leuders, and the arts council's executive director, Rob Ross. The arrival of plumed elephants and male peacocks wouldn't have surprised me.

Daren Gislason had been instrumental in funding and publicizing the show. During the school year, he taught third graders. I imagined him as a pied piper, leading his young charges on forays into the natural world—or perhaps a garden on the banks of the Yellow Medicine River. On opening night, I discovered a bit of P. T. Barnum in this surprising man. Despite the tremendous heat, Daren appeared in a full tuxedo and black top hat to act as chief usher. The old opera house was packed with people on folding chairs and spilling up the walls onto old church organs. I spotted the Rezmerskis near the back. It was a relief when the sun went down, but the windows remained open, attracting a few mosquitoes.

Earlier, Nancy and I had edited the slides into a pre-show prologue lit primarily by a slide projector. Imagine huge heads of cows and other farm images emerging from the giant, painted boxelder bug. In performance, Bob Hindel improvised on the piano, matching melodies to imagery. At the end of the prologue, the interior of Daren's garden settled on the abstract bug, merging bug, trees, dappled shade, and a circle of white rocks. And then we were onstage with the bugs.

I longed for Gusztav to be part of this important milestone for me and the Lyric Theater. He had to be back from Hungary for the opening of classes in Marshall, but I hadn't heard from him. And then he bounced into the theater with a young woman on his arm. He headed to the first row before I could say hello. After the show, he congratulated Bill and Bob, introducing his date as a student that he was encouraging in dance. She touched his arm. Staking her claim? He shook my hand as if I were nothing more than a former colleague. I turned away to accept congratulations from other Holm fans. And then Gusztav was gone down the stairs. No parting, no "I'll call you soon." As night descended, the streets filled with shadows and my heart with melancholy.

Evening shows on September 8 and 9 were performed to full houses and tremendous applause. We took lots of pictures, even some with the actors on the roof of the opera house trying to cool down. We were on top of the world, looking out at the prairie spreading all the way to the horizon.

Atop the Opera House. Rebecca Bringgold, Elizabeth Wiley, Joey Babay, Laura Taswell, Novick Inge Stubbs, Bill Holm, Hector Cruz, E. E. Balcos, Sally Childs, Bob Hindel. Photo by Nancy Campbell.

Critical Response

Niggling worries that Holm's literary allusions would lead to a charge of academic elitism were soon put to rest by Bill's humor and easy connection with the audience. I had sent a press release to Ann Grauvogl, staff writer for the *Argus Leader* in Sioux Falls, South Dakota, providing a framework for the show that "reaffirmed human values, whimsically held up foibles of humanity for investigation, and celebrated the environment as we know it in the Midwest." After seeing the show, Ms. Grauvogl described it less pedantically: "a shifting collage of words and notes, movement and stillness, metaphor and reality." Beautiful.

We returned to Minneapolis for shows running September 21 through October 8, 1988, where we had to face the metro press and other theater people who were mostly still strangers to our little band of artists. The Lyric Theater might be described best by Bill Holm's marvelous paraphrase—"imaginary windows filled with real boxelder bugs." (Based on Marianne Moore's famous line, "Imaginary gardens with real toads in them.") The Lyric Theater could have existed in virtual reality, a term that hadn't been coined yet, at least to my knowledge. But the bugs were real.

Peter Vaughan of the *Star Tribune* gave us a solid pre-show article and a review that was much more positive than I had expected. A capsule of Vaughan's review said:

> A novel blend of music, words, and dance that brings the erudite whimsy of Bill Holm's book, *Boxelder Bug Variations*, to the stage. At its best, it's funny and poignant. At other times, the attempts to link Holm's words to a variety of dance styles is awkward or forced. On balance, though, this is an imaginative, well-executed marriage of divergent artistic forms.

Bill didn't like the word "whimsy," but I thought the review was both accurate and positive.

In 1988, however, along with Peter Vaughan, we were ahead of the times. Maggie Kramm in the *Pioneer Press* said that "the 'Bug' fails to add bite to poetry." She fell into the inevitable trap of comparing the work to Garrison Keillor:

> This Lyric Theater production is a modest, sincere but mostly unsuccessful effort to re-create the homespun charm, the understated humor, the delight in simple things that gave Garrison Keillor's *Prairie Home Companion* its great popularity.

Wrong. With Holm present, no one dared to breathe Garrison Keillor's name. Bill had filled in for Keillor on public television several times but read from his own poetry. From then on, he was strongly associated in people's minds with Keillor's down-home, folksy style. Bill felt his own style to be unique—he felt stigmatized by his association with *Prairie Home Companion*. Had Maggie been present, she would have been skewered by those amazing blue eyes.

Margaret O'Donnell in *The Minnesota Daily* used her review to show off her own creativity:

> *Boxelder Bug Variations* is like a cross between *The Far Side* and *Doonesbury* written by Whitman and Thoreau on an afternoon when they were feeling a little more loose than is usually acceptable. The Lyric Theater fails to preserve the sense of honesty and amusement found in Holm's original work... the actors were unable to deliver the lines convincingly, in part because they're dancing, they take the subject too seriously. With huge elliptical, inaccurate representations of boxelder bugs propped up on the stage, they perform modern abstract dances with frowns fixed on their faces. The only magic left in the stage version was Holm himself, the Norwegian [she must have meant Icelandic] poet from Minnesota [did she mean Minneota?] playing his harpsichord in honor of his pet subject, boxelder bugs.

Had Ms. O'Donnell interviewed Bill, she might have applied her creativity appropriately. Had she also interviewed Randy Scholes, the art director from Milkweed who designed the abstract bugs used in Bill's book—the basis for the stylized bugs on the set—she might have understood that Holm's pet subject wasn't boxelder bugs, but rather a metaphor for living like a proper American transcendentalist.

Hector and Novik in Birdsong. Photo by Nancy Campbell.

After the dust had settled, Bill said, "With little praise and even less funding, we did an elegant production!" Yes, elegant. Bill's musical pieces were abstract and whimsical—the "Boxelder Bug Tango," "Boxelders on Parade," "Birdsong," etc. Bob Hindel's additional music grounded the polka and the blues. Many of Bill's numbers demanded molded expressions to pay respect to earlier times featuring the minuet or the waltz.

From bottom to top: Laura Taswell and E. E. Balcos; Novik Inge Stubbs and Hector Cruz; Elizabeth Wiley and Joey Babay. Photo by Nancy Campbell.

Bill did not attempt to emulate or copy Keillor's homespun style. He was just Bill, educated in the classics, totally engaged in everything around him, a world citizen with a gentle but lively spirit, larger than life. But people carry their own baggage into the theater, so we had to live with the consequences.

Bill was enormously pleased with every move the dancers made. Peter Vaughan described Bill as having a "playful spirit that impels his artistry." Vaughan expanded on his appreciation of Holm: "He is frequently self-deprecatory, often funny and never puffed with self-pretension." Bill also shed light on the human condition.

Bill Holm. Portrait by Nancy Campbell.

I loved this show deeply, but it was an experience designed to toughen me up. The show didn't fit preconceived ideas of form, which carried huge risk. I remain deeply grateful to Peter Vaughan, who was far thinking and ahead of the times.

Boxelder Bug Variations was performed again on May 13, 1989, as part of a writer's festival at Southwest State University in Marshall. One of the actors was unable to join us this time, so we had to reorganize some of the lines and dances. We had a videotape of the show as performed at the Theater Garage, so we set up rehearsals in the Andahazy Ballet Studio in St. Paul, and I collaborated with the remaining five performers to restructure the show. Gusztav had called, and we were back together, so at the Marshall performance, I added a solo for him, which filled out the show. He performed well, and I was still unaware that his department was demanding that he take on teaching assignments that would activate his post-polio syndrome to a level that taxed him to the point of collapse.

The minute the show came down in Marshall, the actors and technicians headed out for other commitments, and I was left amid this amazing set with a few male volunteers, including some SSU administrators. As we moved the set into the scene shop, I pleaded for efficient stacking of everything in the least amount of space possible. In the process, a hurried administrator commented that he had never seen anyone bend so far to accommodate other people. I flinched and thought *typical male response.* When we finished, the platforms resided in a large unruly stack. Later I fielded negative feedback from the tech staff, and my skin thickened a little more. But I was locked into my type—who liked to please others and willingly put forth extra effort to do so. I wasn't just being female.

I left Marshall in darkness, driving a large, empty Ryder truck back to Northeast Minneapolis where my car was parked. At five foot three, I had to sit partway forward on the seat in order to push the clutch all the way to the floor, and my arm was barely long enough to push the stick into third gear. The three-hour trip tested my strength and coordination. There was no radio. Only a few stars were visible between small towns. As I slowed to 35 mph in Buffalo Lake, I looked for lights in back rooms, imagining the occupants engaged in foreplay.

Back under city lights, I pulled next to a building with Ryder written in large letters on the side. I parked, exhausted and relieved and also a little scared as I gauged the distance from the truck to my car in a transitional part of town that housed many large vehicles and businesses closed for the night. I gathered my courage, and with a heightened sense of caution, crossed to my car and drove home.

My life was transformed again—the first time at the Bread Loaf School of English in an abundance of fireFlies, the second time in Minneota, Marshall, and Minneapolis among boxelder bugs.

In 1987 I met Don in the Skyway after work to tell him that I would file for divorce soon. My attorney advised me that I was entitled to half of Don's retirement account and was adamant about including that in the divorce agreement. Don's eyes widened, and he inhaled until I thought he would burst. "You will never see a cent of my retirement money."

I can still see him turning on his heel and stalking off, disappearing around a corner into the labyrinth. Shortly thereafter, he retired early on a mental disability, bought a pick-up truck and fifth-wheel camper, closed out his teachers' retirement account, and toured the United States for over a year before he ran out of money. In 1957 I had pledged, "Till death do us part." I thought I was entering a partnership. It wasn't. Perhaps I should have felt guilty. I didn't.

My oldest daughter told me that her father's biggest worry was that he would be left out of family celebrations. I asked Beth to assure him that would not happen, and I stayed true to my word. Don filled the role of father and eventually grandfather as my children grew to middle age. I straddled a fence, playing different roles as dictated by circumstances. It felt a lot like acting.

Hunting Cockroaches

With four years of production history, a mixed bag of reviews, and funding granted by the Regional Arts Council in Southwestern Minnesota, it was time to submit another grant to our local Regional Arts Council, MRAC. In workshops, I learned that grantors liked collaborations between artistic entities. Surely I could find a collaborator. I gathered my courage and called Peter Moore to talk about a shared production. He liked the idea, especially when I said I would write the grant proposal for submission to MRAC.

Peter was both artistic director and managing director of his theater, just like me. But the resemblance stopped there. New Classic produced contemporary plays in rented spaces and worked only with Equity actors. Peter started the theater to provide work for himself and his Equity colleagues. He made his living as an actor, director, and teacher, specializing in stage combat. He mounted productions when he had the time and felt he could afford it. I don't know what his mission statement said or even if he had one, but New Classic fulfilled the basic requirement for legitimate begging—incorporation as a 501©3 not-for-profit organization. Because Peter was well known and respected and did good work, audiences and funders would see our partnership as a wonderful opportunity for the Lyric.

Peter was looking for money to produce the area premiere of *Hunting Cockroaches*, a dark comedy by Janusz Glowacki. It was about an immigrant couple from Poland having a hard time in New York. Anka, a well-known actress in Warsaw, couldn't get work because of her accent; Jan, a writer, suffered from writer's block. The story unfolded with these two people in bed. As they tried to get some sleep, flashbacks brought characters from their past crawling like cockroaches from beneath the bed. The New York production was called "mordantly funny" by *Newsday* and "quintessentially brash" by the *New York Times*. We planned to do a joint production in the Theatre Garage from June 2 to 25, 1989. Unwittingly, the play gave people who had seen *Boxelder Bug Variations* an opportunity to tease me about being the "bug" theater.

Sure enough, MRAC granted $6,500 to the Lyric Theater for a shared production with New Classic. I took on the producer's role of providing space, marketing, and managing the budget. Peter hired actors under his AEA contract and paid them from grant money that I transferred to New Classic as needed. Publicity carried both the New Classic and Lyric Theater logos.

Peter and I hired Lou Salerni to direct the show. Lou left his position as artistic director of the Cricket Theatre in Minneapolis to head the

Theatre-Directing Graduate Program at Memphis State University. He agreed to direct the show at a vastly reduced fee—he called it a paid vacation—and set about hiring some of his favorite actors from his days at the Cricket—all members of the Actors' Equity Association. I still heard Bob Moss asking, "What makes you think you can control union actors?" Maybe Lou would show me the way.

We rehearsed at Mixed Blood Theater where Peter's brother Charlie worked. Located on the West Bank of the University of Minnesota, it had once been a fire station. The actors and staff arrived and fell into the easy banter of long-time colleagues. Peter pulled an afghan and a camera from his bag and set up publicity shots before the rehearsal got underway. Then, in two sentences, Peter laid out what he wanted them to do. The whole procedure took about six minutes. It was a significant learning moment for me.

A "cockroach" (SteveHendrickson) claims space in bed with Polish immigrants Anka Krupinski (Camille D'Ambrose) and her husband Jan (Bob Davis). Photo by Peter Moore.

I fell easily into the role of facilitator and relinquished decision-making to Peter. Lou, Peter, and the actors seemed to speak in shorthand with wonderful results. I stopped attending rehearsals to take care of administrative chores. At about this same time, my day job at the law firm changed to a supervisory level. Briggs was converting to personal computers, and I would attend classes along with the secretaries.

When we moved into the Theatre Garage for tech week, Lou surprised me after the first tech rehearsal when he stopped at the counter where I was sorting photographs for display and told me that I should take charge of scheduling reviewers in time to bear fruit. Very quietly, he said, "Peter talks the talk, but he expects you to follow through." And then he caught up with Peter and left me staring at their backs as they walked the walk through the front door, engaged in animated conversation. True to type, I had found my spot, working behind the scenes, taking care of details, acting like everyone's secretary or assistant. I must have been a serving wench in some other life.

The reviews were excellent. With an all-union cast, most everyone saw it as a New Classic production. I didn't object. The Lyric was seen moving in the inner theater circle, leading to more success. But I was naive. The Lyric was still a long way from executing our own Equity contract.

1989–90: Bridges to Cross

The theater was entering its fifth year. We had produced seven shows, and I was tired. I had been at the law firm for three years. The Lyric had survived for four. I ran on an empty plateau, not a hill in sight. What next for the Lyric?

Now that the Lyric no longer managed a booth at the Metrodome, we pursued other fund-raising ideas. We rounded up board members and friends to work alongside hundreds of other volunteers at an all-night inventory count at Dayton's Department Store. We had book parties for Tupperware and Discovery Toys, held another annual garage sale, and asked actors to help us with another gala at Nancy Campbell's home, all female-driven ideas with modest results. Everett now had three male colleagues on the board, joined by eight females, a 2:1 ratio.

In September 1989, I bought my first computer, with advice from Kate Schultz of the Word Processing Department at Briggs. She took me to a computer warehouse in Bloomington, where I bought an unbranded CPU, keyboard, monitor, and printer. Kate remained my go-to person for years.

In August, we held a board retreat to try to establish a clear direction for our productions and how we were going to finance and market them. Over time, our board stabilized to include Sally Anderson (Dain Bosworth), Everett Janssen (president, private business owner), Carol (Bronski) Michels (office clerk, secretary/treasurer), Marge Stanton (bond analyst/legal secretary, marketing director), Susan Slack (finance), and me. When Laurie Rivard Montanez (Norwest Financial Advisors) joined, she became our treasurer and trained me to produce financial reports using Quicken software. The board never dipped below six, and the longevity of these people provided stability as others came and went. We kept seeking a stable mix of business folk and theater artists.

Chapter 7: Curves in the Road

A New Partner – Cyd

Cyd McKuen Haynes, a much younger director, recently married and new to town, asked for a meeting. Tall, with auburn hair and an air of competence, Cyd volunteered to work with me—no money but a great title—Artistic Associate. We would select plays and alternate as directors. Our director's stipend would give us a sense of professionalism—and a little money.

Cyd's day job (Managing Director for Northern Sign Theater for the deaf) meshed well with volunteering for the Lyric. My day job didn't mesh at all. I had become the office administrator for the secretarial staff at Briggs and Morgan (Minneapolis branch) and walked a fine line to keep it all balanced. Now that Don and I were divorced, I felt free to spend more time with Gusztav, that is, when he was available. He was well into middle age and still wanted to create his own family, which took him out of my circle of friends and often back to Hungary. His letters were eloquent and deeply personal but skirted the subject of love. He focused on researching his family history, which took him into the Făgăraş Mountains in Transylvania. His castles were real and very old. Mine were about 450 square feet of stage space that I hoped to rent at the Hennepin Center for the Arts or the Theatre Garage.

My parents lived nearby. They were in their eighties, but Dad still managed the household. My free time was split between walking along Minnehaha Parkway to maintain my health and stopping by their house to help maintain theirs. Mother was losing ground to crippling arthritis and macular degeneration, legally blind, and no longer able to drive. Carol Michels performed housekeeping chores. Dad stuck to caretaking and selling real estate. I still enjoyed thinking about the day Mom learned to drive and all that she had taught me by that simple act—don't be afraid; act first; you can apologize later.

I thought about money all the time. I followed Dad's cash and carry rules. My financial worries were personal as well as professional.

Leah

Bob Hindel's associate, Marius Andahazy of the Andahazy School of Ballet in St. Paul, passed along a script he received from an unknown woman with the suggestion that the story might become a ballet. The woman was Leah Bernstein, the script, Bernstein's "The Frog Princess." I didn't see a Russian fairy tale as a Lyric production, especially given the lessons learned with Nessie, but I was intrigued by Bernstein's unique storytelling.

I visited Leah at her home near Theodore Wirth Parkway in north Minneapolis. She came to the door wearing a cotton print dress, shapeless beige cardigan, long cotton stockings and slippers, her gray hair captured beneath a print scarf wrapped turban style atop a wrinkled face suffused with warmth. Her brown-spotted spaniel squeezed between us as she pulled me into the overheated living room. A well-used baby grand stood in front of a small bay window, with music stacked haphazardly on shelves and atop the piano. I had stepped back in time by about sixty years.

"Come, come," Leah waved me to the dining room. "Just leave your coat on that chair," she said, pointing to a wing chair. "I have chicken. You like? Just tell me what you like." Leah was a Russian-American Jew, and it was reflected in her speech.

While I filled up with baked chicken, rolls and canned peaches, Leah poured out her life story. Her cadence leant a sense of rote memorization, a litany that she had repeated many times. When the last word dropped into place, she stared at me, her eyes gleaming.

I visited Leah again with composer/pianist Bob Hindel in tow. Leah fed us more chicken accompanied by green beans and cookies, told us stories, played the piano and then asked Bob to play. He settled in at the piano, and her face lit up as music poured from his fingers.

"You have brought me a real pianist!"

Bob's eyes were riveted on Leah as he played, drinking in her enthusiasm and laughing softly to himself.

Leah's life and music were inseparable. She spoke of the difficulties she experienced as a young Jewish girl during the Revolutionary years in Ukraine, her arrival in Minneapolis with her parents and sister in 1923, how she discovered her gift for music, how family ties affected her choices in life, her first job dancing with her sister in musical shows at the Orpheum, the scholarship to Julliard that could not be used due to crushing financial reasons—and her marriage to Pincus Bernstein. There was certainly a play to be pulled from the stories she told, and it would have to include live music. Maybe even dance. Since Leah was beginning to show signs of dementia, her story needed to be captured and told very soon.

I talked with Richard (Dick) Rousseau, a local writer who turned history into dramatic form for the Science Museum. Leah agreed to let Dick write the play. She gave us a tape she had made of her musical compositions along with copies of the original scores, and I asked Dick to look for ways to incorporate music and dance into the script.

An informal reading of the first draft was held in March 1989. A second, more formal reading was held at the Theatre Garage on May 22. Heidi Arneson, a tiny actress with a big talent, read the part of Leah on both occasions, and a local piano teacher provided piano accompaniment and underscore pulled from Leah's music.

A roundtable discussion followed the reading, which included dramaturg Michael Lupu of the Guthrie and Tessa Bridal from the Science Museum. Leah was too ill to attend. Our discussion circle numbered about ten. We kept trying to turn our little band of volunteers into an orchestra of new recruits with little success.

The playwright arranged a more formal reading at the Playwrights' Center, and we received lots of positive feedback. Major funding could provide a stipend for the playwright and launch a production.

I submitted a proposal to the Metropolitan Regional Arts Council (MRAC), hoping to ride the coattails of our previous award for *Hunting Cockroaches,* as well as our increased visibility and reputation. I attended the adjudicator's panel discussion, seated with other applicants lining an outside wall. I thought our review was going well until one panelist raised her hand. She sat with arms tightly folded across her midsection, the elbow of her raised arm resting in the palm of the other hand, nesting close to her body. She asked, "What made them think that Leah would agree to this?"—an echo of Bob Moss—"What makes you think you can …" This time I had the answer, and I could barely silence my tongue. The rules governing the panel discussion allowed only panelists to speak.

I was appalled. I had stated in my description of the project that Leah was involved from its inception and was delighted to have her story told. The temperature plunged as other panelists responded to the question. Proposal denied. Was it possible the woman responsible for the denial had not read all of the proposal? Did she feel that we were the wrong people to produce this because she assumed we had no Jews working on the project other than Leah herself? Was she a Jew defending her own territory? I wanted to weep. We had so much invested in the project, and our small fundraisers could not cover our needs.

When I delivered the news to Dick, he said he could go no further without a stipend. We had reached the end of the road.

Leah's increased dementia put her into the Shalom Nursing Home in St. Paul, and her house was sold to help pay for her care. Leah and I had to let go of our dream.

My self-confidence leached down into my shoes—heaviness dragged at my feet. I retreated into production chores and yielded the directing reins to Cyd.

1990: Wordplay Antics

Cyd pitched a small cast musical to the Lyric board, *The Texas Chainsaw Manicurist,* by her friend, Scott Warrender. The show originated in 1985 as a smattering of funny songs—witty, wacky, and delightful. Cyd had been directing at the Texas Shakespeare Festival when Scott was concocting this craziness upstairs in a very small office with nothing but a very large grand piano—and Scott. At the end of the summer, some of Cyd's Shakespeare actors performed a few of the songs for an invited audience, and Cyd fell in love with the material immediately. In addition to the title song, musical numbers included "I Love Her Creamy Nougat," "Nightingale by Night," "Mr. Potato Head Married My Mother," and "My Barbie was the Tramp of the Neighborhood," to name a few.

**Dorian Chalmers, Joey Babay, Steve Sutherland, Colleen Everitt.
Photo by Greg Trochill.**

**Dorian Chalmers, Colleen Everitt, Joey Babay, Steve Sutherland.
Photo by Greg Trochill.**

For five years, the show remained a collection of funny songs. It opened in New York and Seattle, and each production was revived by popular demand. Meanwhile, audiences in Orlando, Houston, and Anchorage also enjoyed this bizarre mix of familiar scenarios and pop images. Cyd and Scott began making the show more cohesive, dropping a few songs, adding new ones, and coming up with a production that would premiere in Minneapolis.

Warrender shipped all the props and costumes to Cyd, and a talented cast went to work, including Joey Babay (from *Boxelder Bug Variations*) and Dorian Chalmers (a veteran of the shows I directed at Mankato State). Pat Danz (*Boxelder Bug Variations*) designed a set made up entirely of paint and large rolls of paper in primary colors, even painting large red circles on the old upright piano.

We opened in the Theater Garage and ran from January 19 to February 25, 1990. Vaughan's review in the *Star Tribune* bore the title, "Fresh musical revue's gentle satire laments our loss of innocence." Roy Close in the *Pioneer Press* said, "Manicurist abuzz with humor." Cyd and Dorian garnered praise from both reviewers. Our costs totaled $12,267, which needed only a little supplementation at closing. Our tickets were a modest $9.00. We listed thirty-one donors in the playbill; many were current or former work colleagues, family, and one foundation. We talked about a remount, but we couldn't pull everyone together for a second round.

Prisoners of Conscience Strut the Boards

I first heard of *When the First 200 Letters Came* from Jane Wager, the same woman who doubled Don's crazy bridge bid years earlier in Ely. Jane had moved to Colorado and volunteered at the Arvada Center for the Arts just outside of Denver. The Arvada Center had commissioned Marie Cartier to write and direct a play based on Amnesty International's letter-writing campaigns for people in Third World countries who were "disappeared" by soldiers representing totalitarian regimes. It was staged as part of Arvada's month of activities based on the theme "Prisoners of Conscience." Jane knew I was drawn to unusual scripts that demanded creative staging, and she knew I had great sympathy for the peace and justice movement. Since Minneapolis was the home of the Center for Victims of Torture, it seemed worth exploring a Minneapolis production of the play. Jane gave me Marie Cartier's contact information, and I talked to David Stamps at the local chapter of Amnesty International regarding co-production.

Cyd was interested in directing this piece, but we both worried that our Midwestern audiences wouldn't be able to tolerate a visceral production as suggested by the playwright. We wanted them to feel empathy for the characters and to embrace the letter-writing program sponsored by Amnesty International. Cyd's director training had focused on Shakespeare's plays, a playground that tolerated a great deal of experimentation. Marie Cartier's play was a clarion call for experimentation to someone with Cyd's background.

Amnesty International offered to buy out one performance in Minneapolis and one in St. Cloud at $1,800. They also asked for permission to video the production for educational purposes. The University of Minnesota liked the idea of scheduling a fall production with a performance on both the Minneapolis and St. Paul campuses.

This show required targeted marketing, especially to churches and peace and justice activists. Press releases would include Amnesty president Jack Healy's belief that "music and the arts are the most effective means of spreading Amnesty's word," a statement that correlated well with the Lyric's mission.

Cyd received a small grant from the Composer's Forum and hired her husband to formulate a musical track for the show. In a show this experimental, he assumed free rein to experiment with dissonance. As a result, the "music" elevated the pain of the storytelling.

The show ran from September 28 through October 5 at the Theatre Garage and for two performances on October 12 and 13, both at Coffman Memorial Union at the University of Minnesota. The St. Cloud performances never took place. The video was made, however.

Playwright Marie Cartier came to see Cyd's production and was not pleased. Her production in Denver had attacked the audience—throwing objects, loud aggressive delivery of lines, etc. She had also included lines that tied America's death penalty to the act of torture, a secondary issue. After discussion with her actors, Cyd cut those lines, which would further alienate the audience with what many would call propaganda. Cyd improved the structural arc of the script by adding a scene that told the story of Terry Anderson, an American journalist for the Associated Press, who was taken hostage by Shiite Hezbollah militants of the Islamic Jihad organization in Lebanon and imprisoned for 2,454 days before his release in 1991.

Marie was unhappy with Cyd for cutting something without her input, so that became another whole issue. Cyd felt that her production was true to the intention of the script and the playwright. She had accomplished her goal—that an audience member could not leave without feeling changed somehow. In the program, Cyd included in her "Notes From the Director" a quote from Franky Schaeffer's *Sham Pearls for Real Swine:*

> The Arts ask hard questions. Art hurts, slaps, and
> defines. Art is interested in truth: in bad words
> spoken by bad people, in good words spoken by
> good people, in sin and goodness, in life, sex,
> birth, color, texture, death, love, hate, nature,
> man, religion, music, God, fire, water, air, and
> earth. Art tears down, builds up, and redefines. Art
> is uncomfortable.

Writing for the *Star Tribune*, Peter Vaughan said, "Making torture dramatic needs little effort. Making it palatable in a play is a different story." In his review, Vaughan felt the play "with its litany of pain and humiliation numbs the senses."

Roy Close from the *Pioneer Press* said that *When the First 200 Letters Came* was "a bad play that espoused a good cause." He called it a litany "as undramatic as a laundry list." The litany, "when the first 200 letters came," was intended by the playwright as a call to action.

The previous two shows shared several elements: They were both episodic, intended to provide food for thought, and were developed by young playwrights with current events in mind. But where *Chainsaw* had music composed by the playwright, *Letters* gained lyricism only through language. Where *Chainsaw* poked fun at current events, *Letters* pointed to blackly tragic events. *Chainsaw* told us to laugh; *Letters* told us to cry. *Chainsaw* was an evening of fun; *Letters* was a call to action.

Many people brush aside reviews with the comment, "It's only one person's opinion." I would add "read by thousands of people." Reviews are not intended as marketing tools, but they provide warnings and do affect ticket sales, especially for theaters that cannot afford expensive ads. Before I started directing plays, I read reviews to weed out shows that would waste my limited money and time. Critics educated and honed my developing tastes. I still had lots to learn.

The Critic's Role

After years of reading reviews from a director's point of view, I learned that the role of the critic is much more. The critic anchors the play in its historical context, sets standards, and provides a thoughtful and reasoned analysis. A good critic will never intend to cause harm or base comments on taste, which is personal and subjective and not a fair basis for analysis.

Michael Evans, writing for the *Houston Chronicle* (chron.com), quotes from definitions by famous critics:

> Alfred Kazin (twentieth-century critic): Critics are thinkers whose opinion is valuable to the artist; the critic understands the past, processes the present, and shapes the future.

> Randal Jarrell (children's author and literary critic): A critic is an instrument of seeing and conveying the truth about it.

> Oscar Wilde (nineteenth-century critic, playwright, writer): A participant in art who reshapes or adds to a work of art in ways not intended by its creator.

In the past, critics represented an elite class, people with access to museums, literature, and theatre. Their point of view originated from their place at the intersection of past and future cultures. With the advent of computers, websites, and the proliferation of blogs, anyone can be a critic, whether or not they have ever read a book—or another review. In my opinion, the worst kind of review is self-indulgent—an exercise in cleverness and verbal gymnastics—often unsupported by research or education. Knowledgeable people may still be able to sift the chaff from the wheat, but the role played online where anyone may claim to be a critic has robbed criticism of its veracity.

The first time I watched Cyd's production, I became deeply involved with the material, and since litanies are an accepted convention in works of art, neither of us recognized the effect that they would have until the audience was in their seats. In the program, I invited audience members to linger after the show to talk with representatives of Amnesty International, the Center for Victims of Torture, and the Minnesota Lawyers International Human Rights Committee, who were available at every performance. Our diverse group of actors also stopped in the lobby on the way out. As one of them said in her bio, "I wish this show to be a celebration of awareness…in the words of a recently released hostage, 'It's time to talk. It's obviously time to talk.'"

We had to cover a $2,900 deficit; we had learned some expensive lessons.

It was time for me to direct again. The next play would bring the Lyric's work into focus and point us toward more success and stability, or I would hang up my shingle. Night after night, I had worked alone, reconciling box office reports to bank statements. I was wearing out. I could not reconcile myself to this routine on an ongoing basis.

We moved into home territory with Minnesota writer Jon Hassler, a writer with a fan club.

A Trip to St. Cloud – Jon Hassler

Jon Hassler started writing his first novel, *Staggerford*, in 1970 when he was thirty-seven, and it was published in 1976. His very funny second novel, *Simon's Night*, came out in 1979. I devoured Hassler's books the moment they were published. In 1989, when a story appeared in the Sunday *Star Tribune* about a St. Cloud production of *Simon's Night*, I devoured that too. Within the hour, photographer Nancy Campbell phoned and said, "Let's go to St.Cloud." Our mutual friend, visual artist Laurel Gregorian, offered to drive, so we were on our way with only minutes to spare for a 2:00 p.m. matinee.

The play had been workshopped at both the Playwrights' Center and the Cricket Theatre over an eight-year period. It was scheduled for production and then canceled by the Cricket, next by the Chimera, and finally by Theatre 65 due to financial restraints that led to the closure of all three theaters. Mr. Hassler finally turned his back on the Twin Cities and invited the Inverted Pyramid Company, a community theater in St. Cloud devoted to producing new plays, to mount *Simon's Night* for the first time.

The play centers on Simon Shea, a retired English professor who escapes into the Norman Home for the elderly, seeking a haven. Instead, he encounters the home's quirky residents who have succumbed to proprietress Hattie Norman's notions of what is appropriate behavior for older people. The only holdout is Mr. Smalleye, a Native American whose fierce independence is asserted by his determination to shoot one last goose. While Simon struggles to adapt to the Norman Home, his estranged wife Barbara returns unannounced. Since she fled with the art teacher twenty-five years earlier, Simon's only contact with his wife has been an annual exchange of Christmas cards. Simon tries to convince Barbara he belongs at the Norman Home by telling her, "If I could sell poetry to twenty-year-olds, why shouldn't I be able to sell purpose to the elderly?" Barbara counters with, "There's more to life than television and cookies." Simon prevails with both disastrous and hilarious results and is changed in the process.

By intermission, I knew that I wanted to direct *Simon's Night*. After the show, my friends pointed me towards a group of people gathered around a middle-aged man, smiling as friends showered him with congratulations.

"That's him. Go, go, talk to him." They herded me closer, one on each side.

Jon Hassler wore a white turtleneck under a black pullover sweater as if he were a man of the cloth. His rounded shoulders suggested much time bent over a book or a manuscript. I hovered just outside the edge of the group, but my brain froze, silencing my tongue. I turned to my friends and said, "I'm not ready. I'll write to him in the next few days. Let's get back to Minneapolis."

In my first letter to Mr. Hassler on November 23, 1989 (Thanksgiving morning), I explained the mission of the Lyric Theatre—to provide a forum for collaboration between theater and music artists. I told him I wanted to explore musical possibilities inherent in theater outside of the typical uses in musical comedy or as pre-show or intermission music. I pointed out that I liked the St. Cloud director's choice of a local composer for introductory music. I suggested that the show might have been more interesting had the music been integrated into the show instead of living outside of it. So, I invited Jon to meet over a cup of coffee and talk about these ideas.

Jon replied that he was interested. I wrote again:

> I think there is a delightful and gentle humor in
> the novel that doesn't carry over to the play. The
> humor has almost a lyrical quality to it. It stems
> primarily from the situations and dialogue. Thus,
> it has a more farcical feel. That is as it should be,
> and you are to be congratulated. But that doesn't
> preclude incorporating the humor contained in
> Simon's commentary on himself and on the world,
> which is so evident in his prayers and thoughts in
> the novel. I prefer to hear Simon in prayer rather
> than direct address to the audience. I also tried
> to envision Simon engaged in conversation with
> another resident at the home—one who never
> speaks, but plays a musical instrument—a violin,
> cello, whatever would be appropriate.

On January 16, 1990, Jon replied in a handwritten letter that he was tempted to "cast his lot with the Lyric Theater" and asked me to meet him for coffee at Sebastian Joe's on the west side of Lake Harriet. He added a P.S., "What if God were a cello?"

At the meeting, Jon agreed to some rewriting and to the integration of live music, so we ended with Jon saying, "Let's do it!" Then he recounted the production history of the play in the Twin Cities. Both the Chimera and The Cricket had agreed to produce it but then closed their doors for financial reasons. Theater 65 completed rehearsals right up to tech week, but then their director/manager was killed by a city bus while riding her bike on the Nicollet Mall. Without her, the theater closed and used the remaining money to stage an opening night party in lieu of an opening night. Jon had only one stipulation for me—that he would not attend a party unless there was an opening night.

Chapter 8
Steady On...

Simon's Night

I had always thought John's female characters were less substantial than his male characters, with one exception—Agatha McGee (a schoolmarm who did not appear in *Simon's Night*). I entered a discussion with board member Dick Rehse, who also produced and directed for another theater. We asked Jon to flesh out the character of Barbara (Simon's wife).

I followed with a letter making more requests:

1. that Simon would appear in the last scene of Act I;

2. that the social worker, Jean, reappear in Act II; and

3. that Simon's prayers be incorporated with musical underscore.

Jon agreed but said he was not at all eager to bring in a composer who would claim royalties. As an alternative, he enclosed Scarlatti piano pieces that brought Simon to mind for him. He still liked the idea of a cellist.

Jon also began the negotiations with his agent, Patricia Karlan, who suggested 7 percent of the gross ticket sales with a guarantee of 70 percent of the seating capacity. Dick Rehse and I countered with an offer of 7 percent applied to a guarantee of $500 per show. We told him if he needed more, he should be talking to the Guthrie. We had paid 6 percent for *Texas Chainsaw Manicurist* with no guarantee on the seating capacity.

I assured Jon that using music in the public domain would be fine, and I liked the idea of a cellist. I also told him I wanted to direct the show.

Lady Luck smiled on us, first with a grant of $7,500 from the Metropolitan Regional Arts Council to stage *Simon's Night* and again when I attended a show featuring Mary Jo Savage, who had appeared in a summer show that I directed at Mankato State. She had started a small acting company in Minneapolis called "Outcaste." Her theater colleagues had trained together at the University of Minnesota in Morris, Minnesota, including Alva Crom. Al needed money, and I needed a stage manager. He was a perfect fit for the Lyric. He had experience in lighting, acting, sound, and every aspect of the production process. Al's day job was graphic design for his family's business, which gave him scheduling flexibility and gave the Lyric a discount on printing costs.

With Al's help, I went ahead with auditions in Northern Sign's small basement space at Lake and Bloomington. As I entered the building, I spotted two gentlemen wandering around in the shops. They looked like potentials for Simon and Mr. Hatch. I was relieved when they showed up minutes later with resumes in hand, joining the line already formed in the stairwell leading downstairs. Sure enough, I cast them both. Larry Roupe played Simon, and Tom Carey played the old farmer, Mr. Hatch. Both men carried enough age to play the roles with just a little help from costumes, make-up, and physicalization of old age.

Mr. Smalleye (Bruce Murray), Mr. Hatch (Tom Carey), Mrs. Biggs (Kay Bonner Nee), and Hattie Norman (Kristen Mathisen). Photo by Nancy Campbell.

Kay Bonner Nee, a seasoned veteran of the stage, fit the role of Mrs. Biggs, a daffy, incurable romantic who flirted shamelessly with Simon. Kay was very small, red-haired, and feisty. I was a bit worried about Kay's short-term memory. She had a long monologue in Act II, which she more or less mastered after great effort. She was so cute and funny; she delighted everyone (except Larry, who rescued her whenever she went up on a line).

The rest of the roster was easier to cast except for Mr. Smalleye, the Indian. I knew Bruce Murray because he was married to Beth Cherne, the Ely director featured in the 1984 article mentioned earlier. He was an unconventional choice, heavy-set, with a long, bushy ponytail. Bruce was a Native American who made his living primarily as a stand-up comedian—and he was not afraid to climb onto the roof of the Norman Home.

**Linda Mayo (Noalen Stampe) and Simon Shea (Larry Roupe).
Photo by Nancy Campbell.**

Simon visits with Evert Metz (Michael Garry), who is about to steal away with Simon's wife. Photo by Nancy Campbell.

We were developing our own stable of actors to carry many of the leading roles. Chris was back in the fold and often joined Larry, Tom, and me for a quick drink and a snack at the Black Forest after rehearsals. I had a social life again. It helped fill the hole left by Gusztav's most recent departure. It also brought me to the point of fatigue that was barely tolerable. The fatigue was exacerbated by Type 2 diabetes, as yet undiagnosed.

The actors presented a reading of the revised script at The Playwrights' Center on January 29, which kicked off the marketing plan. The reading was well attended, and the comments were positive, which cemented our relationship with Jon Hassler and many of his fans.

We rehearsed in the building where we held auditions but moved upstairs from the basement into an empty storefront. The building was in the process of becoming a diverse mini-shopping mall but was only partially occupied. In the evening, we were the last people left in the building and had to lock up. Larry's large German Shepherd, Delores, provided escort service to our cars, so we dubbed her Head of Security. Her mere presence kept people at a distance.

To stage this show, we needed a theater with a high ceiling to accommodate a staircase leading to second-floor bedrooms and the roof of the Norman Home. We rented "The Little Theater" on the second floor of the Hennepin Center for the Arts on 6th and Hennepin in Minneapolis (now part of the Cowles Center and home to the James Sewell Ballet).

We secured an excellent and experienced set designer with Guthrie Theater connections, James Muirhead, who met the challenges of this new script with inexpensive ideas for a two-story house. Muirhead's unit set represented much more than the Norman Home. It transformed into many things when a musical riff underscored changes in lighting or an actor entering with a prop or two—the grounds on a college campus, a hospital bed, and an artist's studio. Lighting director, Peter Leonard, used the largest wall to project images from as far away as Ireland. Here Simon climbs the Rock of Cashel to where a cathedral once stood amidst a loud storm, shouting back to Linda waiting below.

Rock of Cashel. Photo by Nancy Campbell.

At one point, Simon helps Mr. Smalleye to the roof so he can "shoot me a goose" and then departs. The honking of geese is followed by a gunshot. Mr. Smalleye falls off the roof (sliding down the back side of the roof line unseen, onto a platform supported by scaffolding). When Smalleye emerges into the stairwell (having entered a window unseen), holding his bloody head, Simon rushes up the stairs to help him. With enough rehearsal, we could make it work, but that piece of stage business remained a huge challenge every time I mounted the play (four times so far).

Hattie grabs the rifle as Simon helps Mr. Smalleye descend. Mr. Hatch, Mrs. Biggs, and Mrs. Kibbikoski (Annette Fragale) stand by. Photo by Nancy Campbell.

Simon's ex-wife (Lavina Erickson) arrives at the end of Act I i as the residents are leaving to go to the doctor. Photo by Nancy Campbell.

We cast a wide net to recruit an audience. When Jon read from his most recent novel at several bookstores, we were there to hand out bookmarks bearing news of the play. When Jon gave a talk at the Women's Club in April, we were there. We scheduled Thursday matinees to attract seniors and mailed out flyers. *Lifestyle Magazine* and *Good Age* published articles. *The Catholic Bulletin* published a review and carried an ad. Dale Conley and Jim Ed Poole interviewed Jon on MPR's Morning Show and interspersed the actors performing short cuttings, which included little musical riffs. Working from a photograph of Larry, Lucy Rose Fisher, an employee at the Wilder Foundation, designed the image we used on everything—playbills, coffee mugs, and a free ad on the inside cover of St. John's University magazine, which went out to thousands of alumni.

We scheduled a special night for St. John's University Alumni Association, and it sold out. Jon addressed the audience prior to the show while his wife Gretchen and I watched from the lobby doors. Jon was having fun. Gretchen whispered to me, "When we first got married, Jon told me he would never talk to audiences. Just look at him!" We were fifteen minutes into show time. Finally, the stage manager started dimming the stage lights, and another crew member escorted Jon to his seat, where Gretchen joined him.

Regarding music, I got myself into some hot water. An answer to Jon's question—"What if God were a cello?"—appeared on a downtown sidewalk, creating a deep-throated sound on his cello, something classical, and I stopped to talk. I was excited and not thinking clearly. I hired this cellist without checking credentials. An actor (also under contract) knew him from a previous show and refused to work with him. It was more feasible to replace a musician than this particular actor, so I paid out the cellist's contract. I replaced him with, of all things, a trumpet player who played short, mood-setting transitions from backstage, and when the action moved to a pub in Ireland, he appeared momentarily on the set. Phil Holm and Charlie Caranicas split the schedule because they also split the schedule for Twin's games at Met Stadium. Both Phil and Charlie went on to become very well known in their field and were frequently interviewed on MPR.

As the lights ended the show with a blackout on opening night, I felt I was falling into a void from a great height, leaving fully fledged nestlings, a feeling that intensified during the curtain call when Larry Roupe stepped forward to invite Jon Hassler onstage for a warm embrace. I handed a large bouquet of colorful blossoms to Carol Michels to present to Jon onstage, a gesture that finalized the end of my role as director for this show. As the actors left the stage, I stood in the lobby, smiling to cover my loss and accepting congratulations.

As the crowd thinned, Lyric Board Members began herding everyone into elevators or down the stairs to regroup at D'Amico's in Butler Square, a party underwritten by Ballentine Books. Jon's New York agent, Claire Ferraro, joined other Ballentine people to meet the cast and everyone who worked on the show. I often left parties within a half hour because I had no idea how to make small talk. But I stayed to the end, uncomfortably drifting from one conversation to another. We had successfully fulfilled Jon's stipulation that the opening night performance would occur before the opening night party.

The reviews varied. Peter Vaughan had read the book and found Larry Roupe's height and large frame incongruous with the description of Simon in the book. Comparisons to the book were inevitable, but then Roy Close wrote in *Pioneer Press*, "*Simon's Night* is as thoughtful and bland as its central character." He had not read the book but found Larry's Simon to be "recessive" compared to Lavina Erickson's animated portrayal of Simon's wife.

These reviews were offset by comments by older reviewers writing for papers designed to reach the senior community—reviews that found the characters delightful and the story hitting close to home. Jon himself was always fascinated to see his characters take form on stage. They often took on personas that he may not have intended. Jon never objected. He was always charmed.

Publicity shot before rehearsals started. Larry Roupe (Simon); Sally Childs, Director; and Jon Hassler, playwright, at Minnehaha Creek. Photo by Nancy Campbell.

The Demands of Success

The Connection, an early Twin Cities agency, handled ticket sales, although I still used my own phone number as backup and for group sales. I had great commuter bus service from downtown to home, even during the noon lunch hour, so I often jumped on a bus to spend twenty minutes at home. I jotted down phone messages from my answering machine (remember those?) and then returned as many calls as I could before jumping back on the bus with the remaining messages tucked in my purse for return calls after 5:00 p.m.

Once Hassler fans found out about the show, I had to start turning people away who didn't have reservations. They were very angry people! The theater was a black box with risers for seating on one side, and I finally replaced the 120 rather large chairs with close to 150 smaller ones. That number didn't quite fit on the risers, so we reshaped the stage to get some chairs along the sides of the acting area down front. Larry jokingly said he had only one request—that the people who were sitting practically on stage with him be Catholic! I was able to seat almost everyone, but very large people complained that the seats were too small. We were accustomed to audiences numbering 60; now they were closer to 160. We extended our run for one more week until another theater moved in. We grossed $34,854 in ticket sales and sent a check to Jon for $2,440 on June 2, 1991. I paid myself a director's fee. We decided to remount the show in 1992.

We rented a storage garage and took the set apart very carefully. All three of my daughters joked that their boyfriends were acceptable only if they owned a pick-up truck. Everything had to be taken up or down in an elevator with a removable trap in the ceiling. Nothing was easy—and that included finding anything in the storage garage as it filled up.

For the first time, we had money to carry over to our next production. Volunteers set up a bookkeeping system on Quicken software. Carol Michels needed to spend more time with her son and newborn daughter, so she taught me to enter data and generate reports for monthly meetings with help from Laurie Montanez. I had two full-time jobs and the increasing responsibility of aging parents. I was happy but very tired. I tried to get more sleep, but I never gave my blood sugar a thought.

The board discussed offering a season of plays rather than going play-to-play. We could save money by publicizing multiple productions and generate pre-season cash by selling season passes. Season ticket sales provided upfront money needed to open a show and alleviated some of the pressure.

Vicarious Romance

In the past year, I had seen *Catsplay* by Hungarian playwright István Örkény at the Guthrie Theater. The story followed Mrs. Erzi Orban, who had carried on a forty-year love affair with Victor, a corpulent and aging opera singer. After her husband's death, Mrs. Orban's guilt led her to substitute food for love. False teeth and swollen ankles could not prevent her from indulging in grand passions. She introduced her old friend Paula to Victor, only to be betrayed by them both. The play was really an opera, which appealed strongly to me, especially its piquant Hungarian flavor and the main character's bombastic style.

THE LYRIC THEATRE PRESENTS

CATSPLAY
by Istvan Orkeny

SEPTEMBER 6-29
at the Minneapolis Theatre Garage Franklin and Lyndale

**Nancy Gormley with Chester, belonging to photographer
Nancy Cambell, used on the cover of the playbill.**

The play also reminded me that I still had a link to Hungary not only in Gusztav but also to his mother, Iluska, who had visited at Christmas in 1991. They had spent the holiday at my apartment on Diamond Lake Road, where I left them to their own devices to spend Christmas Eve with my family, including my ex-husband, at Carol's house. When I returned at about 10:00, the chicken breasts I had left ready for the oven were still on the counter, and Iluska was raging operatically at Gusztav because she was hungry. I got them fed and then played carols on the piano. "Silent Night" works in every language. On Christmas Day, as the natural light faded, I loaded them into my Honda hatchback, and we toured the Christmas lights in Edina and on Summit Avenue in St. Paul, listening to Iluska's oohs and aahs—her only English words.

Center, Nancy Gormley as Mrs. Orban (Erzi) introduces Paula, her best
friend (Lavina Erickson), to her paramour, Victor Vivelli (Bob Sonkowsky).
Photo by Nancy Campbell.

When Gusztav returned to Marshall, I heard nothing more from
him. Months later, the phone rang, and the young woman who had been
his date at *Boxelder Bug Variations* in Minneota asked, "what is going on?"
I told her I hadn't spoken to Gusztav in some time.

"You know he's married, don't you?"

I didn't.

"He brought back a young Hungarian wife. She can't be more than
twenty-two or twenty-three years old!"

I had known it was coming. I just didn't like hearing it from someone
else.

"You know more than I do. I'm sorry I can't help you."

Within the year, Gusztav's young wife would return to Hungary to
deliver their child. Gusztav would be a new father at age fifty-seven. At
fifty-four, I was the proud grandmother of Sam and Meghan, ages two
years and six months, respectively. We were oceans apart.

Catsplay – The Union Comes on Board

I envisioned Nancy Gormley as the lead in *Catsplay*, scheduled for September 6 to 29, 1991, at the Theater Garage. I had seen Nancy in several plays and wanted to bring her into the Lyric family of actors. Since she was a member of the Actors' Equity Association (AEA), the Union for actors and stage managers, we would have to apply for permission to cast her. I reasoned that a Small Professional Theater (SPT) contract with the Union would contribute to gaining recognition as a professional theater. Actor's Equity had recently developed the SPT to meet the needs of the small-theater community in the Twin Cities.

SPT requirements were modest and negotiable, but it was a giant step for the Lyric. Was it a wise investment? Not only would we have to pay royalties, design fees, director's stipends, material and rehearsal costs, and rent—all up front, but we would also have to pay a guaranty bond to AEA for at least two people since we also were required to hire a union stage manager.

If Al Crom joined Equity, he could only stage manage in union houses, and there weren't many in the Twin Cities. Instead, he chose to run the light and/or sound board for *Catsplay*. I called the Guthrie immediately and, within minutes, had a list of young stage managers who had entered the union through their training program.

We had the summer to prepare for the additional financial burden. Larry Roupe called nearly everyone who saw *Simon's Night* to pitch season passes to the next three plays, *Catsplay*, *Dear Liar*, and a remount of *Simon's Night*. He had a vested interest—he would appear in the last two shows. Larry had a great deal of fun turning on the charm, especially with women ticket buyers. With each order, he asked for a small donation, which often resulted in an extra $10-$25 pledge.

Larry passed along his sales results almost daily, and I made up a letter/invoice which I could mail out with the season flyer. When the money came in, I mailed out the season passes, which I created on my amazing computer. That summer, Larry and I developed a mutually beneficial social pattern as well as a working partnership. We met at a coffee shop to do crosswords in the mornings before work, and on weekends, we went for long walks with his German Shepherd, followed by a movie. If I had no expectations of Larry and asked no personal questions, we had fun. He was well-read and opinionated, and through him, I met a lot of new people. I pigeon-holed Gusztav for the present time. But dreams brought him back at night.

After the wonderful success with *Simon's Night,* I entered thousands of names into a new software mailing program. I generated labels for our bulk mailings which the board and I prepared in the evening in a conference room at Briggs & Morgan.

I still needed coaching on the computer. Kate Schultz needed to step away, so Rita Olk (who played Emily Dickinson in our first production) put me in touch with Don Caba (pronounced Saba), who became my coach and pro bono consultant. Kate Schultz continued to help with graphic design. The computer no longer had the upper hand. Between calls to Don and Kate, I took charge.

As of September 1991, Larry had generated $15,642 in ticket/donor pledges, of which $6,870 had been collected. Collection on pledges continued for a fairly long period. I added a line to the box office report to track the use of season passes.

Money came from unexpected sources. When Outcaste Theater disbanded, they passed along the last $850 that remained in their checking account. We had applied for several grants. McKnight Foundation and Hugh J. Anderson turned us down, but we were waiting to hear from Dain Bosworth and Medtronic. Janet Robert, an attorney married to playwright John Zygmunt, wrote the MRAC grant for the next year. In the meantime, we were talking with Zygmunt about producing his new play *Troy.*

For some time, the Lyric had been talking with other theaters about forming a consortium so we could share some expenses. Cyd represented both Northern Sign and the Lyric at meetings. She and I toured a possible rental space in Northeast Minneapolis with Wendy Knox from Frank Theater. When the space fell through, the consortium idea stalled. Then two competing consortiums of theaters emerged—a Communicators group, which was discussing collective advertising, and the Public Theater Collective, which was more involved with sharing theater space.

The collective idea never bore fruit. We alternated rentals between the Theatre Garage and the Hennepin Center for the Arts. Wendy Knox rented some conventional venues, such as the Southern Theater or the Playwright's Center, and some unconventional ones—an empty grocery store or an empty piece of the old Sears Tower, both located in south Minneapolis.

A Lesson in Lighting

In August, we paid the equity bond and plunged into rehearsals for Catsplay. It encompassed a tempestuous love triangle and tales of self-deception among the over-sixty crowd. I felt that Nancy Gormley outperformed her counterpart in the Guthrie's production, helped by a strong supporting cast.

Roy Close, the critic for the *Pioneer Press*, pointed out the playwright's weakness—using too many monologues that "never failed to brake the play's momentum." As a former English teacher, I was attracted to these very monologues, which functioned as arias—in the world of opera, intended as showstoppers. On the other hand, Close confirmed my choice of leading lady by saying the production "benefits immensely from the presence of Nancy Gormley, whose Erzi is bursting with brassy vitality and *joie de vivre*." He complimented the women, especially Noalen Stampe (Chris Samuelson), "whose portrayal of Erzsi's neighbor, a woman aptly called Mousie, is right on the money." But he also called the performance "overlong."

Erze (Nancy Gormley) comes nose to nose with Mousie (Noalen Stampe), who backs away to share her fears. Photos by Nancy Campbell.

I thought the pacing problem resulted from actors moving too slowly from one acting area to another and pushed them to cross more quickly—to enter more briskly. But the problem lay elsewhere. The following night, I watched closely, and I could see that Nancy hesitated every time she had to cross to a different area to pick up the dialogue in a new setting. I asked her to help me understand why she chose to do this. She said she was waiting for the light to transition so she would not be walking into darkness. So, I watched the next performance with this in mind. I could see it now.

The lighting designer had mistakenly assumed that every transition to a new scene signaled a passage in time, so he had set the cues to <u>follow the actor</u>, waiting for her to enter the new area before bringing up the lights. But time flowed continuously. To denote this continuity of time, he needed to <u>lead the actor</u>, fading the lights up on the new area before they faded out on the old. I had assumed the designer understood the flow of time. Lighting cues had been set on the fly as the actors rehearsed. With this show, I should have spent more time with the lighting staff, even if it meant taking tech week off from my day job so I could work with them before the actors arrived for evening rehearsals.

Once we got the light cues fixed, we immediately chopped at least 10 minutes off the performance time. Not only did the pace of the transitions speed up, but the whole energy level and pace of the dialogue also picked up.

Box office sales were disappointing the first two weekends. The average audience size was only thirty-six, far below budgeted income. Sales picked up for the second half of the run. I can't blame the reviews entirely. Our marketing was not as aggressive as it might have been. We may have rested on laurels earned by the incredible numbers from *Simon's Night.*

Sales and Marketing

The theater had grown significantly from 1988 through 1991. A few numbers from that period of activity tell a story in and of themselves.[3]

At the end of 1991, we were able to carry forward $19,064. But we continued to experience all kinds of growing pains, and no one was getting paid at the level they deserved. For *Catsplay*, I had budgeted $500 for myself as producer and another $1,000 as director. I ended up with $500 for both jobs. The unpaid fees were left in the budget as "in kind" donations which helped get the budgets to a fundable level for foundation support. I learned a lot about balancing a budget, especially when I was willing to take very small stipends. I thought the only thing I lacked was sleep, but I still had lots to learn.

Marge Stanton finally reached a breaking point and could no longer balance her day job with the demands of marketing each show. We were forced to hire an independent contractor to market the next two shows. Susan Runholt, who had done similar work for Park Square Theatre, took the job. Her first demand was that every board member serves on her marketing committee in addition to their other board responsibilities.

We started having shorter board meetings in order to move immediately into marketing discussions to keep everyone on task. We shared some marketing projects with the Twin City Consortium Two, which combined three organizations—Northern Sign Theater, the Lyric, and the Minnesota Academy of Stage Combat Skills (MASCS). Through Susan Runholt, we formed a marketing relationship with Park Square Theatre in St. Paul, exchanging mailing lists and ad space in programs. Press releases, posters, postcards, newsletters, flyers for senior buildings— all were in progress. Susan had everyone working on something. A group sales letter was prepared and sent. Printed materials were still the norm in 1991. How different it would be with today's technology.

Play Practice vs. Rehearsal

Both Larry Roupe and Nancy Gormley had become my closest friends, and we often socialized together. As actors, they had many followers, so it made sense to bring them together in *Dear Liar* by Jerome Kilty. The play was based on the romantic and witty correspondence exchanged between Irish playwright George Bernard Shaw and Mrs. Patrick Campbell, the actress for whom he wrote *Pygmalion*. When Shaw saw "Mrs. Pat" in *The Second Mrs. Tanqueray*, he claimed to have fallen "head over heels in love in the first 30 seconds." She nicknamed him "Joey the Clown" and told him, "If I could write letters like you, I would write letters to God." Their letters only masked lover's quarrels. The masks came off when the onstage battle between Shaw and Campbell became adversarial offstage as well.

I pondered the role played by rehearsal in the theatrical process. The terms "play practice" and "rehearsal" are not wholly interchangeable. Theater people generally don't say "play practice." Football players practice. Doctors and lawyers practice. Actors go to rehearsals.

The terms have one important shared trait. To do either one, the player must repeat, repeat, repeat. We have all heard that "Practice makes perfect." But who has heard that "Rehearsal makes perfect"? It lacks alliteration, but there is more to it than that.

Practice puts the focus on perfecting technique, holding the player to an outside standard, getting it right. Rehearsal puts the focus on discovery, finding the truth—mostly through interactions with other people, other characters. Actors discover inner truth through behaving as someone outside of themselves.

In rehearsal, the outside standard is the integrity of the script. This is where the director enters. They must demand that the actors are true to the script as interpreted by the director. In rehearsal, a director may say to an actor, "I don't believe you. Do it again."

Getting back to Larry and Nancy, Larry had previously played the role of George Bernard Shaw and came to rehearsal to practice what he already knew. Nancy was playing Mrs. Patrick Campbell for the first time and was coming to rehearse—to discover, to find the undercurrents that drove her character.

Nancy learned her lines in smaller pieces, tying words to movement as we rehearsed various scenes. Her pace was often halting during this phase of rehearsal. Larry used rehearsal time to test his memory and wanted to run without stopping.

Nancy made no secret that she substituted wine for water with her lunch. Larry ascribed her slow pace to the wine. He wanted me to call her on it. I wasn't so sure. Rehearsals took place many hours after lunchtime. Larry's impatience grew. One night he blew his top—not at Nancy but at me. I had to end the rehearsal and thought I was going to have to cancel the play or replace one of the actors.

Either action would have derailed us financially. I had to figure out what to do without playing favorites. I talked with each actor, and they agreed to talk it out together—so we continued. Nancy curtailed her lunch libations, and Larry grudgingly allowed her to use rehearsal time to process her characterization. It was an uneasy truce.

Nancy Gormley with Larry Roupe. Costumes by John Woskoff. Photo by Michaelle Sparrow.

Dear Liar

My love for language carried me forward once again. As Susan Runholt pointed out in her eloquent press release, "Shaw's and Campbell's love/hate battle clearly was waged with rhetoric and embraced by vocabulary."

The challenge for the playwright had been to develop the relationship of these two remarkable people, Shaw and Campbell, through the words found in letters. The playwright began with actors as themselves—readers of letters. They took on the personas of the characters as they moved physically into the playing spaces and became Shaw and Campbell. I saw no need to apologize for the fact that neither actor physically resembled the people they represented. This wasn't *Man of La Mancha*, where Cervantes opened his trunk and, with wig and goatee, turned himself into Don Quixote.

My challenge was to determine just how stylized the production should be. I opted for the logic suggested by the script—with set and costumes that were elegant stylizations of the period they represented. At times the letters were spoken as if to a mirror over the audiences' heads where they were reflected back to the person for whom they were meant (a convention of Reader's Theater). But once established, we slowly broke the convention, and the letters became dialogue, the scenery receded, and the intriguing relationship took center stage—or at least that was what I was aiming for.

Nancy Gormley and Larry Roupe. Costumes and upholstery by John Woskoff. Sets by Jerry Boeve. Lights by Peter D. Leonard. Photos by Michaelle Sparrow.

The critics had their usual fun. They agreed that they wanted Nancy to be more over-the-top, to give us a display of the histrionics that Mrs. Pat was known for. Roupe was quite formal, playing his part as a reader (of letters). Peter Vaughan ended his review with praise:

> While it takes some time to get used to this rather dispassionate approach, it bears fruit in a moving second act when each character begins to leaven the laughter with the increasingly noticeable signs of age, infirmity, and death. When Gormley reads Mrs. Campbell's letter announcing the death of her son in WW I, it rings with pain and truth. Shaw's angry reply, damning war and its makers, is delivered by Roupe with similar conviction and power. In the end, the audience is treated to an affectionate and involving look at two noble souls finding solace and worth in each other.

Writing in the *Minnesota Daily* (U of M), Penelope Morgan gave Roupe high praise but asked more from Gormley. Morgan commented on the sexism inherent in the historical context:

> The script is excellent and the performances do it justice. Sally Childs… has created two multifaceted characters, foibles and all, who reveal our own humanity. Admittedly, Roupe carries the play… but I suspect Shaw would have expected it that way.

Mary Anne Welch, writing in *City Pages*, hated the script. From her strong feminist viewpoint, she claimed the story to be dishonest:

> *Dear Liar* mimics the habit of history, drooling again over the great Bernard Shaw. Severely edited and artificially arranged to hype Shaw's brilliance, these "letters" round out into a story of the playwright and the actress who served his genius; the play only pretends to hail Campbell—just as Shaw's plays only pretend to hail women.

Phew! That was a surprise. I certainly had feminist feelings of my own, but I thought the play gave Campbell plenty of opportunity to reveal Shaw as a typical blind male—a product of his time, an image of manhood that women have been prone to comment on as long as I can remember. This was part of the Shaw/Campbell combat—and it was historically accurate. The play certainly held up "the habit of history" described above, which is also accurate.

As always, readers of reviews were left to their own opinions. We were "Critic's Choice" in the *Star Tribune* and garnered a large picture in the *Skyway News*, so I felt pretty good about the reviews altogether.

Small Disappointments

Dear Liar came down on February 9, 1992, and a remount of *Simon's Night* opened on March 12. The Lyric dropped its option to use the AEA contract until further notice. I thought it might be good to get another director's perspective. Cyd was not available, so I hired Brian Martinson, the artistic director of the New Tradition Theatre in St. Cloud, Minnesota. I met him when I directed his wife in *South Pacific* at Mankato State in 1983. In the interim, he had built a solid reputation as a director.

Since my first reading of *Simon's Night*, I had longed to play Barbara. I wanted to test myself as an actor, apply all that I had learned since grad school. I asked Brian if I could audition. He said yes, but then cast Lavina Erickson, who had played the role in the first production.

We did not have the trumpet players available this time around, so I took on the creation of sound from backstage, playing short riffs on the piano and incorporating wind chimes and various other live sound effects as needed. Five actors returned from the first production, and we found solid replacements for the others. The director had the same script and the same set, but it was a different show.

Mr. Smalleye (George McCauley), Simon (Larry Roupe), and Hattie Norman (Kathleen Hardy). Photo by Michaelle Sparrow.

Remounts never achieve prior audience numbers. There isn't the same excitement, the same curiosity about the unknown, or the same generous marketing offers. The show did well, but the numbers did not match the first production.

The Ravages of *Troy*

Troy by John Zygmunt had been brought to my attention by Chris Samuelson. Although Chris had returned to grad school, I wanted to honor her earlier role as one of Lyric's three originating directors. Susan Runholt's description in the season brochure promised laughter permeating a tale of war:

> It's the last days of the Trojan War. The gods are
> getting quirkier, the warriors are whining, and the
> women are ready to mount a rear-guard action of
> their own to get the men to call off the fighting.
> Amid the sound of clashing egos and misplaced
> erotic desires, *Troy* explores the humor of men's
> aspirations to glory and immortality. The futil-
> ity of war, the vagaries of beauty and the joy of
> life's unpredictability are just a few of the themes
> explored in this sharp-edged and fast-paced com-
> edy—a world premiere by one of the Twin Cities'
> most talented new playwrights.

Troy promised to fulfill our mission by including music and development by local artists. The playwright wanted Steven DiMenna to direct. Steven had led the Fuller Young People's Theater but left the Twin Cities when it was forced to close for financial reasons. Now he was back, so I met with the two of them at my apartment on 46th and Bryant. I can still see these dapper young gentlemen sitting on my couch. They promised to put the Lyric on the map, so to speak, and introduce me to a whole new set of actors. This implied a negative image of the Lyric Theater, but I decided not to be offended.

Indeed, John and Steven did cast strong actors—including several who are now well-known Equity actors. Michael Crosswell, an emerging

139

sound designer, developed an inventive musical score. All these people were getting solid reviews for their work at other theaters. The set was interesting—lots of flag-like canvas drops that could be moved to create various spaces. The elements for a good production were in place, although I did not feel any personal involvement in the piece. I chalked this up to a lack of discernment on my part and perhaps a gender bias. The men all seemed enthused. The show opened on October 16 at the Hennepin Center.

In the seven years since we started as the Lyric Theater in 1985, Mike Steele of the *Star Tribune* had never reviewed us. He ordinarily reviewed dance productions and big Equity shows. When he called for tickets, I wondered why he had chosen to see *Troy*. I was worried. Was there a hidden agenda? On opening night, I gamely played my part, selling tickets, setting up coffee and cookies, and helping with a party in the lobby after the show.

Steele's subsequent review compared John's script to skits in a varsity variety show. Another self-important critic gave the show a scathing review in a smaller newspaper. It was accompanied by a full-page picture taken from our program cover. The Lyric couldn't afford so much as a 2-inch ad buried on page 6, but now we were given a full-page picture. I was incensed and devastated. I chided myself for not trusting my female sensibility, which had put me at odds with this script.

With the infusion of money from the playwright and his wife's families, we kept the show running. When a harsh review throws ice water on a production, it often produces a rift between the actors/running crew and the production staff. A few actors who were personal friends made a point of talking to me, but I did not feel welcome backstage and depended on my stage manager, Al Crom, for backstage communication.

Several months later, I had lunch with the playwright, and he humbly confessed that his parents paid for his college education, but the Lyric Theater (me in particular) paid for his theater education. I couldn't help but like the guy, but it was an expensive lesson for all concerned.

Chapter 9: Rainbow on the Horizon

Enter Erica Zaffarano

The next show was a small cast musical, Carol Hall's *To Whom it May Concern*, which Larry Roupe was slated to direct. But Larry had leapt at an offer to portray Herbert Hoover in a one-man show called *Chief,* commissioned to mark the expansion of the Hoover Library in 1992 in West Branch, Iowa, and then run at the Riverside Theatre in Iowa City. When the Iowa show was extended, he was unable to return in time for auditions. I took over the direction. I needed to heal, to restore faith in myself. The brochure proclaimed *To Whom it May Concern* to be:

> A joyful, musical look at what happens in the
> hearts and minds of people participating in a
> church service. With music that's alternately
> foot-stomping and lyrical, poignant and witty,
> members of the congregation consider elements
> of their lives: birth, death, love, tolerance, and the
> nature of the divine. It's a celebration of commu-
> nity and compassion, an exploration of faith and
> the beauty and uncertainty that surround it.

The script pushed the exploration of faith when the priest's monologue revealed that his doubts were driving him to mental anguish.

I continued to work with Alva Crom as our stage manager and Peter Leonard as our lighting director, but I lacked a set designer until the eleventh hour. In desperation, I called Tom Bliese, my set design prof from Mankato State, hoping to find a talented student. He said he could do better than that and gave me a phone number for Erica Zaffarano, a set designer with whom he had worked at the University of Iowa, Ames. Tom thought Erica and I would be a great team, and I called her immediately. She was in her car, heading home to Minneapolis from Iowa, with her three-year-old twin sons in the back seat.

"How did you get my number?" she asked.

I replied, "Tom Bliese."

"Really," she said, "I just got off the phone with him." She was interested in designing the show and agreed to meet with me within a day or two.

Finding Erica was a stroke of luck. She created a setting out of fabric pillars that provided a palette on which the lighting director could paint and project—and she came in under budget. Erica and I continued to work on other shows until my retirement. She has built a solid reputation in the Twin Cities and other midwestern cities based on her amazing talent and ability to think outside the box.

To Whom It May Concern

The show itself was formatted as an Episcopalian service. Everyone in the church—fourteen, including the priest and choirmaster—had short monologues and/or songs that revealed their interior thoughts. At midpoint, the service was disrupted by a stranger off the streets, and the rest of the service was used to reunite this small band of congregants with communion at show's end. A pretty good metaphor for life.

Although the show was framed by the service, it was not a religious piece per se. Carol's characters were called The Child, The Stranger, Bob the Dog Owner, The Grandfather, and so on, thereby giving them symbolic significance. Mike Bond served as music director/pianist, and together, we cast diverse and extraordinarily talented actors/singers, which included Peter Rothstein, whose youth and sincerity moved me every time he sang about the loss of his younger sister.

Peter Rothstein shines amidst Angie Drahos, Jennifer Santoro, Skip Connolly, and Jennifer Adams. Photo by Nathan Sorenson.

When this cast sang at full power, they nearly lifted the roof of the Little Theater right up into Zenon Dance Theater's studio space directly above us. The cast worked hard and took risks. I put a young actor into a wheelchair. His monologue was about his divorce and visits with his small daughter, from which he created some interesting movement and added heart-breaking depth to his performance. The cast pointed out that I had grounded our best dancer, but once I asked him to juggle during "Skateboard Acrobats," they forgave me.

"Skateboard Acrobats" sprang from the imagination of a young woman identified only as Sister. Her first word grew out of her throat as she arose from a pew singing, "Here they come down the sidewalk on a beautiful day," roller skating to the center space between the seating and the altar, where she was joined by the rest of the cast playing children's games such as jump rope and hopscotch. One character rode a unicycle, and another came down the center aisle on a skateboard, flipping it up barely in time to avoid the audience. The whole show was filled with surprises and gorgeous music.

Joe Rux, George Farr, Skip Connelly, Kathleen Hardy, Suzanne E. Heller, D. Pittam, Jennifer Santoro (removing roller skates, as the music starts to heat up), Jewel Rae, Angie Drahos, Jennifer Adams. (Back Row) Peter Rothstein, Bob Otto, and Mike Bond at the piano. Photo by Nathan Sorenson.

"When I Consider the Heavens," opening number with Suzanne Heller, Joe Rux (wheelchair), Skip Connelly, Jennifer Adams, Peter Rothstein, Angie Drahos, and Jewel Rae (the child). Photo by Nathan Sorenson.

I was in direct contact with Carol Hall's husband and ordered cassettes to sell in the lobby. He told me Carol was coming to Minneapolis to attend a friend's Saturday night wedding. She agreed to come to the theater on Saturday afternoon to hear a couple of tunes and have a picture taken with the cast. All but one cast member was present when Carol arrived in white cowboy boots and lots of turquoise jewelry. Out of curiosity, I asked if the show was "a trunk show." She said yes, the songs had been sitting in her apartment collecting dust for quite some time.

Carol's time was limited, so the cast clustered onstage and sang the opening number, "When I Consider the Heavens," followed by a production number led by the Stranger called "In the Mirror's Reflection." The latter was the most modern and most difficult piece, with lots of dissonance. Everyone moved independently at a rapid pace and then froze for spoken lines embedded in the music.

Carol swayed a little at the edge of the stage, entranced. After the singing stopped and the sound died away, she said we had an even better combo of singers than her own production, which was performed in a small Episcopalian church in Manhattan. Both Carol Hall and Gretchen Cryer (best known for "I'm Getting My Act Together and Taking it on the Road") were in that New York production, so I was dumbfounded by her comment. I still have a coffee mug emblazoned with the cast pictured with Carol Hall, which Jewel Rae (The Child) gave each of us at the end of the run. The picture has faded into a dim memory.

Carol Hall died in 2018, twenty-five years after that picture was taken. The biographical material in her obit did not mention this lovely and very personal nugget of creativity, *To Whom it May Concern*.

Peter Vaughan reviewed the show. He generally handed off musicals to other reviewers, so I was both worried and pleased. He said the show received a "sharp staging," and as always, his understanding of the form and content of the show was right on the money. A huge burden was lifted when he said, "The Lyric production, under Sally Child's direction, is absolutely first-rate, the best work this theater has done in years. The ensemble singing is precise and rich, filling the theater to its rafters." He gave kudos to many individual singers, including Kathleen Hardy, Jennifer Adams, and Peter Rothstein, people who have reappeared throughout my directing career.

L to R, Front: Paul Reyburn, D. Pittam, Carol Hall, Sally Childs, Jennifer Santoro. Row 2: Peter Rothstein, Angie Drahos, Jewel Rae, Kathleen Hardy, Skip Connelly, Bob Otto. Row 3: Alva Crom (Stage Manager), Mike Bond, and George Farr. Photo by Nathan Sorenson.

Communion "Walk in Love," George Farr, Jewel Ray, Skip Connelly, Peter Rothstein, Kathleen Hardy, Suzanne Heller, Angie Drahos, Jennifer Santoro, Jennifer Adams, Joe Rux, Mike Bond (piano), D. Pittam, Bob Otto, and Paul Reyburn. Photo by Nathan Sorenson.

The review also praised the work of lighting designer Peter Leonard and set designer Erica Zaffarano. Vaughan did not mention the incredible work done by Mike Bond, who played the role of Choirmaster, accompanying and directing from the piano and even singing my favorite song, "Who Will Dance With the Blind Dancing Bear?" Mike made it look so easy that Vaughan missed the importance of his role. Every time Suzanne Heller sang her song about needing miracles, I wanted to jump up and shout, "Yes!"

We used every marketing tool we could think of. We appeared on *The Morning Show* on Minnesota Public Radio, hosted by Dale Conley and Tom Keith (Jim Ed Poole). They gave us the full half hour to drum up enthusiasm for the show. Later on, Dale Conley brought his wife to see the show and chatted with the actors afterward. That was a first for us.

We also contacted St. Joan of Arc, a very liberal Catholic church with a huge congregation that often invited guest speakers and musicians to share material as part of their service. St. Joan's congregants worked with St. Stephen's parishioners to run a soup kitchen for the homeless on a regular basis, so I suggested to the priest that he might ask us to sing and use homelessness as a theme for his homily. He accepted and incorporated a segment of our show that featured Bob Otto, The Stranger, and his jazzy song, "Ain't Nobody Got a Bed of Roses." The cast sang another number during the offering, "Walk in Love." Its strong gospel feeling generated the rhythmic clapping and swaying beloved by the St. Joan crowd. We sang at both services (masses), which were held in the gym of the attached school, with about a thousand people at each service. At our matinee performance that Sunday, we had some tired actors running on adrenaline, actors who were both gracious and generous with their time.

These two marketing events paid off for us with many sold-out houses. It was a happy cast—and a very happy director who enjoyed reconciling the ticket sales on a nightly basis. We extended the show for an additional week, and then we stored the set for a remount in our next season.

As a side note, two marriages came out of that production: Paul Reyburn and Suzanne Heller, as well as Jennifer Adams and Skip Connelly. Both couples continued to pursue the craft of theater.

At about this time, I pondered the importance of having powerful alliances and name recognition, especially when doing a play that was new or not well known. We got our first MRAC grant through an alliance with Peter Moore for *Hunting Cockroaches,* we gained financial support in Southwestern Minnesota by producing Bill Holm's *Boxelder Bug Variations,* but we were turned down by MRAC when we proposed *Leah,* which lacked any name recognition but then succeeded when we did a play by noted author, Jon Hassler. With every choice, I weighed in on this component, looking for possible connections to recognizable names. I wanted to shout UNFAIR! It also seemed un-American, elitist, and so on. I even wondered if subliminal racist or gender-driven feelings were built in; a woman producer of a play about a local Jewish immigrant woman. Given the current environment in 2022, I can't help but raise these questions long after the fact.

A Change in Fortune

While I was enjoying success, my father, at age eighty-seven, was struggling with caring for my mother, now legally blind. He had become a hard-nosed pragmatist, and when macular degeneration plunged Mom into darkness, he started preaching in favor of euthanasia. Dad loved a cold beer at about 5:00 p.m., which often turned into a sermon at the supper table, mostly about Responsibility. As a kid, my brother had heard Dad's fishing buddies tease him by calling him "The Preacher." Now, Dad's habits drove away old friends, so I dropped by often to see how my mother was holding up in this environment. Dad was an active proponent of Dr. Kevorkian and studied *Final Exit* by Derek Humphry, a British-born American journalist who founded the Hemlock Society and later cofounded the Final Exit Network. Dad also wrote diatribes on his IBM Selectric typewriter with each idea a one-sentence paragraph. His conversation became litanies of rehearsed pronouncements (often a symptom of oncoming dementia). I escaped into home ownership with the help of Nancy Gormley, realtor by day and actress by night. From my home office, I cocooned into planning the next theater production.

A year or so earlier (1992), Larry Roupe had seen a show at The Brave New Workshop where Carol Connolly performed several poems. After the show, Larry turned his charm on this savvy, middle-aged blonde and learned much of her story. Carol Connolly became a writer at age forty in 1976. Her eight children were leaving the nest, and her marriage was falling apart. She tried to sign up for a fiction-writing course at the Loft from novelist Judith Guest (author of *Ordinary People* and a fan of Jon Hassler). The class was full, so she signed on for a poetry class. Although she had never written a poem, she took to it naturally and gained recognition for her collected work, *Payments Due*, published by Midwest Villages and Voices and subsequently staged in Los Angeles. Upon returning home to St. Paul, she wanted to see it staged in the Twin Cities.

Larry Roupe and Carol Connolly.
Photo by Michaelle Sparrow and Nathan Sorenson.

Larry and I met with Carol and her long-time partner, pianist Bill Eden, at a posh restaurant near her condo on Selby Avenue in St. Paul. The story she told us landed her in our line-up of challenging pieces built on the work of Minnesota writers.

Payments Due

When Carol's marriage ended, she left her comfortable life on Summit Avenue, a parkway lined with stately old mansions occupied by wealthy people. In 1972 she visited Washington, DC, where she saw a production of Ntozake Shange's *For Colored Girls Who Considered Suicide When the Rainbow Was Enuf*—Shange's first and most acclaimed theater piece, nominated for a Tony Award in 1976. Shange coined the term "choreopoem" to describe her series of twenty separate poems choreographed to music that wove interconnected stories of love, empowerment, struggle, and loss into a complex representation of sisterhood. This choreopoem opened Carol up to the power of live presentation. She continued to write, and her dry wit led her to try stand-up comedy.

In 1988 Carol took on a gossip column for the St. Paul *Pioneer Press and Dispatch*, leaving little time to write poetry. Four years later, she lost the gossip column. By chance, C. Bernard Jackson, director of the Inner City Cultural Center in Los Angeles, was getting on a plane at MSP in Minneapolis to return to LA, and someone put a copy of Carol's book into his hands. By the time he arrived in California, he had decided to dramatize it. He adapted it for six women, and Carol's only request was that the cast be multicultural and represent all ages. In 1992, Jackson gave *Payments Due* a full production at the Ivar Theatre in Hollywood, a former strip joint and porno palace that he had converted to a legitimate theater.

In LA, Carol heard a local legend that claimed the Ivar was haunted by a stripper who committed suicide in the theater. Actors allegedly heard her wailing in the dressing rooms. So Carol wrote a long poem about the stripper in all of us and about women who are man junkies. She called it "Fantasy Dancing." Her partner, Bill Eden, a composer and professional pianist, set it to music, and it became part of the show. The review of the LA show was terrific. Sylvie Drake, the *Times* theater critic, said,

> For a woman who became a poet at 40 and claims
> to have stumbled into poetry only when another

writing class was too full to take her, the results
are impressive: at once down to earth and in touch
with feelings, with a stinging knack for aphorism.
Call it pragmatic *panache*.

The May 1992 issue of *The Ladies Home Journal* carried an article about Carol's transition out of marriage and into her new life in their "Woman to Woman" column—"frank talk about the most intimate aspects of our lives." Carol entitled the article "I was dumped—but I got my revenge." The piece concludes with an announcement of the LA production (wow, nationwide publicity!). Carol's last statement in the magazine article was, "Despite warnings to the contrary, life can be beautiful after divorce. And living well truly is the best revenge."

After hearing Carol's story, *Payments Due* sounded better and better. It fit our newly rewritten mission—"life-affirming, potential for music, lyrical in nature, utilizing a local writer." I was back in familiar territory, working with a very smart woman. Carol was able to get a tape of the LA production for Larry and me to watch. I agreed to produce it, and Larry wanted to direct.

We auditioned people early and weathered a couple of changes in the casting. We started with a multicultural group representing a span of ages: Rita Olk, who played Emily Dickinson in our first show as well as a wheelchair role in *Catsplay*, would play the older characters. Kathleen Hardy and Brenda Brown represented African Americans in mid-life, and Donna Glennie, a proficient pianist, would create musical bridges. Emily Stewart was our youngster at twenty-something. We took a lovely picture at the Loring Bar and Cafe, and then Brenda Brown dropped out. A call to Jennifer Connelly (nee Adams of *To Whom It May Concern*) filled the hole, and we retook our poster picture.

After the first rehearsal, Donna Glennie came to me and asked, "Is this the way all of the rehearsals are going to be?" I thought *oh, dear,* and asked if she could give me a little more information. She stuttered a little, shrugged, shook her head, and said something that sounded like "never mind." "What?" hovered on my tongue, but she turned and walked away quickly. I was worried.

151

That evening Donna called, and I released her from her contract. I stepped into my first acting role for the Lyric Theater. A show directed by Larry Roupe was both a worry and an advantage. We had a familiar team in place with Rita, Kathleen, Kristin, Jennifer, and me. Emily Stewart was brilliant—she was also the daughter of Gary Stewart, Larry's old friend from Utah who taught and directed at Indiana State University. Emily would not quit with Larry directing. The poster picture included Donna Glennie, but there wasn't time to reshoot it. The multicultural and age ranges were maintained.

Most actors step into the director's shoes rather easily, and if anything, they tend to give too much direction. In Larry's case, as I was about to learn, he gave very little direction. I thought I was getting a glimmer of what Donna Glennie had been asking earlier. Larry wanted rehearsals to start with small talk followed by a run-through, maybe a brief discussion, and then go home to walk the dog, eat a sandwich and enjoy a stiff drink before bed.

In rehearsal, we adjusted and found ways to discuss what was necessary. I was on the horns of a dilemma, but the women supported and protected me. They understood that Larry was a close friend, and I had honored his request to direct because he was instrumental in the success of the Lyric Theater. The actors all had enough experience to create their own interpretations and blocking patterns, so Larry really did not have to do much. Carol Connolly was at the early rehearsals. She could hardly refrain from jumping in with comments, so she excused herself before Larry's raised eyebrows turned verbal.

Erica Zaffarano gave us a setting that Peter Vaughan described as "an open, upscale cabaret; a place of fun, energy and occasional introspection." Most of the forty poems were delivered solo, sometimes one person addressing another, sometimes addressing an imaginary companion, and sometimes using the space simply to dramatize or underscore the meaning of each poem. Some poems were underscored by piano music, and often they were tied together with little piano riffs. The show started to cook. It became a choreopoem.

Kristin Mathisen steps out in "Fantasy Dancing."
Photo by Nathan Sorenson and Michaelle Sparrow.

I lacked credentials as a music director, but I reached into my limited background, creating music with little or no comment from Larry. Bill Eden and Jack Carter were available as advisors. Among the actors, I had the least experience. It had been a long time since my acting gigs in Ely, so I needed encouragement. I also had one poem that I did not fully understand. When I asked for help, Larry promised that we would come in early and work together in the next day or two. But when I offered to pick him up early to give him time to coach me, he always put me off.

I suspect he was uncomfortable giving me direction—or he didn't know what to do with the poem either.

The other actors thought I was making sense of the words in this mother-daughter poem, and Larry told me just to talk louder. I already felt I was shouting, but he was hard of hearing and kept asking me to come farther downstage. I was losing confidence.

Emily Stewart helped more than anyone. One evening during a rehearsal, she mimed smoking a joint, which she then passed to me. I went along with the fun, taking a toke as I had seen in a movie somewhere, never having smoked a joint (or anything else). Emily was the only one who didn't know this, but when everyone started to laugh, I got the giggles and we had to stop. It was a freeing experience, and Emily became my partner in the poem, playing the daughter receiving advice from her mother. From then on, I pretended in my head to be a little high and not able to quite make sense, and everyone thought it made great sense.

Emily Stewart and Sally Childs.

AND THEN IT'S WHO YOU KNOW
for Brigid on her eighteenth birthday

The moon dances tonight
swings her veils in a wide circle
her smile is bold, full of promise
for she knows

the first and most perfect
of figures is the circle.
Even as you embrace this
incontrovertible wisdom,

contemplate the effect
of gravitational forces.
Begin to cultivate
a defiant attitude.

Question everyone. There is
a vanishing point. Ask
would your method work
if the circle passed through

its origin? Would it be
consistent with everything else
you know? Will it remain
constant over the years?

Perhaps you will become

a pacifist to passionate

inquiry, but even if you

slip into this category

continue to cultivate

a defiant attitude and keep

in mind, that in spite of forces

beyond your control,

the circle is infinite.

**Kathy Hardy, Kristin Mathisen, Sally Childs,
and Emily Stewart pursue the infinite circle.**

Emily Stewart, Jennifer Connelly, and Rita Olk.

After many performances, I confessed to Carol that I never arrived at a consistent interpretation of the poem. She laughed, said she would never have guessed, and to just keep doing what I was doing.

Peter Vaughan opened his review by saying:

> Poetry isn't necessarily the most dramatic stuff,
> but it certainly sings in the Lyric Theatre's skillful
> staging of *Payments Due*, a collection of whimsy
> and pain by St. Paul poet Carol Connolly.

He pointed out the strengths of each performer and concluded:

> *Payments Due* may be a woman's play, but its
> humor, insight and bravery should make it every
> bit as entertaining to men. It's common ground
> Connolly is traveling: a warning to the young and
> a reminder to the old.

Carol's hard-edged poetry lent itself to performances filled with energy based in anger. She was bothered when audience members commented on her bitterness, which she denied—bitterly. She claimed that these people were projecting their own feelings into her poems. But isn't that how we "make believe?"

Women who represented different lifestyles and points of view— many of them Carol's acquaintances or personal friends— attended performances. Carol, at one time the "Duchess of Dish" for Channel 11, still wrote for the *Journal of Law and Politics* and knew every prominent Democrat, male and female, in Minnesota. One night Carol introduced me to Amy Klobuchar, who had just finished her law degree. Now Amy is one of Minnesota's state senators and made a bid for president in 2020. I am still amazed at how well-connected Carol was in St. Paul.

We scheduled many Q and A discussions, especially after the matinees. Our list of discussion leaders included:

1. Ann Bancroft, leader of the Women's Antarctic Expedition

2. Joan Growe, Minnesota Secretary of State

3. Norma Jean Sims, Psychotherapist and social activist

4. Dr. James Shelton, Director of Affirmative Action for the Minneapolis Community Development Agency and past President of the St. Paul Urban League

5. Dudley Riggs of the Brave New Workshop and his wife, Pauline Boss, Professor of Family Social Sciences at the University of Minnesota, and

6. Sister Mary Walter Duvall, Principal, Academy of the Holy Angels, among others.

Carol and Larry joined the discussion leaders at the front of the stage, facing the audience, and we actors sat to one side. There were often some hard-core feminists in the audience. Carol fielded most of the questions, but if Larry was pushed too hard by these women, he often deferred to the actors. Later in the dressing room, the older actors commented on having to carry the ball.

We asked a lot from this team of Lyric women. When the Duluth YMCA invited us to present the show in honor of its centennial on September 11, 1993, five out of the six actors signed on. Emily Stewart had left Minneapolis and had to be replaced. Each actor received a stipend of $125 and expense reimbursement for housing and gasoline. The Lyric received a fee of $1,600 to cover these expenses. We performed in the Duluth Playhouse in the Depot to a small but enthusiastic audience. Several of my Ely friends drove over one hundred miles to see the show in Duluth and then stayed for Carol's post-show discussion despite a two-hour trip home.

Carol wanted to hold writing classes in prisons that might lead to the publication of poetry by women prisoners. She thought that a presentation of *Payments Due* at a local prison might get her foot in the door. Her friend, Millie Beneke, Director of Project Interaction, Inc., set up a performance for us at the women's prison in Shakopee on Mother's Day in 1993. When we arrived, we discovered that nearly every inmate had children visiting and lacked interest in listening to poetry. We performed in a community/lunchroom for about ten to twelve people, including the kitchen staff, who appeared to enjoy themselves.

In May, I received a gracious letter from Ms. Beneke with a check enclosed, which I was happy to share with the actors. It had been a day of great learning for all of us.

Carol Connolly died on November 21, 2020, just a few weeks short of her eighty-sixth birthday. She had become a St. Paul icon.

Strategic Planning

In the meantime, the board was working hard to develop the theater on all fronts—funding, community reputation, recruiting volunteers, and board members. In March and April 1993, we met several times with Carol Vantine of General Mills, who helped us write a formal strategic plan. Carol was poised and professional and shared a great deal of knowledge. She also interrogated all of us, writing keywords on huge flip boards that turned my dining room into a proper board room. As she jotted, she put thematic headings at the tops of the lists and crossed out words as she moved them under a new heading. With a practiced eye, she sorted our history and intentions into three pieces.

Our mission became three-pronged: "to select plays that affirmed positive values and relationships in life's joys and pains, incorporated lyrical dimensions to support/enhance the script, and showcased regional writers/composers when appropriate and consistent with other selection criteria." We set goals and attached specific dates and amounts so we could measure each production and each fiscal year's outcome. We listed specific goals for the upcoming year (1993), such as developing job descriptions for board members and volunteers, recruiting two to three new board members by September, defining board functions and staff functions, etc. We laid out key issues to be addressed in the next three years:

> 1994 - Financial stability, consistent administration, identifying/attracting an audience, and board size/roles;

> 1995 - Profitability, consistent marketing, growing audience, paid staffing, and

> 1996 - Permanent site, long-term fundraising.

I felt like a butterfly pinned to a corkboard. The word "consistent" nailed down a big flaw in my management skills. But board members were getting more and more involved, and we were counting on this plan to make our meetings more structured. We were looking for consistent results. It all took an enormous amount of imagination.

Larry turned his attention to what he did best, acting and sales. He remained a vital part of the Lyric team and continued to help us stretch our boundaries. He developed personal ties to many season ticket buyers and donors. This base of supporters often attended fundraisers, whether at Rita Olk's home in Eden Prairie or Sally Anderson's home in Southwest Minneapolis.

Supporters mingled with Jon Hassler or Bill Holm, John Rezmerski, Carol Connolly or Dave Moore (Peter's father and well-known TV news anchor). Larry also put me in contact with many student actors and teachers from Holy Angels and Benilde-St. Margaret's (where he worked as a substitute teacher), as well as many people from the community at St. Joan of Arc. We were developing a "following."

Sally Childs between poet John Calvin Rezmerski and Dave Moore at the home of Rita and Ben Olk.

Sally Childs backed by Bill and Sally Anderson, Paul Mohracher, Jon Hassler, and Ron Duffy. At the Anderson home.

Based on our first season brochure designed pro bono by the Monica Little Agency, we now had a format that we were able to replicate in subsequent years. Our stage manager, Alva Crom, a graphic designer by day, worked with our marketing people to design a good-looking brochure that Larry could use to market the next season during his 1993 summer sales campaign. Season tickets had risen from $8 to $9 per show (as opposed to our regular adult ticket price of $12 to $15).

Doris Overby, who managed the Hennepin Center for the Arts, and John Linnerson, Technical Director for the center, wanted us to be ongoing tenants and helped us get to know Bonnie Morrison and Michael Robbins at Illusion Theater, the permanent tenants on the eighth floor. Since the Little Theater was not always available when we needed space, this was a critical relationship. The first two shows of the 1993–94 season were in the Illusion space, where we had a larger seating capacity. I felt at home. This was the same space occupied by the Cricket when I did my internship.

Most of the cast returned for the remount of *To Whom It May Concern*, but even a few substitutions resulted in a different show. Mike Bond was unable to return. His replacement did not want to sing as well as play, so I handed off "Who Will Dance With the Blind Dancing Bear" to Joe Rux, the single parent. He stationed his wheelchair right in front of the altar, topped by a large suspended cross. Joe's sensitive and soaring rendition of the song elicited tears. I will never forget a comment by a friend from Briggs & Morgan who told me the show could be a "cash cow." Sadly, it wasn't a big money maker, nor did it fill the larger seating capacity, but it remained among my favorites, and I produced it two more times—in Plainview and in Ely, Minnesota.

Herbert Hoover in the Flesh

The upper Midwest was poised on the cusp between fall and winter in October 1992 when I set out for Iowa City to see Larry Roupe's last performance of *Chief,* a one-man show by Rebecca Christian, an Iowa playwright commissioned to write the play based on Herbert Hoover. As I crossed into Iowa, I drove into heavy rain. At Cedar Rapids, the highway widened. My small Honda hatchback pounded alongside one huge semi after another, water spraying up with such force that I white-knuckled the steering wheel to avoid swerving. Visibility was less than a quarter mile. I wanted to change lanes and exit, but it was easier to stay in the chute created by spray from the trucks.

When I finally arrived in Iowa City, Larry and Dick stepped out on the porch of Dick's large Victorian home.

"Well, I'll be damned!" Larry often peppered his personal dialogue with hell and damnation, befitting his bushy black eyebrows. "I thought you would call and cancel your trip."

Dick was at most 5'6" with a small mustache that could have been cut from sandpaper adorning his top lip. Pale blue eyes sparkled behind his gold-rimmed glasses. "Welcome to Iowa, also known as the Bible Belt or the Snow Belt. I'm Richard Houston, but just Dick to friends."

"Thank you..." My winter coat was over my arm, and I tried to control the shaking induced by the cold rain. Dick grabbed my suitcase and ushered us inside, where every inch of wall space was occupied by original paintings. I turned to Dick, "Are the paintings all yours?"

Dick waved in self-deprecation. "Oh, pay no attention." He was already heading upstairs with my suitcase. The stairwell was also filled with paintings.

"But attention must be paid," I exclaimed, wondering if Dick would recognize the line from *Death of a Salesman.*

"I'm no Willie Loman," Dick said as he set my suitcase inside a bedroom door. He gestured to more paintings, which offset the handmade quilt. "I've sold very few paintings."

We returned to the living room, where the remnants of a cribbage hand spread out on a card table. I looked at Larry. "Do you feel like you died and went to heaven?"

Larry laughed. "Dick is a fabulous cook, too."

When the weather cleared, we spent a delightful weekend visiting West Branch, Iowa, where Larry had performed *Chief* at the opening of the Hoover Memorial Library before a crowd of dignitaries, and then we returned to the Riverside Theater in Iowa City to see the show. Larry gave a stellar performance, and the next day we left for Minneapolis in another rain storm. As we crossed the border into Minnesota, the rain turned to snow, and within a few miles, we were driving in deep ruts. It would have been smart to pull off the road, but once stopped, I knew we would be caught for the night. We kept going, slower and slower, the wipers going faster and faster, until we drove into big city traffic that carried us all the way home.

"Chief"

I didn't want Larry's portrayal of Herbert Hoover in Iowa to go to waste. In the upcoming season, *Chief* played in repertory with the remount of *To Whom It May Concern*. According to our season brochure:

> In the era of the Great Depression, they either
> loved him or hated him. Herbert Hoover was
> popularly considered one of the worst presidents
> and greatest humanitarians of the 20th Century.
> Surprisingly, Hoover, a Republican, embodied
> many of the ideas of the current Democratic Party.

Ironically, in Larry's boyhood home in rural Wyoming, Herbert Hoover's name was never spoken aloud. Only two pictures graced the walls—F.D.R. and the Sacred Heart of Jesus. So, Larry had to delve into researching Hoover, a Republican, in order to develop the role. Despite being a strong Democrat, he became very sympathetic to Hoover's story and loved to lead post-show discussions for groups of students.

Peter Vaughan interviewed Larry for a pre-show article entitled "Hoover Gets Overdue Credit in *Chief* at Lyric." Larry told him,

> (Hoover) was a remarkable man who accom-
> plished a great deal and brought his Quaker
> background to all that he did. As president, he was
> bracketed by two major catastrophes, the stock
> market crash and the Great Depression, which he
> could do very little about. As president, he was in
> the wrong place at the wrong time.

Larry believed that Hoover had one of the best minds of any

president, matched by a big heart. Hoover and his wife Lou put much of their own wealth into feeding other people. Very few audience members were familiar with the fact that Hoover ran the Belgium Relief Agency in 1914 and prevented starvation in that country. To commemorate that fact, a statute was donated to the Hoover Library by Belgian survivors who had been children in 1914. After World War II, President Truman put Hoover in charge of famine relief in Europe. Peter Vaughan's post-show review said the play was overly reverential to Hoover, but ultimately, Hoover emerges as a decent man out of touch with the gravity of the Depression who retreated into inaction because he couldn't understand that hard work and faith in the capitalist system alone might not cure the economic malaise.

Vaughan's parting comment was money in the bank:

> Lyric's production, directed by Sally Childs, is always interesting as Roupe spins out Hoover's recollections, projecting intelligence and compassion tinged with the paternal air the rich often adopt toward the less fortunate.

Larry knew the material so well; he needed little direction other than new blocking and loads of positive reinforcement.

We played *Chief* downstage of the Act curtain during the day for student and senior groups and cleared it for evening performances of *To Whom It May Concern*. We capitalized on Larry's popularity as a substitute teacher, and the show sold moderately well, maximizing our ticket sales receipts.

Larry Roupe as Hoover. Photo by Sally Childs.

Sometimes good fortune smiled on the Lyric in unexpected ways. My success directing *To Whom It May Concern* and Larry's success portraying Herbert Hoover gave us both a chance to do what we did best.

We toured *Chief* in the summer of 1993 to Ely, Minnesota, where we performed at Vermilion Community College under the sponsorship of the Northern Lakes Arts Association, which was managed by my old friend and artist, Cecilia Rolando. I still had many close friends in Ely, and they all attended the performance. Several said afterward that they had no expectations of liking a play about Herbert Hoover, but they found it to be remarkable.

Hoover visiting in Ely. Make-up and photo by Childs.

Chapter 10: Cramps and Recovery

1993: An Implosion

The Lyric Theater was gaining traction, but I was losing traction at my day job. When I joined the firm as a legal secretary in 1986, I was told that Briggs & Morgan was known as a prestigious St. Paul law firm. By 1993, it had grown, especially the Minneapolis branch, and the attorneys decided to add an Executive Director to reshape and streamline the administration and to free them from daily chores of administrative responsibility.

For five years, I had been the Secretarial Coordinator—part of the Human Resources Department and the only administrative person in the Minneapolis office. The Human Resources Director asked me to work on projects that required writing skills, projects such as a daily bulletin and detailed job descriptions, including my own. I liked most of my assignments, and I saw myself as an advocate for the secretaries. But the secretaries saw me as representing the "bosses." Ironically, my annual review in September included a warning that some of the attorneys did not feel I was always supportive of their demands. I was in a no-win position. Or maybe just the wrong position, one for which I was unsuited.

One day in November, I was incredibly busy with orientation for a newly hired Head of Word Processing. In the morning, my boss arrived from St. Paul and said she would be working all day in an empty office across from my tiny office and would like to see me by the day's end. No hurry, however. At 4:30, I finally dropped into a chair next to her desk. She wasted no time in chit-chat and told me she had bad news. The new administration had decided that going forward, my job description would list a new requirement—a degree in Human Resources. I had a B.S. in English education and an M.F.A. in Theater. My H.R. degree was informally obtained on the job in this very firm. I finally understood the admonition: There is no loyalty in the workplace.

My boss thanked me for the insights I had provided when she recently waded into the politics and personalities of a large law firm. I asked if I could remain long enough to qualify for my annual 401k contribution. January 3, 1994, became my formal date of separation. I was transferred to the St. Paul office (to save face? or to appease the attorneys?), but other than writing up and distributing a daily bulletin, I didn't have enough work to keep me busy. My boss moved to an empty office in Minneapolis to handle my responsibilities, but it was a crushing load. A week later, I asked to return to Minneapolis, and she was grateful. I assumed the news of my leaving had spread like wildfire, but no one said a word. By mid-December, my unused vacation time covered the time remaining until January 1, so I cleared out my office after 5:00. The next morning, I completed some paperwork and left during the noon hour without ceremony, carrying a small Christmas cactus from a secretary who sat right outside my office. I was happy no one was required to escort me out.

A severance package gave me several months to figure out how I was going to cover my new mortgage. This window of opportunity invited new light into the dark days and teary nights that lay ahead. Figuring out how to parlay my choices into a workable lifestyle took months of scurrying from one temp job to another, leaving me little time for theater planning. I relied heavily on Larry and other friends to give me ideas.

The Curate Shakespeare

Larry had played the Curate in Gary Stewart's production of Don Nigro's *The Curate Shakespeare* at Indiana State University and said the audiences absolutely loved it. The play follows a ragtag group of seven actors as they prepare to perform at least twenty different roles in *As You Like It*. While the temperamental cast bungles through rehearsals, the beleaguered Curate insists the show must go on.

When I read the script, it seemed sarcastic and raunchy but also farcical and funny, so I thought it might succeed in drawing a younger audience—something we talked about a lot at board meetings. I hired Peter Rothstein (who had appeared in *To Whom It May Concern*) to direct—his first directing job in the Twin Cities. Peter was enormously creative, and he was enthused. I told him that the usual Lyric audiences would probably be turned off by anything terribly raunchy, so I asked him to tone down that aspect. Peter said that would not be a problem. But I had laid a restriction on Peter that could unfairly tamper with his own interpretation.

We were back in the more intimate Little Theater on the second floor of the Hennepin Center, where all of the colorful detail in the props, set and costumes stood out against the black floor and walls. Rothstein staged the show out of a Comedia Dell Arte style wagon designed by Erica Zaffarano. Peter brought in Irma Mayorga as the costume designer, who underlined the poverty of this troupe, according to Peter Vaughan, "with an eclectic collection of motley, from Elizabethan lace to grunge." The photos of the show were gorgeous. The reviews were not.

**Larry Roupe as The Curate and Kathy Hendrickson as Audrey.
Photo by Michaelle Sparrow.**

The headline on Peter Vaughan's review pronounced that the "Lyric Staging of 'Curate Shakespeare' is Leaden." Ouch. Vaughan attacked the script, describing the Curate's pep talks as a string of locker-room cliches about doing one's best and meeting the challenges life offers. Despite enthusiasm and skill that produced moments of humor and insight, much of what's being presented is a deplorably leaden staging of an ethereal Shakespearean comedy.

He berated the playwright for not providing the actors any personal histories: "We need to know what lies behind their theatrical facades, what drives them as people and as thespians."

Vaughan ended with kudos to Lisa Randolph for her "dotty, iconoclastic portrait" and Kathy Hendrickson's "skill and breadth" as Audrey. The costumes also received kudos.

Despite heavy marketing, the show didn't sell. I asked Larry about the Indiana production, why it had been a crowd-pleaser. He said that Gary Stewart was a friend of Don Nigro and had a really good feel for Nigro's work. He also said that Stewart's production was very raunchy, pushing the boundaries of farce over the top. Larry liked raunchiness, and I wondered why he hadn't told me this when he first suggested the show. Perhaps he thought I would reject it immediately out of concern that it would not be welcomed by our Hassler fans.

I realize in retrospect that Peter Vaughan and I made the same mistake in thinking this was a play within a play—a staging of a Shakespearean comedy. It was not. It was a staging of a comedy troupe that did not know how to stage a Shakespearean comedy. But my mistake in toning down the raunchiness went much further. The raunchiness apparently drove the show and made it funny. I was trying to mold a play to fit my perception of the Lyric audience. Had the internet and Google been available, I might have been saved from making such a serious mistake. This was a year to grieve my losses. I thought seriously about closing the theater and looking for a more mundane job that would sustain me financially until retirement.

**Larry Roupe observes Lisa Randolph as Rosalind.
Photo by Michaelle Sparrow.**

I was sorry that Peter Rothstein had to weather a negative review for his first directing gig, but it didn't get in his way. In 1998, he co-founded Theatre Latte Da with Denise Prosek as music director. Peter has subsequently directed at the Guthrie Theater and produced some of the Latte Da shows at the Ordway's McKnight Theater and the Hennepin Trust (Pantages). Since 1998, Latte Da has grown from an itinerant organization to a thriving company with a national reputation for innovative and impactful musical theater, a robust new works development program, and a permanent home at the historic Ritz Theater. By the end of June, Peter will assume a new role as Producing Artistic Director of Asolo Repertory Theatre in Sarasota, Florida. (Information online at info@latteda.org.)

The Doldrums

The Octette Bridge Club by P. J. Barry was in rehearsal and would run in tandem with late-night performances of *Payments Due.* These shows bespoke my own struggle with women's issues—the issue of independence versus interdependence linked to marriage, divorce, family, career—in a world changing and adapting, but not fast enough to break through the gender lines firmly entrenched in our culture.

Lyric's finances were in worse shape than the rag-tag motley characters in the previous show, and the board entered into a serious discussion of whether or not we would be able to proceed. Ironically, my fear of debt, bred into me by parents who married during the Depression, was threatening us with failure as surely as if we were seeking a loan and siphoning receipts into loan payments. The common denominator in the plays that were least successful was MONEY. Never enough to hire administrative or clerical staff or to sustain the AEA Contract. Never enough to pay myself a sustainable wage.

When I should have been reading plays and seeing new work in New York or St. Louis (the Humana Festival), I was wearing my fundraising cap and writing grants—or producing another show or registering for unemployment compensation or looking for temporary work. In the beginning, I had chosen plays with budgets that relied primarily on the goodwill of my many talented friends. Since I paid myself last, if at all, I rationalized that it was okay to divvy the money equally, little that it was. Only once did I select a play that was financially underwritten—with disastrous results. So, why? Why was I still chugging up a hill that grew steeper all the time? Because I was tenacious? Is that a positive or a negative word? Or was the answer because, taken individually, I was pretty good at all of the pieces (except the tech stuff) and so used to shifting hats, I just kept going? I liked to think it was because I preferred working in a field that benefitted humanity over working hard to satisfy corporate greed. My teacher's heart still beat in imaginative rhythms.

I was in the lobby of the Little Theater chewing on this problem when Kristen Mathisen asked what was afoot. Since she was in both *Octette* and *Payments Due*, I dumped it all into her sympathetic ear. "Oh, noooo," she wailed. "How much do you need?" She offered to loan us $6,000. At first, I couldn't get my head around borrowing from one of the actors, but she said the money was just sitting in an account and earning very little interest. I took her offer to the board, and they accepted. Were we only buying time?

The Octette Bridge Club **and Its Sister**

Pairing *Octette Bridge Club* and *Payments Due* had been a no-brainer. I wrote in the press release,

> Whether you bid, pass or double, bridge is a game
> of communication. How families communicate
> with various partners—or fail to communicate—is
> the underlying theme of both plays. The results are
> enactments of a woman's emerging independence.

The Octette Bridge Club (a comic drama) was a nostalgic view of eight sisters who play bridge, gossip, and sing together. Act I takes place in the more innocent 1930s and Act II in the 40s. Betsy, the youngest player, asks her sisters to look realistically at their marital relationships and help her understand the struggle taking place within her own.

The late-night show *Payments Due* fast-forwarded the audience to the 1990s, whereby relationships broke down due to failed expectations. In the title poem, Connolly said that she was born "late, yelling and struggling into the real world of debits and credits, bid and ask, payments due or else." Like the eight sisters in *Octette Bride Club*, Connolly grew up in an Irish Catholic environment. She once remarked, "When you come from mostly an Irish family, it's hard for a young woman to be heard." This is Betsy's problem in *The Octette Bridge Club*.

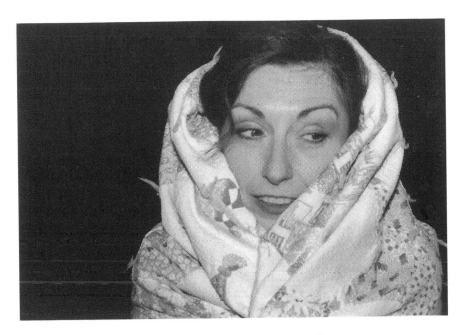

T. K. Lumley as Betsy. Photo by Michaelle Sparrow.

The two plays provided a forum for women's voices. I still wanted to do a little acting and approached Cyd about auditioning with the caveat that I would not hold her to any expectation of being cast. But I won a role—one based on my own merits. I wasn't just stepping up to fill a last-minute vacancy.

Directors are often encouraged to take on an acting role from time to time, forcing them to walk in the actor's shoes when they are giving direction. Cyd's directing style included individual meetings with each actor, and I looked forward to this eagerly. I asked if these meetings were part of her grad training at SMU. She said no. She made a habit of meeting with each actor early in the rehearsal period to find out more about them as people and as actors. She then used this information to guide her direction, thereby helping each actor get closer to the result she desired. I have no memory of my meeting with Cyd. I do remember the outcome.

At the first Sunday matinee, Peter Vaughan was in the audience, notepad in hand. On stage, trapped in a wheelchair as the result of a stroke, my big monologue came near the end of the play. The sisters were being snarky, and in an adrenalin rush, I put them all in their places. It was a breakthrough moment of utter silence except for my voice, flying freely to the top tier of the audience.

**Kristin Mathisen offers Halloween treats to Sally Childs.
Photo by Michaelle Sparrow.**

Peter Vaughan titled his review "Lyric gives 'Octette' a well-done airing" and went on to say the play was "a modest, charming character study receiving an entertaining production by the Lyric Theater." He said of the actors,

> T. K. Lumley deftly establishes Betsy's instability and then, as the play jumps ahead 10 years, reveals her strength and capacity for growth. There is an endearing resilience and intelligence in her wise, consistent portrait. Other fine performances are given by Lavina Erickson as the devout, repressed Martha, Sally Childs as the kindly spinster and Barbara Humphrey Barker as the most perceptive of the group.

The eight sisters at Halloween, left to right: Kristin Mathisen, Lavina Erickson, Betsy Husting, Barbara Humphrey, T. K. Lumley, Sally Childs, Gail Hammerschmidt, Shirley Wasilaukas. Photo by Michaelle Sparrow.

Well done, Cyd! No asides for the weakest member of the cast or any such well-placed needle. Vaughan also pointed out that Cyd "zipped through the story but allowed each character to emerge and grow... finding humor, pain and immense potential in these withered lives."

The *Star Tribune* featured us in a "Spotlight" space with a picture and blurb—the first time in two years. We were selling tickets again!

One goal of our Strategic Plan was to target more marketing, in this case to senior groups, with offers of a special afternoon—"See a PLAY and PLAY bridge on the set following the show." A game of bridge and a theater performance share many words—board, play, set, leg, hand, but didn't share definitions. I PLAYED with words, dangling them like carrots in front of group leaders. It was darn clever. We were even prepared with prizes and refreshments. We never had a group take us up on the offer—

senior groups usually try to get home before the commuter traffic snarls up the streets and highways, but group bookings increased.

We were also featured with a great picture in "Do the Town," a publication of the Marketing Committee of the Minneapolis Downtown Council, which was published every two weeks. We were breaking barriers.

On Being an Actor Again

In retrospect, the shows that worked best shared an important element— strong ensemble acting. I started thinking about this when reading *The Boys in the Boat* by Daniel James Brown about the crew of rowers from Seattle who triumphed at the 1936 Olympics.

I examined theatre in the light of Brown's analysis. He said that in the boat, every person "must recognize his or her place in the fabric of the crew, accept it, and accept the others as they are." When it all comes together (becomes an ensemble), the "<u>intense bonding</u> and the resultant sense of exhilaration are what many oarsmen row for." I believe that actors <u>bond</u> through <u>intense</u> listening (rehearsing instead of practicing). When they experience the "resultant exhilaration," they are able to replicate it over and over through intense listening—which keeps the material fresh, as if they are doing it for the first time. When I appeared in *Octette Bridge Club,* I no longer heard Don Bronski saying, "I bid 'em, you make 'em."

We ran performances of *Payments Due* at 10:15 on Friday and Saturday nights after *The Octette Bridge Club.* It felt good to be home in our intimate space on the second floor of the Hennepin Center for the Arts. Despite needing to recast several roles, the new ensemble had great range. Although we lost the racial diversity, we retained the age span, and the poetry worked just as well.

As usual, I felt awkward in the dressing room, especially right after the show when actors were still riding on the adrenaline remaining in their systems. This was when people spoke without thinking—it was like a truth serum. I often heard other directors talked about in very unflattering terms and wondered what was said about me in dressing rooms all over town.

Back Row: Kristin Mathisen, Lavina Erickson, Lisa Randloph, and Suzanne Koepplinger. Front Row: Sally Childs and Rita Olk. Photo Michaelle Sparrow.

One night after a late performance of *Payments Due*, I was seated between Kristen Mathisen and Lavina Erickson, both strong supporters of the Lyric and close friends. Kristen made the comment that what I needed to do was to hire some <u>really good directors</u>, and Lavina agreed. I smiled and asked for a little more input, which I got from both of them. It was a heart-stabbing moment.

I had directed eight of the Lyric shows, and Cyd had directed three. I told myself that the comment was based historically in some of our reviews—simply advice for moving forward—not meant as a comment on Cyd and me. By "really good directors," I think they meant people who had solid reputations in the acting community and good notices from critics. They were aware that directing fees could be prohibitive. The going fee for a well-known director was minimally from $1,000 to $2,000. What the actors didn't know was that the most I had ever paid myself as a director was $500, and the remainder of my directing fee converted to unearned income as a pro bono donation.

Cyd and I were so busy with the Lyric and our day jobs that we were not directing for other theaters, thereby limiting our exposure in the acting community. Cyd was about to leave the Lyric and Northern Sign to manage Chautauqua, a new organization that would perform on Harriet Island in St. Paul.

Once these two shows closed, we started paying off our loan from Kristen, and we even paid a little interest. As we got stronger financially, we were able to borrow small amounts from a government agency for non-profits.

Starting Here, Starting Now

The criteria for the next Lyric production demanded low risk. I was in the Director's chair, my confidence shored up by success with *To Whom It May Concern*. I looked beyond Minnesota connections and selected a small-cast musical, *Starting Here, Starting Now*, with lyrics by Richard Maltby and music by David Shire. Maltby won the 1978 Tony as Best Director of a Musical for conceiving and directing *Ain't Misbehavin'*. He was better known, however, as a lyricist of *Miss Saigon*. Shire had composed forty feature film scores, including an Oscar for the song "It Goes Like It Goes" from *Norma Rae*. Our press release for *Starting Here, Starting Now* described the show as "rich with upbeat melodies and charming moments that develop into some real beginnings, some false starts and many small discoveries." I'm sure that sentence came from the Music Theatre International catalog. That sentence also seemed to describe my life as I scuttled from temp job to theater to parent's home, just the old Energizer Bunny beating my drum.

Joey Babay, who appeared for us in *Boxelder Bug Variations* and *Texas Chainsaw Manicurist*, had joined Actor's Equity Association. Since we lacked the money to reinstate a union contract, he could no longer perform for us but was willing to step in as the choreographer. Erica was available to design the set. The three of us staged it as a journey that required a large steamer trunk which we filled with props. Suitcases were carried up or down a z-shaped ramp that provided sitting

180

space or additional height for standing. We pulled spare suitcases from my basement and painted them red, green and tan. An old-fashioned street lamp lit the way up the ramp. Erica used her wizardry to create intimate spaces within the ramp and a dance floor to suggest stops on the journey.

Dana Farner, Norah Long, and David Anderson.

The show was essentially a revue featuring three singers—one man and two women. Mike Bond was back as Music Director and Pianist. I cast Norah Long, Dana Farner and David A. Anderson as the performers. Norah was already what is known in the industry as a triple threat, equally good as a singer, actor and dancer. Nora trained under Ben Krywosz of Nautilus Theater to learn to use the techniques for actors/singers as taught by Wesley Balk, a professor at the University of Minnesota. She went on to become a union actor appearing at major Twin City theaters, including the Guthrie Theater, the History Theatre and Chanhassen Dinner Theatre.

Dana Farner and Norah Long. *Today is the Last Day of the Rest of My Life.*

David Anderson, a conductor and baritone with The Sentimental Journey Big Band, added balance and ballast. The dancing was a stretch for him. His day job was as a cabinet maker for a family-owned business, so after hours, he cleared away the sawdust and put in lots of extra hours working on his dance numbers. It paid off. Part way through the run, an audience member approached me during intermission, asking where I had found a professional dancer who could also sing. I could hardly wait to tell David after the show.

Again, we were invited to fill a spot on MPR's "Morning Show" with Dale Conley and Tom Keith. Mike Steele reviewed us for the *Star Tribune* and said that the show was at its strongest musically:

> The cast, supported stylishly by Mike Bond at the
> piano, blend nicely—Anderson with a ringing
> baritone, Long with a pleasant soprano and Farner
> with a great character voice full of personality.

David Anderson with pizazz.

He also pointed out that the songs were complete in and of themselves and "didn't need any 'artificial' movement or to be oversold." Did that imply we had kept the movement pleasantly simple—or that we had used too much movement? He ended the review by saying the songs were "all big league, the trio singing them with ebullience and charm."

Ironically, I had worried about finding enough movement in the piece to make it interesting. The journey idea shaped the show. My favorite song, "Just Across the River," had spurred some of our movement ideas. The song received great comments from Dale Conley on MPR radio—without any movement at all. There are so many ways to "call a spade a spade."

Norah Long, Dana Farner, and David Anderson.

Dana, David, and Norah high stepping.

Bit Parts

The day I separated from Briggs and Morgan at the end of 1993, I went directly to my first commercial gig as an actor at the second-floor restaurant in the IDS building, which overlooked The Crystal Court, a huge atrium connected by a skyway to all the other office buildings downtown. The restaurant was well known as a scenic element on the Mary Tyler Moore Show which ran on CBS from September 19, 1970, to March 19, 1997, and customers often asked to sit at the Mary Tyler Moore table. I had been hired to appear in a commercial advertising the newest cuisine available in the restaurant's most recent reincarnation.

I arrived with several wardrobe bags trailing from my left arm. I was paying back a debt. The videographer was Todd Gross, a former student of Larry's, who had filmed *To Whom It May Concern* for the Lyric Theater's archives at no cost. The moment I appeared, a wardrobe specialist looked over my choices and settled on something blue. Within minutes, I was memorizing a few lines, and I became a person with no name. "The talent will enter from here and cross to…" It took a moment to realize I was "the talent" and had missed my first direction. I stepped into this new world and did everything Todd asked for, including quacking like a duck over a featured entree.

I had recently registered with a couple of talent agencies and gone on a few auditions. Now, nameless but "talented" with duck-quacking capabilities, I had launched a new slice in my life, absurd and unpaid. After the shoot, I descended to street level and waved at the statue of Mary Tyler Moore tossing her hat into the air in front of the flagship Dayton's Department Store at South 7th Street and Nicollet Mall before stepping on a bus to go home.

My next temp job was as an interviewer and scheduler of secretaries for Templeton & Associates, a temp service that specialized in legal secretaries and paralegals. I was welcomed to the job by two former Briggs employees.

One morning Lisa Dunham, the paralegal scheduler, walked in looking like a supermodel in an elegant black and white tweed knit pantsuit topped by a full-length duster that accentuated her long legs.

Her flawless skin, blue eyes, and cropped blonde hair completed the picture. I fell in love with the outfit and signed up as an independent fashion consultant for Weekender clothing with Lisa as my manager. I would never have agreed to sell non-essentials like Tupperware or jewelry or crystal glassware, but everybody has to wear clothes. So, I bought my sales pack and started booking in-home sales events, demonstrating a line of knit clothing made in the U.S.A. and Canada. For the first time in years, I could afford to visit friends in Ely and Denver and write off my travel expenses by demonstrating clothing. I loved both the clothing and the perks, but selling and booking in-home demonstrations was difficult for someone who would rather work backstage. But as the sole employee of a theater, I needed to learn salesmanship, and when women tried on clothes together, there was enough fun to offset my discomfort.

My dear friend Pam, who managed the Lyric box office for years, also worked as the Office Manager for Sprenger & Lang, a law firm practicing employment law and managing class action suits. Pam had no history with temp agencies, so eventually, she hired me directly as a part-time receptionist and typist at a better wage than I could get through an agency. Life settled into a pattern that allowed flexibility for theater work, looking in on parents, selling clothes and theater tickets, and seeing the grandkids. Everywhere I went, women admired my beautiful knit clothing, so I learned to talk more readily with strangers, a win-win situation.

Chapter 11: On a Wintry Hill

The Murphy Initiative

Over several years of calling our patrons, Larry Roupe developed a friendship with Mark McCartan, a Hassler fan who shared a connection to The Academy of Holy Angels where Larry subbed regularly, and Mark's sons were students. Mark and his wife had traveled to Ireland where they saw an Irish play that Mark had recommended to the Lyric Theater. While in Ireland, the McCartans called upon the playwright Niall Williams and his wife Christine Breen and discovered the couple had met while living and working in New York. When Niall's wife inherited property in Ireland, they crossed the Atlantic and began a new life. It was rare for a theater patron to suggest a play, so I investigated further. I was looking for a Minnesota connection. It came in the plot line.

The Murphy Initiative is set in a village in western Ireland full of Murphys. A county councillor concocts an initiative (scheme) that would save the parish from dire poverty and keep his son from emigrating, a common problem in this part of Ireland. The plan is to lure gullible Americans to Ireland where they will stay at the original decrepit Murphy homestead for an exorbitant fee. Justin Murphy, <u>an American actor from St. Paul</u> who is desperately seeking his Irish roots, arrives in Ireland with his daughter, a newly graduated psych major. The American Murphy could quote line for line from every Irish play written before 1968, while Irishman T. B. Murphy could do the same for the American film *The Magnificent Seven*. The comedy often spilled over into farce. According to the playwright, "Situations are pushed to the nth degree to demonstrate that 'we need you and you need us.'"

**Irishman, Connie Murphy (Tom Sherohman) takes advantage
of the ignorant American, Justin Murphy (Walter Weaver).
Photo by Michaelle Sparrow.**

I signed a license agreement with Niall Williams on July 24, 1994, for a Lyric production in February-March 1995. Director Joe Sadowski started working with Williams via phone calls to reshape and improve the script. Williams and Breen would see the play when they arrived on a stateside book signing tour for the fourth book in a series recalling their experiences in settling on the family farm in Ireland. The Irish American Cultural Institute coordinated the tour to include a reception at Kiernan's Irish Pub in Minneapolis for the playwright following the March 11th performance of *The Murphy Initiative*. Prior to the show that night, the McCartans hosted Larry and me, along with Williams and Breen, for dinner at The Loring Bar and Restaurant, rounding out a very special experience. But before we reached opening night, this production became even more special.

Peter Vaughan's review noted, "The show must go on" as the "rallying cry" at the Lyric Theatre during tech week. Indeed. Bob Otto

(T. B. Murphy) was to play a major part. Two days before opening night, Bob was caught in the crossfire of a gang shooting in St. Paul just as he was getting out of his parked car. He was treated at the St. Paul-Ramsey Medical Center where the doctors advised him not to return to acting for at least a month.

The only possible way to open the play on time was for the director, Joe Sadowski, to step into the role. I spent the next day arranging a three-performance contract with Actor's Equity for Joe while he stuffed the lines into his amazing memory. *The Murphy Initiative* opened on time and received a very sympathetic review. Then my parachute deflated with Niall Williams' lukewarm reaction to the performance. The farcical elements must have worked much better in Dublin where actors spoke with authentic Irish voices, and the Americans were no doubt portrayed as foolish romantics. Crossing the Atlantic may be the acid test for playwrights.

By the second weekend, Galway McCullough, a young actor who recently returned to his Minnesota roots, took over the role vacated by Bob Otto. We were blessed with Irish names. Molly Delaney portrayed a spirited young Irish woman and got the best mention in the review.

Bob Otto eventually recovered enough to become a speaker on gang violence and then moved to recover with his uncle in Iowa. As far as I know, he never returned to acting.

Bob Otto

At the time of this writing, Niall Williams has become a major Irish novelist with eight novels to his credit. When I researched his website, I found no mention of plays.

Too Big For Our Britches?

For several years we held an annual fall fundraiser—the Harvest Celebration. These events had raised modest amounts and were informal at-home parties held at Rita Olk's or Sally Anderson's palatial homes. Everett suggested we risk a gala and used his membership at the Calhoun Beach Club to rent The Boulevard Room on November 5, 1995, from 2:00 to 5:00 pm. Built as an apartment community on Lake Street facing its namesake, Lake Calhoun, the building was an iconic landmark for the wealthy. I imagined myself a princess in 1955 when I attended a prom held in the lavish second-floor ballroom. Having passed through several phases, including housing for the elderly, it had returned to upscale apartments and club facilities.

We mailed an invitation to all of our six thousand ticket buyers. We culled out a second list of about two hundred people to receive a personal phone call. Ben Olk offered the offices at National Checking, his St. Paul printing business, for an evening round of calls. As enthusiastic as the board was for other activities, only a couple volunteered to call. We still weren't very good at tailoring our efforts to the personalities and time constraints of our small working board. We reached a few people that evening, but future calling chores were left to Larry Roupe.

Rita continued to spearhead the Harvest Celebration planning, looking for donors to help cover printing costs. I visited the Calhoun Beach Club to view the lush lobby, which led through large double doors to an expansive mirrored and marbled room framed by French doors and a graceful grand staircase. But my most salient memory was being a small seashell in a very large aquarium. The club agreed to cater the event for $12.00 per guest, and we had to contract for one hundred servings. I signed the agreement but planned to keep a board member at my side in case I lost my voice (as I had at my daughter's wedding).

Guests arrived in elegant outfits, wafting perfume. They paid a minimum donation of $25.00 at the door. Then they entered the Boulevard Room, where a lectern and grand piano sat in an alcove shaped by the bottom of the curved staircase. A cash bar and long table of sweet and savory morsels drew people to the farthest side of the room.

The Potted Palms, a jazz trio, which included Kathy Hardy's husband on string bass, provided background music. Once a sufficient crowd was in place, I introduced the next season, and Jon Hassler read from his most recent novel, *Rookery Blues*. Then Kathy Hardy and David Anderson (*Starting Here, Starting Now*) sang musical selections from the Big Band Era, the music featured in Hassler's new novel, *Rookery Blues*.

The event was lovely, but the room was a little too big for the seventy or so people who attended. If my elderly mother had come, she would have told me I was getting too big for my britches. After the bills were paid and pledges collected, we cleared $22. A year later, Barbara Davis of Resources and Counseling told me that was fantastic. Galas rarely made money.

Soldier Boy

True to our history of investigating ideas offered by our growing family of artists, at Carol Connolly's suggestion, we talked to a St. Paul playwright, Paul Mohrbacher. His recently published play, *A Chancellor's Tale*, was getting good press. But Paul felt that play was not particularly well suited to the Lyric audience and asked us to consider his second play, *Soldier Boy*, which was rooted in the meat packing strike at Hormel in Austin, Minnesota, ten years earlier. As the playwright pointed out:

> This is not a play about the Hormel strike. It's a
> play about some people in a small (fictional) Mid-
> western town torn apart by a psychic fault line.
> Each of them is singing a song. But ... the fault
> line has spread so wide that nobody else is listen-
> ing. It's about singers deaf to each other's song.
> And into this mess steps the outsider, to shake up
> the fault line and restore community.

The characters and locale may be fictional, but Paul Mohrbacher's inspiration came from events in Austin. Not only was he interested in the "us and them" attitudes that tore families apart, but also what happened to the voices that urged accommodation. *Soldier Boy* had as its central character a wise, elderly man, modeled on Paul's father-in-law, a dentist who had experienced the strike and died in 1990 at age ninety-five.

The underlying themes were understanding and conciliation. It even had a song supplied by local songwriter Richard Wilson. Cyd was back after Chautauqua closed and signed on as director. A little spade work led us to Dick Welsbacher, who recently retired after thirty years as Director of Theatre at Wichita State University. Dick was the father of local playwright, Anne Welsbacher, and was able to prolong a visit with Anne to take on the role of Doc Dooley. In the play, Dooley's daughter, Sarah, works for The Company and is a struggling single mother of a teenaged daughter. Enter Tony Guzman, a union organizer who lives in Doc's building and becomes a friend. Four people and several levels of conflict.

**Dick Welsbacher in the title role of "Soldier Boy"
with his granddaughter played by Christi Cole.**

Soldier Boy tied for third place in the 1993 Jewel Box Theatre Playwriting Award, a national playwright's competition sponsored by a community theater founded in 1957 in Oklahoma City. The play had gone through readings at The Playwright's Center, where Mohrbacher was an active member. Cyd and I thought it was seaworthy enough to be launched in a full production. Peter Vaughan disagreed, however; he found the characters interesting and lauded Mohrbacher's "keen ear for dialogue" and his skill in finding humor at will. But Vaughan called for tightening, focusing, a fuller exposition of the major concerns, and fixing some hard-to-believe moments. The play had tremendous promise and was certainly worthy of the rewriting that Vaughan was calling for.

Ticket sales remained fairly good, despite Vaughan's comments. Mohrbacher's wife, Ruth Murphy, and her brother, Tom Meany, marshaled their large family to see the show and push ticket sales.

As far as I know, *Soldier Boy* never got that rewrite, and when I checked recently on Mohrbacher's LinkedIn page on the internet, only *The Chancellor's Tale* made it into his list of playwriting achievements. In my estimation, Doc Dooley, a crusty sage with the wisdom to promote conciliation to resolve a conflict, is a character we can still learn from in a country with an "us and them" mentality so well demonstrated by current events.

Hoover Crosses the Prairie

Meeting Larry for morning coffee may have started with a crossword puzzle, but much of our time turned into brainstorming ways to parlay the Lyric's successes into continuing sources of income. As a natural extension of our group sales efforts, we chose *Chief* to take on tour to schools. In 1995 I received permission from the playwright to pare down the two-hour show to fifty-five minutes, and Larry relearned the shorter version, the perfect project for Larry and me, a couple of seasoned educators. I researched the cost of a short tour to include ten schools and kept the budget under $6,000, which included some pro bono services.

The Lyric Theater received a grant of $5,000 from U.S. West. We also received technical and marketing support from the Southwest Arts and

Humanities Council (SMACH), so we limited our tour to southwestern Minnesota. We swapped rehearsal time at the Academy of the Holy Angels in Richfield for a kick-off performance for their students. The rest of the tour went to Hutchinson, Dawson, Benson, Minneota, Pipestone, Luverne, Windom, Lake Benton, and Delano, starting on February 9 and ending on March 6, 1996. Rob Ross of SMACH made the arrangements with the schools, and I sent a confirmation letter, press information, and study guide to the contact person at each host school.

On a very cold February morning, Larry and I loaded furniture and suitcases into a small rented van. He played his role (star of the show) while I chauffeured. Our first stop was Hutchinson, a town with some interesting history located about sixty-five miles west via Highway 7.[4]

We pulled up to the high school, an old-fashioned dark red building, and I entered the front lobby to check-in. The principal greeted me, looking perplexed, apparently unaware that we were coming. I handed him some paperwork, worried that we would be turned away. After an awkward half-hour of discussion, he invited us in and set the wheels in motion. I set up the stage with the help of students and a stage technician while Larry spent time talking with students in history classes. After the show, we still felt like intruders, but the teacher thanked us and wished us well.

As soon as I got to a phone, I started calling principals to confirm our arrangements in person. For the most part, throughout the tour, Larry worked with sophomores who studied American history as part of the curriculum. I kept driving and sparred with the schedulers and receptionists, carrying paperwork and furniture as needed. Larry had become my big brother, competitive and protective simultaneously.

In Minneota (Bill Holm's hometown), while Larry visited a classroom, I was asked to lecture in an interactive televised women's studies class that included students connected by satellite cameras in Marshall and Canby. I talked about Lou Henry Hoover and read from *First Lady Lou*, another script written by Rebecca Christian. I had taught high school English/Media for twelve years in Babbitt, Minnesota, but this was my first experience teaching on camera.

At the end of the day, we received a handwritten note, an action unheard of in today's electronic culture. It was from a Minneota teacher, who thanked Larry for his strong performance and thanked me for visiting the women's studies class. He also thanked Rob Ross of SMACH for his interest and involvement.

We traveled west, all the way to Lake Benton, an agricultural town on the South Dakota border, where Larry performed for the whole senior high school at the old-fashioned Lake Benton Opera House.

We ended the tour with some wonderful ideas for future school tours, but this would have forced us to hire a staff person dedicated to this aspect of production. We couldn't afford to siphon off funding needed for our regular season, so we put it on hold and finally jettisoned it.

Beyond Performance

1995 became a pivotal year. Cyd and Nate were expecting a child. They sold their home in North Minneapolis, withdrew from further theater commitments, and moved to a northwestern suburb.

Joe Sadowski shared time and expertise, but board membership would have created a conflict of interest since he was auditioning for other theaters. His main advice was to create a bigger board, fifteen to twenty people strong. Our strategy was two-fold: to start inviting any friends or colleagues who had shown interest in the Lyric Theater to board meetings and to hold regular readings and discussions of plays under consideration so board members or prospective members could feel more involved in the artistic side of running a theater.

Everett Janssen stepped down as President, so our new slate of officers included me as President, Kathy Hardy as VP, Laurie Rivard Montanez as Treasurer, and Deanne Levander-Larson as Secretary. Sally Anderson, Barbara Strandell, Carol Michels, and Rita Olk completed the board roster. Many people served beyond the number of years suggested by our by-laws, but we couldn't afford to lose them when they brought so much expertise and Lyric history to the table. Kathleen Hardy and Rita Olk not only appeared in several Lyric shows but also provided connections to the business community.

We continually looked for more fundraising opportunities. Kristy Barnes, an old colleague from Ehlers & Associates and now employed by

Honeywell, willingly shepherded a grant proposal through the Honeywell Foundation, resulting in a $3,000 grant. Sally Anderson had left Dain Bosworth for locally owned Kopp Investment Advisors, where she garnered a $2,000 donation. Kathy Hardy took advantage of St. Paul Companies' employee program for matching donations. For the second consecutive year, Everett's business had been awarded the T-shirt concession at Taste of Minnesota, celebrated on the Minnesota State Capitol mall on July 4. In 1994 Lyric volunteers staffed the booth for three days, resulting in $900 for the Theater. Everett asked for volunteers again in 1995 and offered me a small stipend to act as manager so he could be free to print and deliver t-shirts as needed. A few stalwarts agreed to work the event again.

An annual grant writing calendar was in progress, and I kept up with the application schedule. I still lacked the time or skills to enter into the social aspects of fundraising, the handshaking, and the cordial schmoozing to increase the chance of clinching the deal. I left this to Rita Olk, who was good at it, partly because she and her husband Ben were contributors to many non-profits favored by Ben's clients. Rita also played golf, and the 19th hole was a great place to land a contribution, as an executive of CIGNA soon found out.

The Lyric had become a major tenant in the Hennepin Center for the Arts. To get the most bang for our buck, we decided to stage two shows in repertory between January 20 and March 24. Joe Sadowski would direct one, and I would direct the other. Joe selected *The Decorator,* a zany farce by Donald Churchill, and I selected *The Golden Age,* a comedy by A. R. Gurney. We also incorporated several matinees of *Chief* to be targeted for school groups. We focused on audience development and ignored two aspects of our mission statement, the Minnesota connection and the inclusion of music.

By the spring of 1996, planning could be based on more than just hope. The donor page in the playbill finally listed four foundations as donors: Doherty, Butler & Rumble; Honeywell Foundation; McKnight Foundation; and U.S. West Foundation. Six corporations also made donations of over $500. MRAC continued to fund a show every year, and more ticket buyers were making good on their pledges. *The Southwest Journal* did an article about the tenth anniversary of the Lyric Theater and mentioned that our annual budget had grown to $90,000.

I was still trying to solidify a niche for the Lyric Theater. At about this time, Dave Moore stopped by the ticket counter and complimented me on my willingness to take such amazing risks. Apparently, it was part of the reason he and his wife Shirley kept coming to see our shows and making donations. It was a lovely compliment, but it was not a niche. The Lyric's production history was more roller coaster than prairie locomotive.

We were devoting a lot of board time to marketing discussions. Joe felt the public should have been made aware of our first repertory season when we produced two to three shows in tandem (on alternating dates). Spoken like a true theater artist. I wondered if our audience could define repertory, or even spell it, much less care. We couldn't afford to pay for newspaper ads—a Friday ad in the *Star Tribune* cost at least $450. We knew we had to spend money to make money, but we were already in debt and unwilling to risk more.

I met with Linda Twiss, the Marketing Director for the Cricket Theater. She said that the Cricket spent around $3,000 for advertising per show, alternating between the *Star Tribune* and *The Reader*, starting two weeks prior to opening night and continuing through the run. She felt that this level of advertising helped increase attendance. Linda's office was in the Skyway system not far from the Hennepin Center. We agreed to keep meeting so I could continue to learn from the marketing experience she gained from working for various arts groups, including the History Theater and the St. Paul Chamber Orchestra.

In April, I stopped taking a stipend and spent more time on increasing my sales of Weekender clothing, the sideline that maintained my cash flow when times were tough. As a result, I needed more help with the theater. Again, board members stepped up, especially Rita Olk, whose prior fundraising work for the Eden Prairie Community Theater prepared her to hit the boards running.

The Decorator and The Golden Age

We renewed our contract with Actor's Equity so that Joe Sadowski could cast Steve Hendrickson in the title role of *The Decorator* by Donald Churchill. The play was a farce—a love triangle—with two women at cross purposes with the Decorator. Peter Vaughan said of the play,

> There are plenty of easy laughs, many generated by Steve Henkrickson's daffy and energetic portrayal of a would-be actor who gets the role of his life impersonating the husband of an adulterous wife. Nuff said. It's a hoot.

A daffy scene with Steve Hendrickson, Janet Hanson. and Sandy Johnson. Photo by Nancy Campbell.

The Golden Age by A.R. Gurney also required three actors. The show had been suggested to me by Wendy Lamphear, the marketing expert I met at Briggs and Morgan, who volunteered to write our first season brochure. She had seen the play in another city and thought it would be a good choice for the Lyric. After reading it, I could see the comic possibilities and thought it could serve as a companion piece to *The Decorator*. Again, a love triangle of sorts. Isabel, an aging muse of the salons of the 1920s with a squeamish granddaughter to unload, has an unpublished manuscript to use as a bribe. Tom, an itinerant academic, offers to write Isabel's biography. He wants the book but not the girl— and then he flip-flops, opting for the girl.

More shenanigans: Alan Sorenson (the writer) transports Marilyn Murray (Isabel), which amuses Molly Delaney, her granddaughter.

I worried about having my work seen in repertory with Joe Sadowski's, a worry well founded. Vaughan told his readers that *The Decorator* "was the type of easy, transatlantic comedy that has been filling the Old Log Theater for years. You will search in vain for a strand of relevance or social commentary, but you won't have to look either long or hard for laughs." A critical SUCCESS! Vaughan said of *The Golden Age* that it "was sheer nonsense from its silly beginning to its transparent close." Whereas Joe's direction was "effective," my production had found "moments of humor, but never became even slightly credible." He absolutely hated the script. Vaughan's review was essentially the kiss of death. We had very small houses for *The Golden Age*.

On the other hand, John Townsend, writing for *Lavender Lifestyles*, said wonderful things about both plays and added *Chief* into the mix, calling them a "Delicious Triple Treat." He said *Chief* was "terrific" and my direction was "effective." Of *The Decorator*, he said the pace and timing were "impeccably brisk." Of *The Golden Age*, he said that my results were "specific and magical." *Lavender Lifestyles* was a magazine directed at the gay community. Townsend's review was not read by the general theater audience, but I read it with interest.

The set designer, Roger Skophammer, received kudos from several reviewers. All three plays used the same basic room that could be quickly and easily dressed and re-dressed as we moved from one play to another. The set for *The Decorator* was contemporary, with a small grand piano and a chair with a cane seat that had to give way and trap one of the actresses in every performance. The piano carried over to the set for *The Golden Age*, and the chair was replaced by a chaise, a set which was described by Vaughan as "a feast of knick-knacks, bric-a-brac, curios and overstuffed remnants of another age." Roger was the Technical Director at the History Theatre and was able to plunder their prop storage area at will.

Alan Sorenson looks down the wrong end of Isabel's rifle with Molly Delaney clutching her robe in *The Golden Age*.

**Sandy Johnson contemplates Janet Hanson's
foolishness in *The Decorator*.**

We lost $6,000 on each show. Eight hundred and ninety people
attended the twenty-three performances of *The Decorator*; six hundred
and twenty-five attended the eighteen performances of *The Golden Age*.
Averaged, only three tickets separated the two shows. Our repertory
experiment was adversely affected by the coldest Minnesota winter since
the turn of the century. The city was virtually closed down for a weekend,

including four shows at our theater. Add to that a dying parent of one of the cast members, and we were forced to drop a couple more shows. I wrote to Dramatists Play Service asking if they would consider refunding the prepaid royalties for the six canceled shows ($60 per show). They graciously sent us a check for $360.

Chapter 12: Jogging South, Down River

Rural Roots and Small-Town Values

Chris Samuelson was back in town, tucked into a bedroom in my home, where she began working on an adaptation of Jon Hassler's most autobiographical novel, *Grand Opening*. Set in Plum, a fictitious name for Plainview, a small town twenty-three miles northeast of Rochester, Minnesota, the story was based on Jon's family buying a small grocery store in 1943 when he was ten years old. Chris had recently seen *To Kill a Mockingbird* at the History Theater, which used a narrator to frame the story. But narration (telling the story as opposed to showing the action) is not a dramatic device. She was determined to adapt *Grand Opening* without a narrator, a difficult choice for a novel that was told in first person by a young boy. While we were still producing in the Little Theater, she told me she had a first act, but she was stymied. Hoping to break through, we asked a few actors to read the first act for Jon Hassler and a few other trusted people on a Monday (dark) night.

Jon Hassler loved the script and offered to complete it. Chris gave him her blessing, and four months later, the script was ready for a fall production. Since Hassler's previous script had put the Lyric on the map, it seemed a good choice. I was happy to go "home"—to get back to Minnesota writers and what they represented for me. The University of Notre Dame summed it up when it conferred the degree of Doctor of Letters, *honora causa,* on Jon Francis Hassler:

> A Minnesota storyteller whose novels plumb the
> placid depths of small towns, quiet loves, and
> muted yearnings, searching them for avenues of

grace. Living, working, teaching and dreaming
in Midwestern towns occasionally overlooked by
mapmakers, he guides his readers into similarly
neglected regions of the human soul. A realist in
matters spiritual, he aims his narratives at the place
where human folly encounters divine mystery, and
so becomes an artist of the sacramental.

I asked Joe Sadowski to direct again. The Little Theater was already booked, so we sublet the eighth floor at the Hennepin Center for the Arts from Illusion Theatre, the full-time tenant.

By July, I was back to full-time hours for the Lyric just in time to launch a many-faceted marketing plan that targeted school audiences for morning matinees. I whipped up a study guide for *Grand Opening* with contributions from Hassler's long-time friends—Dan Lange, a high school teacher; Joe Plut, Jon's colleague from Brainerd Community College; and Larry Roupe's colleague, Tom Bakken, an English teacher at Benilde-St. Margaret's High School who implemented Hassler into his curriculum. They all became marketing channels to reach students. The State Department of Education provided us with labels for every school in Minnesota. After the mailing, the marketing committee followed up with phone calls, and Larry Roupe fired up his fingers to call donors and season ticket buyers.

The high schools filled several 10:00 a.m. matinees. Students were well behaved with one exception—the day that several schools arrived right on time, but the last school got sidetracked when the bus driver thought he was going to the Hennepin Government Center instead of the Hennepin Center for the Arts. When they finally arrived, I announced, "We have to get you up to the eighth floor as quickly as possible. Students need to line up in front of the elevators, but if there are any athletes up to the challenge, you may jog up the stairs to the eighth floor. Now let's go." From the laughter in the stairwell, I think the eight-floor climb was the most fun some of them had all day.

We partnered with Barnes and Noble to create "Book Fairs," whereby we brought materials and people to the store to provide readings or other entertainment and hand out information. In turn, the Lyric advertised the book fairs, earning a small percentage of the book sales while we were present. The first one was at the Galleria in Edina, where Jon read from *Rookery Blues*. As Hassler fans lined up for the book signing, a friend and I handed out Lyric Theater bookmarks which people automatically stuck into their books for later use. The Lyric received $472 for that event, so we went on to participate in other Barnes and Noble Book Fairs.

Jon's publisher, Ballentine Books, graciously provided us with artwork from the book jacket and the paperback cover of *Grand Opening*. They also bought out the performance on September 5, which they filled with people from the publishing and book-selling businesses as well as a few dignitaries from their own publishing group. Much of this was started before Jon even finished the script. Rehearsals began July 29, and a mass mailing went out on August 1. We were already halfway to opening night.

The Play, *Grand Opening*

Hassler's *Grand Opening* covers the nine months in 1944 that led up to D-Day in Europe. The characters were vintage Hassler, quirky as always.

Rufus (Duane Koivisto) suffers the attention of Wallace Flint (Richard Jackson). Photo by Michaelle Sparrow.

Without a narrator, as in the novel, the play begins when Jon's fictional counterpart, ten-year-old Brendan Foster, leads his family onstage. Brendan's Catholic parents struggle to restore a failed grocery store and turn it into a profitable business in a town where a grocer on the opposite side of the street is a proud Lutheran, setting up a major conflict that characterizes Plum, a small rural town. The Fosters find Wallace Flint asleep on some gunny sacks in the back room, where he rests when he feels an epileptic fit coming on. Wallace claims to "come with the store."

Brendan Foster (Matt Harris) preps flyers, while Dodger (John Stillwell) exchanges a flyer, and a friendly moment with Rufus (Duane Koivisto). Photo by Michelle Sparrow.

Brendan's somewhat senile grandfather fleshes out the family and provides much of the humor as he connects with the neighbors—Mrs. Ottman and her mentally challenged son Rufus, who live next door—and several blocks away, Mrs. Clay, the loneliest woman in Plum. Dodger Hicks, a teenaged outcast, latches onto Brendan until Brendan figures out that Dodger is a social liability, but Dodger keeps returning to the Fosters over Brendan's objections. Stan Kimball, the local undertaker and furniture store owner, encourages the Fosters while his judgmental Lutheran wife watches through binoculars from her window next door. Only one other character is plucked from the novel, the most disconnected priest ever to serve a parish.

Stan Kimball (Clark Cruikshank) coaches Hank and Catherine Foster (Chuck Deeter and Laura Wiebers) in marketing groceries. Photo by Michelle Sparrow.

As in other Hassler stories, the small town plays a major role as the Fosters try to fit in, especially when Catherine runs for the school board—and falls prey to a Lutheran plot. Then the Fosters' store is destroyed by fire, and Dodger is found dead in the basement. When the Catholic priest refuses to lead the funeral mass, Catherine Foster delivers an eloquent speech celebrating Dodger's life but damning the townspeople who sat in judgment on him. In the closing monologue, Brendan overcomes his fear of Rufus, reaching for his hand as he finalizes his feelings about Dodger.

Joe Sadowski continued editing the script, with Jon Hassler's help, right into the rehearsal period. We were in the first of the last four rehearsals when Joe wanted to make some changes to the ending. I grabbed the new pages and headed to a bookstore in suburban Wayzata where Jon was signing his new novel for buyers lined up six deep. I had to break in. After reading Joe's changes, Jon was not pleased. I headed back to the Hennepin Center with this news… Joe was not pleased. Forced to abide by Jon's wishes, this transaction drove a wedge into their relationship.

In his review for the *Star Tribune*, Peter Vaughan compared the story told in the novel with the story told in the play. Vaughan commented that Hassler novels "gain their vitality and vision from their well-drawn, off-beat characters far more than their slender plots." He went on to say that in a play, "plot takes precedence over character, and figures who stir the imagination on the page become flat and underdeveloped on stage."

Joe Sadowski understood these challenges, and in casting Larry Roupe as the grandfather, he met the challenge head-on. But Vaughan reminds us that in the book, the grandfather is "a fascinating mix of wisdom and dependence, likely to wander off on some personal pursuit, forget his way and have to be brought home like a lost dog." He goes on to comment that Roupe "creates a memorable portrait but he fails to suggest the grandfather's failing mental powers." Roupe chose to play Grandfather as slyly opportunistic but easily sidetracked. When he wanders off to deliver a sales flyer to the turkey grower's lonely wife, he finds her in the garage brewing some hooch, an opportunity to flirt a little and join her in a drink. Hassler never objected when actors abandoned the characterization in the novel to interpret the character they found written into the script—as long as it didn't alter Jon's plot.

Grandfather (Larry Roupe) distributes flyers for the store, leading to a neighbor's garage and a casual drink with Mrs. Clay (Delta Giordano). Photo by Michelle Sparrow.

On the other hand, Hassler himself willingly altered the plot line out of necessity when he had to tell the story with fewer characters. For example, Hassler reassigned the Christmas Eve kiss under a streetlight to the turkey grower's wife and Grandfather, eliminating the need for the telephone operator, another male character in the novel. Roupe and Sadowski mined the moment for comedy—a delightful moment that led the audience back into Act II after the intermission.

Grand Opening was attended by 5,343 people, grossing $56,827 (including tickets, playbill ads, donations, and concessions). Once all the bills were paid, we expected to net about $23,000. We could finally pay off our loan from Kristen.

Despite financial success, I felt dissatisfied. I could not decide whose story was being told in the play. Was it Brendan's? Dodgers? Catherine's? Hank's? Too many choices. If we were to do the show again, this issue would have to be resolved.

"Hello... Lyric Theater"

On Monday morning preceding the closing weekend of *Grand Opening*, I perched on a stool in my office, a family room sized for no more than a family of three that opened off the back of my kitchen. I was reconciling box office statements when the phone rang. I marked my place with my half-full coffee cup and grabbed the phone from its cradle.

"Hello. Lyric Theater."

"Hello. I don't know if you remember me, but my name is Ken Fliès and I live in Plainview, Minnesota—you know, the town that Jon Hassler used as a basis for Plum in the play... the play I saw in the Twin Cities last weekend. I talked to you in the lobby after the performance."

"Yes, well, I remember talking to quite a few people... but tell me why you are calling today."

"Okay. There's going to be a reunion of Jon Hassler's high school class here in October, and we expect Jon to attend. I don't know how these things work, but we think people would be excited to have a performance here on that weekend."

My mind raced. *Is this guy for real?* I bought a little time to think.

"Does Plainview have a theater facility or auditorium large enough to stage *Grand Opening?*"

"We do have a large space. There's a stage along one side of the gymnasium, so we can bring down the bleachers and put some folding chairs in place. The high school does plays this way. We just had ..."

I flinched as he drummed on. I waited for him to breathe and broke in.

"Yes, I believe you are describing a gymnatorium. But here's the deal. It's too late in the game to schedule this production for an out-of-town performance. Those kinds of arrangements are made about a year in advance so the set can be designed for touring, and actor's contracts can be written to include those dates. Some of our actors belong to Actor's Equity, and many of them are already in rehearsal for other productions."

Ken's disappointment was palpable through the connecting wire. "I see. Well, will you be doing the play again in the future?"

"Not this play. But next year, we will be producing *Dear James* if all goes well. I'm working on the adaptation myself, so I have control over the process, including deadlines. If you're interested, I could talk to you when we're ready to move ahead. I would not want to perform in a gymnatorium, but you might start looking at other possible spaces—some place with good acoustics and real seating—not bleachers."

"I'll think about this," said Ken. There was an awkward pause. "Do you have any ideas for me?"

"How about a large church? Pews would be better than bleachers. Or a big restaurant?"

I didn't know yet that Ken attended St. Joachim's Catholic Church and owned the local country club with significant seating. He grabbed the idea.

"That is something I can look into."

We agreed to keep talking as plans for *Dear James* developed. Ken Flies wanted to pursue creating a Jon Hassler Playhouse and an Institute for Creative Writing in Plainview. He was playing my song.

Ken Flies and Jon Hassler pose on the future opening night of the Jon Hassler Theater in Plainview with the portrait created from a photograph and donated by Greg and Sally Rademacher.

Finding Plainview

The first mention of Plainview in the Lyric Board minutes was a site visit on October 28, 1996, just one month after Ken's life-changing phone call. He would soon be waiting for me at a former country club called The Tavern on the Green, nearly one hundred miles away. That morning I left Minneapolis and drove south on Highway 52, past the Koch Refinery at Pine Bend, where Highway 55 curved east to dump traffic onto Highway 61 along the Mississippi River. I veered to the right to stay on 52, the corridor that carried heavy truck traffic and a lot of cars going to the Mayo Clinic in Rochester. I passed Hader, where Highway 22 branched off to the southwest, to Mantorville, a small town that loomed large in memories of my grandparent's old house and my mother's childhood stories. I rolled down the window and imagined my father whistling behind the wheel of our old Chevrolet, echoing the meadowlark on the telephone wire ahead, but the fantasy dissolved into the powerful wind whipping my face, bearing dust, pollen, and exhaust fumes.

I closed the window and tuned in to public radio. I was almost halfway to Plainview, a small town twenty-three miles northeast of Rochester, located in the Driftless Area that included a small part of southeastern Minnesota never touched by a glacier. The Zumbro and Whitewater Rivers formed a watershed that emptied into the Mississippi River about twenty miles to the east, between Kellogg and Winona. Plainview served farmers who raised corn, soybeans, dairy cattle, and elk. It also served the Mayo Clinic in Rochester as a bedroom community of a little over three thousand people.

I left Highway 52 at Orinoco, following County Highway 12 until it crossed Highway 63 and magically became State Highway 247. I slowed down for the tiny town of Potsdam, where a prominent butte rose off to the left, a bump on the horizon. About nine miles later, I drove into Plainview, where a vegetable canning factory located across the street from the Catholic Church buffered the prairie wind. Street signs announced that I was on Broadway, a name in small towns almost as popular as Main Street. I drove past the high school where Jon Hassler had graduated in 1951, glanced across to the Presbyterian Church, and completed the ten-block stretch of businesses that ended at Emanuel Lutheran Church and School.

I turned right on Hwy. 42, curving strongly past Lanning's Grocery store, where a broad-shouldered statue of a brown and white steer stood on a triangle of green lawn. I continued past the lumber yard and turned left onto a rural road and then left again onto a dirt road that led through tanks of nitrous oxide used for fertilizer. (Who in their right mind would stage the entrance to a supper club this way?) I emerged from a dust cloud onto a paved drive leading along a nine-hole golf course and into the parking lot of the Tavern on the Green. The glorious sunshine of southeastern Minnesota warmed my face and fanned out over the golf course, nailing the shingles on the roof of the supper club, bathing the changing colors of small maples tucked among the dark green pines. Autumn, a time of renewal and beginnings for a former teacher's biorhythms.

I followed the sidewalk to the entry of the low-lying building, finding a wood-burning stove, unlit but ready for cooler temperatures. The hall led past restrooms to the dining room but also provided entrance to the pub on the right, where pool tables and a long bar waited for thirsty golfers who would arrive after the ninth green. Ken came out of the kitchen located behind the registration desk, a slender dark-haired man in middle age, physically fit and smiling broadly. His wife, Millie, who was cooking that day, entered, her stunning silver hair cut short and spiky atop her vibrant face, welcoming me to the cozy dining room.

Ken and I sat down at a table next to one of many plate glass windows that brought the outside greenery near to hand. The clock read 11:00, so we agreed on an early lunch of sandwiches and Millie's fabulous corn chowder. Ken warmed to the subject of Plainview, his love for his hometown tumbling from his lips as he talked of his family's history as farmers, his wife's family history with the Binder Bus Company, his background with the Peace Corps in Brazil at nineteen, his business background during the years he and Millie raised their family in California, and their return to Plainview to fulfill Millie's dream of opening a restaurant and, finally, Ken's vision for developing an arts complex in rural America.

After lunch, Ken proved to be an excellent tour guide as he turned his car west onto Highway 42 to take me to Carly State Park, just a few miles out of Plainview, where bluebells would bloom profusely in May and campsites were highly sought, even in the fall.

We drove for about three hours, ending up back in town where Ken turned onto a street that curved back to the main street, re-entering Broadway at the Catholic Church. Along the way, he pointed out a charming old house that the Hasslers had rented when they first arrived in 1943 and another old house across the street where the handicapped man who was the model for Rufus in Jon's novel lived with his mother. He pointed to the lawn of the church that Jon had mowed as a boy and the High School where Jon had climbed out of one of the old windows to play hooky with his friends. Ken stopped at the Variety Store, located halfway between St. Joaquin's Catholic Church on the west end of Broadway and the Emmanuel Lutheran Church on the east end. The Variety Store had once been Leo Hassler's "Catholic(-owned)" Red Owl Grocery Store, located across the street from the "Lutheran(-owned)" store. Inside, the store looked like the five-and-dime stores of my childhood, with the large safe that had belonged to Hassler's grocery store tucked behind shelves and display cases filled with craft items, plastic flowers, embroidery thread, magazines, greeting cards, model cars, and balls of every size.

Back in the car, we continued to cruise. Ken pointed out the old Methodist Church, which would soon be vacated when the current congregation merged with the Methodists from Elgin in a new building under construction a few miles out-of-town halfway between the two villages. Ken laid out his vision for a Jon Hassler Playhouse and Institute for Creative Writing. He thought the old church might fit into his idea for an umbrella organization with several artistic partners. Later I returned to Minneapolis with my head bursting, wondering if any of this would ever bear fruit.

For the next year, the Lyric Theater did not produce another play while I tackled my first adaptation from a novel, selling Weekender clothes on the side and temping for Sprenger and Lang.

The arts were doing well in Minnesota. In April 1997, I notified the Lyric Board that Governor Arne Carlson had proposed an arts initiative which would release twelve million dollars to arts institutions. The money would be fed through the State Arts Board out to the Regional Arts Councils. As such, MRAC would gain a share of this money which might, in turn, find its way to the Lyric Theater and other Twin Cities arts organizations. I prepared letters for the board to send to our legislators urging them to support Minnesota Citizens for the Arts through this initiative.

The Lyric could look forward to more regular funding by MRAC. Honeywell and McKnight were open to annual grant requests. But we still needed to raise more money to prepare for a production of *Dear James* in the fall of 1997. We invited a mix of former donors, actors, and friends of the Lyric Theater, Plainview folks, and some of Jon's colleagues from St. John's University to a fundraising party on June 19 at Sally Anderson's new home, which overlooked Minnehaha Creek near Penn Avenue in southwest Minneapolis, a venue well suited to the size of our organization and my limited talent for schmoozing. Guests entered via a shaded walk into a large foyer. An office branched to one side, with copies of *Dear James* stacked on the desk for signing.

Jon Hassler signing books in the office. Photo by Nancy Campbell.

Nancy Gormley and Ron Duffy reading and, perhaps, acting!
Photo by Nancy Campbell.

Nancy and Ron create a special moment from the script.
Photo by Nancy Campbell.

Hosts Sally Anderson and Rita Olk. Photo by Nancy Campbell.

The passage led to a kitchen on the left filled with volunteers setting up food and drink under the direction of Sally Anderson and Rita Olk, both stunningly white-haired with brilliant smiles.

Guests stood or sat with full glasses and plates in the great room, framed by lofty ceilings, creekside windows, a fireplace, large sofas and chairs, and a stairwell to the second floor. The elevated landing at the bottom of the stairs housed a grand piano, a perfect staging area for Nancy Gormley, Ron Duffy, and Larry Roupe, who would read from the unfinished script.

After the reading, high-spirited conversations rose and bumped into each other as Nancy Campbell's camera flashed, highlighting faces and elevating the temperature. An old-fashioned small-town newspaper would have said, "A good time was had by all."

Father James and Agatha in the same moment onstage.
Photo by Nancy Campbell.

Chapter 13: A New Patch of Road

Learning to Adapt

According to Jon Hassler, *Dear James* was born in Rome on Epiphany Sunday (January 6), 1986. Jon was admiring Michelangelo's Pieta in St. Peter's Basilica when he suddenly imagined Agatha McGee and James O'Hannon standing beside him. He wrote in his journal, "*The pieta is marvelous beyond my expectations. Mary is so young, Jesus so dead. Does Agatha see the youth, and James the death? Is James mortally ill?*" From then on, he saw the rest of his trip to Italy with triple vision—his, Agatha's, and James'.

After re-reading the novel, I was faced with bringing the rich, full characters from small-town Minnesota to life on stage in a two-hour time frame. The other challenge was to identify the most important relationships and then find and develop the conflict in a way that was appropriate to playwriting without altering Jon's storyline. Ed Block, who has taught Jon's novels to students at Marquette University, says, "Digression is a key component of almost everything Hassler wrote. In Hassler's novels, conflict was never a straight path leading to a satisfactory conclusion." Adapting this novel would be challenging.

The title of the play suggests that James will be the leading character, but the title also calls for his pen pal as a character. So, Agatha McGee, the upright resident of fictional Staggerford, Minnesota, who regularly sets the town on its ear with her saw-toothed tongue, emerges in the lead.

The Lyric Theater couldn't afford to pay more than a handful of actors, especially if some of them were Equity members. Most playwrights don't worry about the cost of the actors—they leave that up to the theater manager. I was both—always two hats on one small head.

I reduced the town of Staggerford at first to three locals and added in a priest from Ireland. I borrowed a familiar structure from musicals where a primary love story between a beautiful ingenue and her handsome swain is paired with a secondary comic pair of lovers (think "Guys and Dolls"). In my adaptation, the primary love story is between the aging Agatha McGee and her defunct pen pal, James O'Hannon. On the comic side, French, called Frederic by Agatha, falls into the clutches of Imogene Kite, the highly judgmental, nosy, and needy spinster librarian, daughter of Agatha's neighbor and best friend, Lillian. Oddballs all around.

Agatha McGee (Nancy Gormley) and Father James O'Hannon (Ron Duffy) visiting Rome. Photo by Nancy Campbell.

When asked, "How difficult is it to translate or transfer a novel from one medium to another?" Jon replied:

> It's hard to do, I found. It's easier to write a play
> from scratch, which I did last year with *The*

**Imogene Kite (Kari Holmberg) and Frederick (French) Lopat
(Chuck Deeter) house-sitting for Agatha.
Photo by Nancy Campbell.**

> *Staggerford Murders*. It's difficult to cut out all that
> beautiful prose, of course, and reduce the novel to
> its dialogue.

Indeed, I stripped out the dialogue for the four characters, typing it verbatim into a word processing document on my aging computer. But the town, as both judge and jury, needed to be represented by another character. Agatha's neighbor Lillian in her modest way, was a wonderful foil to Agatha's keen mind, but she lacked a sharp tongue. Father Finn, Agatha's close friend and spiritual advisor, was forbidden by the confessional from acting as a jury. I ran through other possibilities and finally landed on Congressman Myron Kleinschmidt, whose actions were always the result of the finger he kept on every citizen's pulse. His job was to represent the town, but in his conniving and needy heart, he literally became the voice of the town. His role was only a cameo, but he brought the plot and Agatha's world to a tempestuous boiling point.

Agatha (Nancy Gormley) loses her volunteer position under attack by Myron Kleinschmidt (Larry Roupe), the incumbent running for Congress. Photo by Nancy Campbell.

The first draft of *Dear James* was read aloud by Lyric stalwarts, and I took note of all suggestions from the actors and a few invited guests, including Jon Hassler. I incorporated many of these suggestions into a second draft, which was reviewed by Joe Sadowski. His advice—SIMPLIFY. I pared down the script. The letters and the Irish stories got shorter and shorter. To get feedback, I met with Jon at his townhouse, which backed up to Minnehaha Creek just east of 35W. His wife Gretchen brought cookies and coffee to the meeting and stayed to socialize. Jon was soft-spoken and terse. Our communication had always been strictly business, so I felt blessed seeing Jon and Gretchen together in a social setting.

When *Conversations with Jon Hassler* by Joe Plut was published later in 2010, I eagerly turned to his interview with Jon on *Dear James*. I held my breath as I read:

> (JOE)-Q. Sally Childs adapted *Dear James* for the Lyric Theatre in Minneapolis, which ran from September 5 until October 5, 1997. Please discuss changes you remember. I know she pared the cast down to five characters.

> (JON)A: Yes, I have to say that was a very good adaptation, too. I think it's the best of my plays, and I didn't write it. She cut out a lot, of course, the part about Ireland—other things in it, but it's a good play. I don't remember what changes were made, Joe, do you?

> Q: Not too many, but I think it was more between James and Agatha. Critic Noel Holston, in the September 10, 1997, *Star Tribune*, opines: "*Dear James* is frequently amusing and occasionally hilarious—more comical, perhaps, than Hassler intended. Dry-witted dialogue from his novel, which Childs has excerpted mostly verbatim, often gains a wicked crackle on stage." Any comments on this or anything more about Sally's adaptation?

(By this time, I was breathing into a balloon of happiness.)

> A: I remember reading an early draft of the play in which she had made up a lot of dialogue. I advised her to use more of my dialogue since I'd worked so hard on it that I perfected it. I knew it was pretty good. So she went back and she put in my dialogue instead of hers. This seemed to work very well.

POP! From my first experience with *Simon's Night* in 1991, I was well aware that Jon's dialogue was perfection. In rehearsal, I insisted the actors get every word, every comma, in its rightful place. As a director, I sometimes cut some dialogue, but I never changed anything that Jon had written unless it was necessary to accommodate a stage direction in some way. When Nancy Gormley was working on memorizing Agatha's lines for *Dear James*, she whined a little, "Nobody talks like this. I need to say it more naturally." I replied, "For Agatha, what is written in the script is natural." Nancy worked hard to get it right, and Jon said of her portrayal, "I like it very much." Terse, as always.

I wanted to telephone Jon, call his memory into question, remind him that he recently told me that a script being adapted by a couple of other people didn't work because his dialogue had been changed, and he could tell exactly where his writing stopped and theirs began. That script never saw the light of day. But I had no recourse. Jon died of progressive supranuclear palsy in 2008, two years before Joe's book of interviews was published. I am relieved to be able to set the record straight at last.

Dear James, the Play

The story begins with an unresolved conflict already in place. We find Agatha in her sunroom in Staggerford, groaning despairingly, writing a letter to James, and then a flashback carries her to a meeting with James in Stephen's Green in Dublin:

>   JAMES: Agatha…
>
>   AGATHA: Father O'Hannon
>
>   JAMES: I've come to apologize.
>
>   AGATHA: For being Father O'Hannon?
>
>   JAMES: For not telling you.
>
>   AGATHA: Who said "there are no snakes in Ireland?"

James begs forgiveness. She grants it but does not
agree to keep writing.

Back at her desk, she resumes writing about the motley crew
of friends gathered at her table for an excruciatingly awkward
Thanksgiving dinner. She crumples the letter, finding no respite
from these small-minded, albeit kindhearted people by pouring out
her feelings to her Irish pen pal, a road now closed due to her own
unbending nature.

Agatha departs on a tour of Italy, leaving French, a Viet Nam vet
suffering from post-traumatic stress disorder, in charge. In Italy, she finds
James waiting for her, pale and ill, and they are drawn together again by
mutual feelings.

Meanwhile, the neighbor's daughter, Imogene Kite, calls upon
French and seduces him in Agatha's sunroom. She later finds Agatha's
correspondence with James, which she maliciously lays on the public
pillory. The action cuts back and forth between Italy and Staggerford,
building tension and producing uncomfortable laughter.

Upon Agatha's return, she finds French gone and discovers evidence
of Imogene's activity. She stands up to Imogene in a wonderful attack
via the telephone, which marks a turning point that leads to revelation,
resolution, and reconciliation.

As I adapted the script, Agatha McGee's voice entered my ear
through the familiar voice of Nancy Gormley, beloved by many in the
Twin Cities acting community. She was tiny but powerful, a pretty face
framed by white hair, open to her emotions—and Catholic. I worried that
her foxy sexuality might be a hurdle for some Hassler fans. Jon, however,
welcomed her many-layered performance. She riveted the audience as she
stood alone in a special light at the end of Act I and cried out from her
heart:

"Oh, Lord, if it's wrong to be the female companion to a priest...
then why does it feel so right?"

Nancy Gormley as Agatha McGee. Photo by Nancy Campbell.

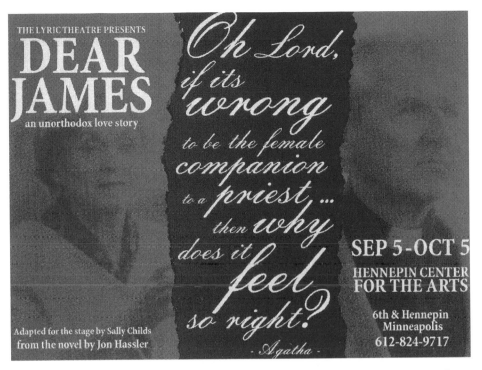

THE LYRIC THEATRE PRESENTS

DEAR JAMES

an unorthodox love story

Oh Lord, if its wrong to be the female companion to a priest, ... then why does it feel so right?

— Agatha —

Adapted for the stage by Sally Childs
from the novel by Jon Hassler

SEP 5–OCT 5

HENNEPIN CENTER
FOR THE ARTS

6th & Hennepin
Minneapolis
612-824-9717

**Postcard and poster for *Dear James* with Nancy Gormley and Ron Duffy.
Photo by Nancy Campbell. Design by Ruby McCusik.**

Larry Roupe played the smallest role in this production, Congressman Myron Kleinschmidt. Larry's towering height and stentorian voice would not be an obstacle, as it had been when he played Simon Shea or George Bernard Shaw in previous shows.

I agreed to bring the play to Plainview for one weekend as soon as it closed in Minneapolis. A loosely formed "Hassler Theater Committee" drove up from Plainview to see the show and figure out how to replicate the set on the cleared altar space of St. Joachim's, the largest "house" in Plainview (seating over three hundred). Ken Fliès led the planning, and his cousin Don Schultz served as tech director, figuring out the logistics and finding furniture, screens, and benches to represent all of the necessary spaces. Lighting was more difficult, and Schultz phoned the evening prior to our arrival in Plainview to ask for advice. Light was needed from a lower angle than what was available above the altar, so I suggested that he make his own lights according to an old tradition, using coffee cans and PAR lights from the hardware store. I enjoyed the pleasure Don and his crew took in figuring out how to implement this time-honored method.

The set for *Dear James* was modified slightly and nested in the altar space at St. Joachim's Catholic Church. Kari Holmberg and Chuck Deeter run a few lines as I check for problems or omissions that need to be solved.

I arrived with the actors on Saturday at 1:30, just in time for a quick run-through before we headed to the Tavern on the Green on the edge of the golf course, where we would kick off the evening with patrons. General admission tickets sold at $10, but donor-level tickets were available at $50, which included an elegant dinner at the Tavern on the Green. During happy hour, cast members read short cuttings from the play and then departed for the church, leaving two local violinists to play classical music while patrons finished their meals. Millie Flies was in the kitchen, so Ken, Dean, and Sally Harrington hosted the event.

The local paper carried two reviews, both enthusiastic. One proclaimed the production to be "magnificent." The second declared the

smacked of Bohemia and connected to the upscale sleekness of the Guthrie Theater, the Walker Art Center, and the Sculpture Garden by a pedestrian bridge crossing six lanes of traffic on Hennepin Avenue.

At first, Peter expressed interest, but after a discussion with his music director, Denise Prosek, he let me know that they had identified their own creative path and were not interested in exploring a merger. I still wonder what would have happened if he had said yes. The Jon Hassler Theater would not have existed. I would not be writing this book. But what else would have happened?

I was still half-way serious about finding other work, so I visited the Resources and Counseling offices in St. Paul. I was looking for some career ideas, brainstorming outside the box, but when I asked a few questions of one of the counselors, she merely directed me to the Job Book. I was totally out of step, much too old at fifty-nine to find a suitable job opening among the youngsters busily thumbing through the listings, mostly for part-time entry-level positions.[5]

Scouting the Territory

I invited Joe Sadowski to suggest ideas for next season. I planned to attend a reading of *Road to Rouen* by Anne Welsbacher on October 26 at a performance studio on 38th and Pleasant, and a few ideas were still available from previous planning sessions.

I needed a new computer and software designed to consolidate my computer work into a program that I could manage—financial, mailing lists, ticket sales, etc. The Lyric applied to MRAC for a capital improvement grant. In October, we were awarded a $750 planning grant, followed by a second proposal for $8,000. I met with consultants Don Caba and Ross Willits. Caba knew our operation, and Willits had provided IT services to The Cricket Theatre. They would tailor the database, train me, and purchase a new computer and software. The program must be so user-friendly that temporary box office people could be trained quickly to enter and retrieve information.

Our board was reduced again to seven faithful and long-serving people, and we knew we should add at least three people as soon as possible. We had worked a wee bit with MAP, the Management Assistance Project, a clearing house for corporate people who assisted non-profit organizations. With money in the bank, we signed up again.

Next year I would turn sixty. The Lyric Board had started to discuss what would happen when I needed to retire. We had learned the value of long-range planning and developing strategies to achieve our goals. We knew we had to have more corporate expertise on our board to achieve longevity.

The Lyric Board agreed to investigate the possibility of relocating the theater to Plainview. In March 1997, Ken Fliès introduced me to Carolyn Ayres, a Plainview native employed by Paine Webber who had volunteered to write a grant proposal that could work as a boilerplate for the Jon Hassler Theater. She also garnered a pro bono consulting commitment from her architect friend, Ron Buelow, who had worked on the plans for remodeling the Children's Theatre.

Ken invited Carolyn, Ron, Erica Zaffarano, and me to come to Plainview on March 19 to look at buildings and meet at the Tavern with other interested parties from Plainview. That morning Erica picked me up in south Minneapolis, and we followed Minnehaha Parkway east, crossing the Mississippi River on the Ford Bridge into St. Paul's posh Highland area. Carolyn's house sat on a cliff overlooking West 7th Street with a breathtaking view that stretched to 35E as it followed the Mississippi River towards the airport. We parked and rang the front doorbell, soaking in the ambiance of an older neighborhood with a strong European flavor.

Carolyn greeted us, elegant in cream-colored pants and shirt, which set off her tanned face framed by stylishly cut blonde hair. She introduced us to Ron Buelow, his crisp gray hair set off by a Navy blazer, who shook our hands warmly. I felt like a mailroom employee in my Weekender knits and wondered how Erica felt in her theater clothes—faded jeans and baggy sweater. We made a little small talk, commenting on the spaciousness of the great room, which recently had been renovated under Buelow's direction, and then entered the garage to climb into Carolyn's white Lincoln. Carolyn drove, Ron rode shotgun, and Erica and I sank down in the back on the off-white luxurious leather upholstery. This promised to be a day to remember.

Carolyn soon headed south on Highway 61 so she could show Ron a house she owned in Red Wing close to Lake Pepin. We stopped for a few short minutes while Ron and Carolyn got out of the car and did a lot of pointing and head nodding.

Once more on the highway, we passed through Lake City and then climbed the bluff, leaving the lush green of the river valley for farm country, studded with wizened corn stalks and soybean remnants, stopping at the intersection marked by the John Deere dealership before turning right on Highway 42 towards Plainview. We skirted downtown to join Ken Fliès and Dean Harrington for lunch at the Tavern and then visited several possible theater sites downtown, including the vacant Methodist Church and the current post office. The church was already of interest to the newly-formed Rural America Arts Partnership (RAAP) as a history center, but the post office was also interested in a larger space.

The only site that had the necessary structure and size was an International Harvester dealership with its tell-tale pylon rising from the roof on the main street, State Highway 247, appropriately named Broadway. The building was owned by Ken's cousin, Don Schultz, whose earlier experience with *Dear James* at the Catholic Church had made him sympathetic to the theater idea. The parts store and implement display area at the front of the building featured a large plate glass window that could yield space for a lobby and reception space as well as a front office. The area where tractors had been serviced was big enough for a black box—a small, intimate theater with about two hundred seats. The tractor dealership needed to sell the building because modern tractors had outgrown the service door and were no longer permitted to drive into town on a state highway. The post office had expressed interest in the building, but we had the upper hand through Ken's family ties.

We returned to the Tavern to join Dean Harrington, a representative of the Plainview Area Development Corporation (PADCO), for a meeting with other interested parties. Dean was a few years younger than Ken, a blue-eyed blonde, calm and quiet in speech and mannerisms. Dean made his life in Plainview, leading the Bank that his father and grandfather had owned and led before him. He and his wife, Sally, had raised five children and been active in community affairs—Dean as a leader and contributor and Sally as an activist, stirring the local waters. The Harringtons were close to coming on board with Ken's ideas.

Ken introduced Marcia Love, the new Superintendent of Schools. She acknowledged the group with a quick "hello" and then excused herself to attend another meeting. The rest of the group consisted of a few business owners and various people with an interest in the arts, primarily teachers.

After Ken outlined his idea to form the Rural America Arts Partnership (RAAP) as an umbrella organization for several affiliates, including the Jon Hassler Theater, the Rural America Writer's Center, and Plainview Area History Center, he invited all four of us—Ron, Carolyn, Erica, and me—to talk about the project from our unique points of view. We had little to say as yet, so we expressed delight with being asked to come for a site visit—patter designed to cover our lack of concrete information.

While the others talked, I scrutinized the Plainview locals. A group of teachers interested in forming a community theater sat in frosty silence. However, at another table, one face, in particular, shone with enthusiasm—a lively, petite, blue-eyed woman who smiled throughout the meeting. I asked Ken about her and learned that her name was Diane, and she had plans to open a restaurant and coffee shop featuring locally grown food. She supported Ken's ideas for a theater.

Ken scheduled a second meeting on April 3 to give me time to share information with the Lyric Board. I reported that I thought there was potential for sharing the building with the school district and recommended we continue to investigate.

The board directed me to attend the second meeting in Plainview, and I asked Larry Roupe to ride along. I wanted his perspective, his charm, and his sympathetic ear. Ken Fliès reported that Dean Harrington had fully committed to the idea of the Rural America Arts Partnership. They had begun working together to promote RAAP and move quickly into production.

At the April 3 meeting, Ken introduced me as the Artistic Director of the Lyric Theater of Minneapolis, where stage adaptations of Jon Hassler's novels had become a regular part of the last several seasons.

He acknowledged Larry as the actor who had played Grandfather in the production he had seen in Minneapolis.

I started with a thumbnail bio of my development of the Lyric Theater and stressed that I had worked for years to gain professional status for the Lyric to provide access to union actors. I concluded by saying, "If the Lyric Theater moves its operations to Plainview, it will remain a professional theater."

A hand shot up quickly. "What do you mean by that? Is it like sports, where the pros get paid, and the amateurs don't?"

"To some degree, it is similar. It means that highly qualified people, people with training and experience, will be hired to perform. Union actors will be paid according to union rules. Non-union actors are generally paid less. This won't be a community theater where actors are unpaid volunteers, although community members would be welcome to audition."

The community theater people lowered their chins and leaned back. I couldn't see their feet, but I pictured heels digging into the carpet.

I added, "The Actor's Equity Association (AEA), which is the union made up of actors and stage managers, stipulates the number of Union versus non-union actors. The Lyric Theater usually uses the Small Theater Contract (SPT), which requires a minimum of only one actor plus a stage manager, and the rest are paid or not, depending on the theater's funding level."

A handsome man with short-cropped salt and pepper hair asked, "What are the chances of local actors being cast?"

"It all comes back to how well an actor reads in auditions and whether he or she fits the physical description of the character... you know, within reason. Auditions will be held in Minneapolis and here in Plainview. Rehearsal time will be split between Minneapolis and Plainview, and all performances will be in Plainview."

Ken asked me to explain what was needed to establish The Jon Hassler Theater in Plainview.

I started with general information: "Theaters designated not-for-profit are still corporations, but unlike for-profit companies, they don't have owners or shareholders. They are governed by a board of directors with officers and by-laws that cover organizational needs. The Board must apply for a tax-exempt status from the Federal Government."

A male voice challenged, "But what happens if they start to make money, if they become… you know, prof-it-a-ble."

"Ahh, well, non-profit corporations are allowed to show a profit on their balance sheet, but it doesn't go to an owner or to shareholders. It is all used to finance the organization."

"So, that means that they have paid employees with benefits and everything?"

"Yes. Most theater companies, big or small, have staff who work either full-time or part-time. But they also contract with independent artists."

"And how would you fit into all of this? I hear you live in Minneapolis." The man looked to his left and then to his right, nodding as if to say, *I think I have her there.*

I took a moment to think. "Well…" I looked at Ken and took a big breath.

"If the Lyric Theater comes to Plainview, the RAAP Board will contract with me to be the Artistic Director. That means I will select the season and then produce the plays. RAAP will also need to hire a manager or find volunteers to take care of the business side—the office staff, including the box office, fundraising, building maintenance, and housing for actors, and so on. board members may voluntarily take on some of these jobs. I will help out as needed."

An older woman asked, "Will board members be paid?"

"No," I replied. "Board members are not allowed to be paid to work for a non-profit. Think about your school board. If a teacher were to run for the school board, it would be considered a conflict of interest."

Ken intervened for a moment. "Sally, I'd like you to describe what your job is with the Lyric Theater."

"Okay. I'll try to be brief. The Lyric Theater is my baby, so to speak. I founded the company in conjunction with two other people who left to return to school after only two seasons. I hung on and developed the Lyric Theater with an active board and lots of volunteer help over a period of fifteen years. I am the only staff member, and I work as an independent contractor, sometimes full-time, if money is available. When money is not available, I contract as a Stage Director, and I volunteer staff hours. As the Artistic Director, I select the plays and then draw up a budget that has to be approved by the board. I am also the Producer. I do the day-to-day work, whether paid or not. This gives us great flexibility and has kept us afloat through hard times. I attend all board meetings and prepare an activity report and financial report, which I e-mail to board members prior to meetings."

"But can you support yourself this way?" asked a young teacher.

"Well… sometimes I have to take on temp work. In the beginning, I worked full-time for a law firm." I shrugged as if to say it was the norm for artists.

Ken interjected a comment to get us back on track. "Sally, why don't you talk a little about how a play gets produced."

"Sure. Each play has a project budget. I see that every line item in the budget gets done. I hire the production staff and actors on independent contracts. Each production costs, on average, about $30,000."

"Ouch," someone muttered.

"Remember that includes big-ticket items like rent, payroll, and advertising. The Lyric's 1998 budget is projected at $90,000. Our goal is to increase the annual budget each year so that we qualify for more grant money.

"Who does the applications? Do you have to do that, too?"

"Yes, but since the board is responsible for fundraising, I won't be *required* to do that in Plainview. But in the beginning, I'm sure I *will do* some grant writing."

"So, where does all the money come from?"

"The income side of the budget is short—ticket sales, concession sales, program ads, donations from individuals and corporations, and foundation grants. The expense side is long and detailed. Remember, a budget is simply a plan. But once you have the actual numbers, once the bills are paid, it becomes a balance sheet. Sometimes money has to be borrowed."

With the introduction of numbers, reality set in. Questions were raised about the use of the space.

Ken Fliès pointed out, "Any use of the theater outside of The Jon Hassler Theater (JHT) will require a rental arrangement. During the summer, the building will be in continuous use by JHT, with one show performing while another is in rehearsal. Summer matinees are important—they generate ticket income from senior groups or other day-trippers from outlying areas, some as far away as the Twin Cities."

The longer we talked, the more easily I could visualize the same problems developing in Plainview that existed in Albert Lea, where Michael Brindisi and his wife, Michelle Barber, had created the Minnesota Festival Theater, a professional (Equity) house, in 1983. The professional theater and community theater battled to share space, especially after Brindisi left six years later to take on the artistic direction at Chanhassen Dinner Theatres, located in a community adjacent to Minneapolis. As we contemplated the move to Plainview, we were advised by many folks with experience at the Minnesota Festival Theater to keep the professional theater separate from the community theater as we developed our plans.

When Ken paused, I pointed out there would be time in the winter and spring months when weather conditions would curtail travel by both actors and ticket buyers. Rentals would be possible during those months. RAAP was interested in working with the school district and community groups to keep the building utilized year-round.

The Plainview arts contingent, who had been formulating plans for a community theater, were clearly disappointed to learn that the theater would be fully professional and would fill the summer season. This division needed to be addressed and resolved by RAAP and other members of the community. Like so many small towns, Plainview had a strong history of splitting into factions, as Hassler had so aptly captured in *Grand Opening,* and newcomers or native sons and daughters returning later in life and stirring new ideas into the community pot would be greeted with raised eyebrows, at best. Sally Harrington had a history of challenging the local school board as her five children passed through the system. But we had an ace-in-the-hole—Dean's many contributions of time, money, and leadership in the community.

I remained skeptical about the feasibility of this project going forward, or if it did, that the Lyric Theater would survive the move. I knew there had been no demographic study, but Plainview was not my town, so I left it to the people in Plainview to work things out. I reported to the Lyric Board that I thought the school's participation would be a key to justifying RAAP's purchase of a building since the school lacked space for theater activities. The new school superintendent did not attend the April 3 presentation, but Ken assured me that she was on board.

After the meeting, I told Ken I'd like to go home on Highway 61, so Larry could see the scenic route that Jon Hassler and his parents had followed when they moved to Plainview in 1944. Ken gave us directions to Kellogg, where we turned North on 61 to follow the Mississippi River to Red Wing and then turned onto 55, which left the river to lead us back to Minneapolis. Before we left, I told Ken and Larry that I thought I had overwhelmed or alienated everyone and probably wouldn't hear from them again.

I was wrong, oh so wrong.

Regrouping

In 1997 Beth wanted to come home from California. She had not survived a third cut in staff at Rancho Los Amigos, a county hospital in Los Angeles where she had been for seven years as an Occupational Therapist. She had tried another job at the Long Beach Hospital but did not like it. She called home on a beautiful summer day.

"Mom, I'm missing out on the last years of Grandma's life. I want to be there to help. And I don't want to miss out on Carol's kids as they grow up. Sam is already seven and Meghan is five, her last year at the Montesorri."

I felt I was missing out, too. The Lyric's move to Plainview loomed on the horizon. It meant more time away from home. I needed Beth and told her so.

"You know you can come back anytime. You can have one of the bedrooms, and Chris can have the other one. I'll fly out and help you with the drive back."

"I'll start looking into a U-Haul. I won't bring furniture, so I think a trailer will work. I'll have to have a hitch put on my car."

"Really? You think your little Mitsubishi can haul a trailer?"

"I think so, but the U-Haul guys should be able to tell me."

"Okay, when you have a date, call me, and I'll schedule a flight to Los Angeles."

When I flew out to join her and saw the overloaded trailer hitched to Beth's little white car, the hitch nearly scraping the ground, I looked at Beth, eyebrows elevated in a question mark.

"I know, it's riding low," she said, "but the U-Haul guys said the car should be able to handle it."

We were leaving tomorrow, one way or another.

In the morning, we settled into the car, Beth driving and me with a map. Beth's little white Maltese, Kenzie, started the trip with back feet in Beth's lap and her face resting on the partially opened window, ready to catch the wind.

The Mitsubishi died in the San Bernadino Mountains, so we had to rent a U-Haul truck, unload the trailer into the truck and pull the car the rest of the way. Outside of Flagstaff, the truck had a flat tire, and we waited three hours for a repair truck to arrive all the way from Mesa to the south. Later, in Grand Island, Nebraska, Beth locked the keys in the truck, which ended our run of bad luck. It was an expensive trip—one that neither of us ever want to repeat.

Beth soon found work and settled into my house. We developed routines that made me feel loved. When she left at 6:30 am, she let Kenzie into my bedroom to curl up at the foot of my bed, ready to greet me enthusiastically when I arose around 8:00 am. When I arrived home late in the evening after a Weekender Sales Event, Beth met me at the car and carried my heavy bag into the house. On days that I drove to Plainview, I knew she would be home by 4:00 pm and would handle any emergencies.

My parents were in their late eighties, and Dad recently had a hip replaced. Mom was crippled with arthritis and scoliosis, brittle from osteoporosis, and legally blind from macular degeneration. The graying out of her sight made her desperate for more light, especially during the winter.

One Saturday in February, after my daughter Carol arrived to clean her grandparents' house, Dad took advantage of having another person around, leaving to run to the grocery store. Mom was settled in her recliner listening to the radio, and Carol pulled the vacuum cleaner into the bedroom, turned it on and was just getting started when she heard a thud. Mom had risen from her chair, walked around her walker, and crossed to an end table. As she reached up to turn on the light, she tipped backward. Carol ran from the bedroom and found her lying on the carpet, moaning with pain and calling out, "Orv, Orv, Orville, where are you, Orville?"

Carol called me and I rushed over there, arriving at the same time as Dad, his hands gripping several grocery bags. Mom was transported by ambulance to the hospital. Several painful x-rays revealed several hairline pelvic fractures. After the mandatory three days required by Medicare to qualify for nursing home care, her doctor released her from the hospital. I saw the fear in Dad's eyes. His mission was to take care of her himself until the end. I gathered my courage and said, "Dad, I think you have to face the fact that you may not be able to bring her home this time. You won't be able to manage all the physical lifting."

Mom was moved to a nearby nursing home where, for nine months, Dad presided at every meal and at bedtime. Now totally blind, Mom never adjusted to her new digs. My daughters and I alternated afternoon visits, giving Dad a few hours at home every day. I started talking to myself whenever I was alone, especially in the car, planning rehearsals, replaying conversations, reshaping my world, which now included a diagnosis of Type 2 diabetes, preparing for the inevitable, forgiving myself for living out my dream while my mother slipped into dementia. She hung on for another nine months.

Dad lived another two years, long enough to see Beth move into her own home and to offer me the job of helping him write a book—a book that would solve all the problems of the world—a job that would mean the end of my theater career. I turned him down. Later I was grateful that he didn't live to experience 9/11 (2001).

In January 1998, the Lyric started the year with $14,000 in the bank and Kathy Hardy as our new Board President. After Kathy attended a MAP Board Training Session, she asked the board to set forth four goals: 1) increase board membership, 2) develop staff to ensure continuity, 3) increase the financial base, and 4) acquire a location and develop space. This put Plainview center stage.

The McKnight Foundation accepted a proposal from us for a $15,000 grant and had promised a response in March. McKnight funding would be the key to achieving our goals.

Kathleen Hardy, our new President of the Board.
Photo by Nancy Campbell.

Chapter 14: Many More Miles to Run

Finding *Old Man Brunner Country*

I fell in love with Leo Dangel's poetry several years after I fell in love with Gusztav. On May 13, 1989, I was in Marshall for a writer's conference, and Leo was about to read.

I stood a few feet from the commuter lounge, a large square conversation pit sunk beneath floor level just outside of the library at Southwest State University. It measured about fifteen square feet with several wide, carpeted levels leading down on all four sides, a place for off-campus students to sit or sprawl between classes. At the bottom, a square floor provided a small performance space. On the edge of the pit, Leo Dangel slumped in his motorized wheelchair, paralyzed for twenty years by a motorcycle accident. The audience, made up of writers and others attending the conference, moved restlessly on the risers and talked in low tones. Leo waited, unmoving, ready to read the last poem from his 1987 publication *Old Man Brunner Country*.

Gusztav shimmered into view, his torso and legs encased in a silver-gray jumpsuit, backlit by windows at the end of the hallway—as if emerging from fog. He smiled and nodded to Leo as he dropped the black sweatshirt that warmed his shoulders and executed a few last-minute stretches. The audience settled as Gusztav descended to the bottom of the pit and struck a beginning pose. Leo read slowly, shaping his words as Gusztav began to move.

Sally Childs

PLOWING AT FULL MOON

Dancer stands tall and still. He shivers increasingly,

The air cold,

his hands tremor, then flutter like leaves.

the hills roll up like unbroken swells beneath the tractor,

He spins, rolling to ground, growing taller, then shorter crossing the floor, straightening into the farmer driving along,

the plow turning a wake wet and black.

then curling up to form the tractor, arms swimming outward to cut a groove, scooping up a sample of dirt, rubbing it through fingers to test if wet, throwing an arm across his eyes to plunge into darkness.

A column of fire gusts up from the exhaust, the roar breaks through finally to a silence felt in the hands and shoulder blades.

As a tractor, his arms shoot out and disperse gusts of exhaust. As farmer he grips the steering wheel, white knuckled—then relaxes back into himself, isolating muscles from neck to shoulder, to arms, abdominals, easing to sit comfortably.

I am with the earth and the dark, alone. And work is being done.

He scoops up clods of dirt, smelling it, flinging an arm across his eyes, then plowing on, across the floor, arms

244

I'll go home and dream of a horse bowing over still water in a cedar tank, drinking the moon.

moving as wheels. He drops into sleep, hands under cheek. Dreaming, he rises to become horse, leaping twice into a forward lunge, head bowing over the tank, arms extended behind his back to form a circle with fingers interlocked, a moon shining over his shoulder, his head moving front to back as he laps the still water.

As Leo closed his book, the audience inhaled together in a single breath. Gusztav walked slowly to the center of the pit and bowed deeply. The applause followed him as he climbed the steps and extended his hand to Leo. Bill Holm also stepped up to shake hands, along with other writers I recognized. When Gusztav finally stepped away, I handed over his sweatshirt, which I had rescued from the surging feet.

**Gusztav Fogarassy rehearsing in his dance studio.
Photo by Sally Childs.**

Gusztav Fogarassy. Photo by Sally Childs.

As Gusztav and I walked back to the dance studio, he gave voice to the imagery that had overtaken his thoughts, "I could see the water in the wooden tank. The moon melted on the surface, rippling with movement from the horse's tongue. I felt nourished, refreshed." His process matched the visualization technique used by many actors. "The experience felt other-worldly. I was part of the universe."

Later that day, I stood in the window outside Rob's office on the SSU campus, lost in thought. As I gazed at the loading dock leading from the Library, Leo emerged and wheeled down a handicapped ramp to the modified car waiting in his special parking spot. He balanced against the car, lifted his chair into the back, slammed the door, and twisted to fall into the driver's seat in one practiced movement. He used his arms to lift his legs into the car and quickly drove away.

I felt a strong attraction to Leo's poetry and thought about it as the basis for another theater/dance staging and mentioned it to Rob Ross, the Director of the Southwest Minnesota Arts and Humanities Council (SMAHC), but the Lyric Theater's finances prohibited serious consideration.

Ten years and twenty-four shows later—including several Hassler scripts—I visited Gusztav in Marshall and dropped by the SMACH office to say hello to Rob Ross. He mentioned that Leo Dangel's health was slipping... if I wanted to base a poetry adaptation on his work, I needed to get going. I was saddened to learn that Leo had lost much of his incredible upper body strength—and his independence.

Leo's collection of poems about Old Man Brunner suggested a homespun story of growing up on a farm. I reread the book with a staging in mind. The poems were "guy talk." They painted a remarkable portrait of contemporary life in rural Minnesota. Each poem added a colorful brushstroke to create layers of unforgettable, yet recognizable, characters—Arlo, Benny, Milo, Wendell and Bernice, Pa, the family pet "dreaming of a cute collie named Jennifer" and Old Man Brunner himself. Not merely nostalgic, Leo's poems were light, sometimes hilariously funny, and often heartbreakingly so. He told us how to "farm in a lilac shirt" or what "a cat can do in Katmandu—that a cat can't do in South Dakota."

Once again, I used the Eudora Welty method of shaping the script. Larry Roupe and Ron Duffy, who was slated to direct, joined in the fun. Each poem was a story in itself. Ron Duffy edited the final version, and I decided to give full playwriting credit to him. I was tired of the fight to be fairly judged. I remember thinking that the piece would probably receive a more positive review if the director bore a man's name. In 1997 there was more support for working women than in 1958 when I returned to work after Beth's birth, but it takes more than four decades to change prejudices. I was dying my hair to prevent slipping into the invisibility of an aging woman. I still had a lot of work to do before qualifying as a feminist.

Each of the five actors became very good at setting up each situation, telling each story, and then landing on the punch line, a requirement for any poem spoken aloud. Duffy staged the piece at the Wolf Creek Country Store. Act I took place on the porch of the store where the characters hung out and interacted, but turned to the audience in presentation mode when the poem/story became intensely personal. Act II played inside the store, so the set revolved during intermission. The switch to the interior made the poetry even more personal.

Chris played the women identified only as "Her," ranging in age from a young child to old age when the widow leaves the home place. Larry Roupe played Old Man Brunner (OMB), curmudgeon extraordinaire:

"Brunnersaurus"

> HIM: Old Man Brunner, with his rough face, shaggy eyebrows, and hooked nose looks like a troll.

> HER: He's gruff with children and says we're spoiled and lazy, but I can't help hanging around him. Tonight at Wendell's place, while the men play cards, I sit on the floor and page through the school book I brought along.

> HIM: Old Man Brunner leans over and asks—

> OMB: "What kind of nonsense they teaching kids these days?"

> HER: I show him the pictures of dinosaurs explaining that they vanished millions of years ago.

> HIM: but Old Man Brunner snorts and says—

> OMB: "Animals like that are still around, living in the mud at the bottom of sloughs."

> HER: He says they come out when a slough dries up to look for a new home, moving at night like a river over fields and across country roads—he knows of cars that slid into the ditch—

> OMB: "on their slimy bodies."

> HER: Riding home later, alone in the back seat,
> I look ahead at the gravel road, trying to imagine
> what huge mysteries might be out in the dark
> fields, hoping, as the car goes over each hill, the
> headlights will shine on a herd of ancient dragons.
> I fall asleep and dream of beasts by the hundreds,
> each one looking like Old Man Brunner, crawling
> across the road, and I wake up knowing he will
> never be extinct.

The dialogue is imaginative and always playful, allowing the audience to connect with these characters, whether they have ever had a rural experience or not. Imagine the audience shifting gears as these actors take on different personas. At times you could smell the heat, the undercurrents, the full-blown lust.

Larry Roupe, well known to Lyric audiences, made prodigious use of the comic timing developed over years of professional work:

"A Farmer Prays"

> OMB: My bank loan overdue, the tractor I bought
> had a cracked block. Lord, you know I'd never
> wish anyone dead, but when the time is up for
> that bandit John Deere dealer, (*adding more venom*) let him be showing off a new manure spreader. Let him fall into the beaters and be spread over
> half the township, amen.

All of this was held together by musical tags—transitions and underscore—performed by David James Carlson, a one-man band with instruments ranging from banjo to cowbell. David set only one poem to be sung, "Saturday was for Cleaning Barns." We simply ran out of time for more, and the show had to go on. The most commonly heard comment I heard from audiences (especially Bill Holm) was, "You need more singing!"

Jason Henning (Young Man), Larry Roupe (Old Man Brunner), David
Carlson (Minstrel), Noalen Stampe (Her), Bick Smith (Him).
Photo by Nancy Campbell.

**Bic Smith and Noalen Stampe, a rural romance.
Photo by Nancy Campbell.**

**Jason Hennings and Larry Roupe in the final moment of the show.
Photo by Nancy Campbell.**

The Lyric Theater scheduled performances for May 1998. It premiered at The Marshall Writers' Festival 5 at SSU with Leo in attendance and then opened in the Little Theater on the second floor of the Hennepin Center for the Arts in Minneapolis for a two-week run.

The review in the *Star Tribune* by Rohan Preston was as delightful as the show itself. Both a poet and critic, Preston was newly arrived to replace the recently retired Peter Vaughan. He called the show a series of snapshots... with improvised games, grinding and monotonous work, not-too-smart farm animals, and, of course, the sexual longings of awkward farm bodies—revealing Dangel's ribald humor—sporting the wiseacre bravura of a cowboy poet.

Despite this excellent review, the audience numbers remained relatively small. Not only were we dealing with rural characters but doing it with poetry! Not a hot ticket in Minneapolis.

I still have Leo's handwritten thank you card. Rob Ross later told me that the production had given Leo a new lease on life. He published two more books of poetry after seeing *Old Man Brunner* on stage. Leo died in Yankton, South Dakota, at age seventy-five on December 13, 2016.

Good News, Fear and Loss

In April, 1998, the Lyric received great news from the McKnight Foundation. We had been awarded $12,000 in general operating funds. Board President, Kathy Hardy, handed out an article called "Opportunistic Fundraising" to encourage us all to become fundraising advocates in social settings.

Even as the Lyric gained financial strength, my mother lost both physical and mental stability as her tenure at the nursing home lengthened. Dad became more demanding, instructing the aids (whose African accents frightened Mom) on how to prepare her for bed. As a result, he was instructed to leave the room as the aids did their job, and then he could re-enter and give Mom whatever care she requested. He was terribly upset but had no choice but to follow instructions. When he told me about it, he said he had accepted the situation but felt it was not good for Laura. He was right about that—the care was not patient-centered. Dad may have accepted the situation, but he never accepted that his beautiful wife of over sixty years could not be restored to her former quality of life. He insisted on trying to make her understand her situation, her reality. But her reality was somewhere in the past.

One day I found her in the community room, stamping imaginary documents. When she saw me, she said, "Sally, I can't decide what number to give this form. I've tried 3 and 4, but those numbers didn't work."

I fumbled for a moment and then said, "Try number 7. Most of your forms are sevens." I held back tears as I curled my hand gently over hers and said, "It's breaktime, Mom, time to quit working. Let's have a cup of coffee and one of the snickerdoodles on the cookie plate."

When I told Dad about this, he shook his head and told me I should have tried to bring her back to reality. He said, "That's what I do when I catch her doing stuff like that." I never asked what other things they talked about during the long hours he spent with her at the nursing home. I'm sure he continued to tout his euthanasia ideas, in which case Mom would cope by going further into the past, spiraling into a litany of depression and devastation—what became "old age" for my once smart, handsome parents.

Back to Work

By June, the Lyric had a new board member, attorney Gordon Gendler. In July, we held another fundraiser at the home of Sally Anderson and introduced our next production, Jemmy, which I was adapting from Jon Hassler's short novel of the same title.

Jemmy told the story of a seventeen-year-old academically talented Ojibwe girl who checked out of school at age sixteen to take charge of caring for her alcoholic father and young siblings after her mother's recent death. The idea came from Hassler's experience teaching high school English in a small town near the White Earth Indian Reservation in Minnesota. He was upset when a sixteen-year-old girl, very much like Jemmy, brought him a notice that she was leaving school. He tried to talk her out of it, but her only response was, "Dad says." Over and over. "Dad says." Jon wrote the book in an attempt to give her story a satisfactory ending. Since he believed that education was her only path to a better life and he knew she would not return to high school, he turned to the arts. Jon was a painter himself, a skill that proved invaluable to him in supplementing his teacher's income. So, in a way, he stepped up to the plate himself, creating a painter and his wife who would offer Jemmy more than a hard life at home.

Jemmy (Emily Omizo-Whittenberg) and Otis Chapman, artist (David Ward). Photo by Thomas Florey.

This couple first met Jemmy when she took refuge in their barn, unable to drive any farther in a raging blizzard. The painter was drawn to her and asked her to be his model for a mural he was commissioned to paint for a large installation in the Twin Cities. When she agreed to sit for him, he used these sessions to increase her curiosity about painting. Jemmy was caught in a cultural clash—between the painter, who offered her an art education, and the culture of the reservation that expected her to fulfill family obligations.

The cultural clash was based on real events, but I feared that the white artist would be considered politically incorrect by today's society. I hoped we could get around this potential obstacle by telling Jon's story honestly and letting the situation speak for itself. Hassler was writing a story from his stance as a high school teacher who was upset at seeing a young life cut short by a hopeless situation.[6] I reasoned that *Jemmy* escaped being a story about a white savior in favor of a story about not losing hope.

I chose *Jemmy* for adaptation partly because it fell into the genre of an adolescent novel. I wanted to increase the Lyric's appeal to school-age groups. And it was a girl's story, so unusual in the world of literature in which I had grown up. The story also had an underlying theme of diversity which might make it more attractive to funders and to a wider audience. So I barged ahead.

Jon Hassler did not like my first draft. I was trying to tell part of the story through singing (chanting) with Indian drumming as background. Jon's wife Gretchen had been to several pow-wows and pointed out that the singing did not use words that could be understood by non-indigenous people, so that idea seemed forced. Jon suggested, "If I were writing it, I would place Jemmy's teacher at the center of the play and call him Mr. Olsen, with a minute or two at the beginning to establish him as Narrator. He could reappear when necessary and address the audience, providing the transitions." Jon had been that teacher, and he even wrote an opening scene to demonstrate his idea.

I wasn't ready to grab at the narrator idea yet. Somehow, I had to learn to create action rather than narrate a story—the plot had to take precedence over the characters. Unwisely, perhaps, I did not use Jon's suggestion. I overlooked the idea that the author, omniscient or not, may be the essence—the central character—in every story. I had taught creative writing to high school students and understood the writer's central role in the creation of the piece but didn't visualize the writer as a physical character. Jon Hassler was a novelist, not a playwright. As a novelist, he may have visualized himself in every story, walking around in the guise of multiple characters. We discussed Jon's stories but never discussed our roles or our process as novelist and playwright. I wish we had.

Jemmy at her easel with brothers, Marty (Nathan Mohammed) and Rollie (Ben Goodlund). Photo by Tom Florey.

I recognized that I would need help from someone with Indian credentials, so I asked Sharon Day to direct. Sharon was the Executive Director of the Minnesota American Indian AIDS Task Force and founder and artistic director of the Ogitchidag Gikinoonamaagad Players. This student-theater's mission was to inform the community about HIV. They toured with six different plays from coast to coast over their seven-year history. Sharon was also an actor, a visual artist, and a published writer. Her written works focused on issues about women, tribal sovereignty, the environment, sexuality and spirituality. Her book of poetry, *Drink the Winds, Let the Waters Flow Free*, was published in 1982. Ms. Day was an enrolled member of the Bois Forte Band of Ojibwe Indians.

Jon had suggested that memories of Jemmy's mother were important, and that was the element that Sharon Day also emphasized. She saw the role of the dead mother as central to the plot. Sharon told Lisa Brock, who interviewed her for an article in the *Minnesota Women's Press*:

> In the parts of the book where Jemmy remembers
> her mother, we just brought her forward as a

character. The dead mother becomes present and continues to help Jemmy figure out her understanding of who she is as a woman and as an Ojibwe woman. And that really fits with Ojibwe culture, where our dreams are as important as our waking moments. People make life decisions based on their dreams, and relatives who've made that journey to the spirit world continue to come back and help us.

Mother (Fawn Wilderson) counsels daughter (Emily Omizo-Whittenberg). Photo by Thomas Florey.

Sharon Day had grown up on a reservation and could speak to all the issues that led to the fact that in 1997 only sixty-seven Natives in Minnesota took the SATs. Day said, "it's because the system is deficient in dealing with our kids."

Neither Sharon nor I wanted the play to be a polemic. We stayed focused on the timeless issues of personal, cultural, and artistic identity as seen through Jemmy's eyes. Jon approved my final draft, and the production went forward. Sharon Day found authentic Native actors.

We did not fare well with the critics. Jaimie Meyer, a playwright himself, reviewed for the *Star Tribune*:

> While Sally Childs' stage adaptation stays true to Hassler's story, it never comes of age itself as a stage play, remaining word-bound rather than rooted in action. The script is weighed down by actionless, word-heavy scenes that drag the play over the cliff to its demise.

Ouch. Would I have fared better using the narrator, as Jon suggested? Meyer also had little good to say about the actors, many of them novices. He did concede that Emily Omizo-Whittenberg was charming as Jemmy—that David Roberts evoked a few laughs, and that Lola Lesheim created a believable character. I felt several additional people also gave solid performances. The young people were age appropriate and believable. Unfortunately, Meyer also held Sharon Day's feet to the fire declaring that the flat characters in the script were flattened even further by her direction. I wish the reviewer had been a woman, someone without testosterone driving their aesthetic comprehension of the world. Better yet, a Native American woman.

I thought we had accomplished a great deal and that the performances had grown in rehearsal. The show was seen by several groups of school-age kids, and they paid attention. They liked seeing people their own age on stage.

I tried to put a good face on things. Many people found much that they liked in Jon's story. I wasn't accused of being politically incorrect. But under pressure, I reverted to type—introvert. While I sought refuge in lobby duty, Sharon led the actors in Native rituals on stage before many performances, but she never stopped in the lobby. I retreated into my other duties, too ashamed of my failed script to seek her out—which I have come to regret. I might have joined the actors in the Native rituals, but I never thought of it. My job was to keep the lobby and theater secure before the show. From then on, I was the ticket seller, bathroom cleaner, costume washer, check writer—all familiar roles. Most cast members remained friendly, and several worked with Lyric/Hassler again. I regret that I have lost touch with Sharon Day.

When I started this memoir, I dreaded dealing with this production, but writing about it has been cathartic. I can't help but wonder what would have happened if I had put Mr. Olsen at the center of the play, as Jon suggested. Perhaps Jon would have taken on the script as he had with *Grand Opening*. Mr. Olsen may have been the lively character needed to make it all work. But then again, we may have been crucified for using a narrator and more word-heavy scenes.

Agatha Joins the Marketing Committee

We had not received MRAC funding for *Jemmy*, so I adjusted the budget. We were pretty much at ground zero financially—again! Jon and I agreed to defer payment of royalties until the end of the next production, Hassler's *The Staggerford Murders,* and I agreed to forgo my stipend entirely. We had some tour dates for *Old Man Brunner*—one in Balaton in southwestern Minnesota and one in Plainview for RAAP. We would have to borrow to get started on the next show. We also had to raise ticket prices by $3, bringing regular adult tickets to $18.

The Lyric added Regina Barr to the Board in October 1998. She made an "entrance" to the first board meeting with her auburn hair carefully coifed close to her head, her eyes sparkling like sunshine on blue water, and a professional demeanor. Regina brought financial and management skills at a time when we needed to create a strategic plan that could carry us into our uncertain future. But the Board was still down one since Deanne Levander-Larson and Sally Anderson resigned in December, leaving us bereft of Deanne's writing skills and Sally's breadth of perception and base of funding contacts over ten years of devoted service. We remained at six members for the time being.

With the prospect of a theater named for Jon Hassler in Plainview, I wanted to involve him in our fundraising efforts. For the first time, we planned to mail a donor letter to our growing list of Hassler fans. I asked Jon if he would channel Agatha McGee long enough to write the letter as if she were writing it. The letter was dated November 10, 1998, and started with this acerbic, funny paragraph from Agatha:

> Miss Sally Childs, founder and artistic director of the Lyric Theatre, Minneapolis, has asked me to write you a letter concerning their next production: *The Staggerford Murders*, a new play by Jon Hassler. I was quite flattered to be asked—until I realized that part of the reason for the letter was to seek money from you. Never in my long life have I lent my name to a commercial cause and would have refused her on the spot except that her second choice of a letter-writer was to be Mr. Hassler—whom I do not trust. Many of you will recall Mr. Hassler's first visit to Staggerford nearly 20 years ago, when he brought in the State Patrol and the National Guard and caused such havoc that by the time he left town, a woman of fragile bearing had been driven mad, her daughter Beverly had been cast into depression, and my dear lodger and SHS's best English teacher lay dead in a muddy farmyard.

The letter continued in this vein for a full page. Agatha became more of a co-conspirator and less of a character in a book. Before sending out the letter, I felt no guilt as I forged Agatha's signature and included a form for donors to complete and return with their check in the self-addressed return envelope. It worked. Our donor base grew quickly. The Agatha donor letter became an annual tradition for the next ten years.

My world was shaped by entrances and exits. Mother was no longer able to swallow liquids without choking. Her water was thickened, which looked loathsome to me, but she didn't seem to notice. When she sat in her wheelchair, an aide watched over her. One afternoon right after Dad had left, she was particularly agitated, trying to stand despite footrests blocking the way. The aide offered her water and turned away to the water dispenser to thicken her drink. Mom tried again to rise and pitched forward. I never heard the details—whether the wheelchair fell on top of her or not. Dad called me later. He had been called to come back and help get her settled. He found her with steri-strips holding cuts together

260

above her eye and bruises that were deepening in color as they gained ground around both eyes. I saw her the next day where she was curled up in a large chair and disoriented. I turned away and wept, although she couldn't see what I was doing. I had been engaged in a long goodbye process for months, but now it took on urgency. No more piano playing, no more walks outside in her wheelchair, just a short downward spiral.

On October 27, Dad called to say the aides had told him that Mom was actively dying. He knew I planned to be there in a couple of hours but asked that I come immediately because he was going to take a break and go to the grocery store. I arrived in a few minutes. Beth was already there. She had sensed that Grandma would have a very bad day and checked out of work early so I wouldn't be alone with her.

Mom appeared to be in a deep sleep, unable to respond to our touch or our words. One of the aides came into the room several times, singing in a rich contralto, cleansing the air. Mom held on, and I called my brother at the nearby high school where he taught biology. After an hour, I called again, and this time he understood the urgency and arrived around 3:00. Mom died holding Beth's and my brother's hands while I gently held her feet. Beth and I then drove to Dad's house, and he drove up a few minutes later. He swung both legs out of the car and rose slowly. We looked at each other for a moment across the shaded street. "It's over, then," he said. Beth and I nodded. "Yes," I said.

Now that Laura Nelson, nee Childs, had died at age ninety, my father was entering the most difficult two years of his life at age ninety-two. I was sixty.

The Hustlings

I shelved the script of *Jemmy* and moved forward with the work of the Lyric and its growing interest in moving to Plainview. The Lyric Board met with representatives of the Rural America Arts Partnership (RAAP) in November. Ken Fliès shared the history and future plans of RAAP, stating that in 1999 they would like to sponsor performances in Plainview of *Old Man Brunner Country* in January, *The Staggerford Murders* in May, and *Grand Opening* in the summer or fall. RAAP asked me to begin grant writing on a consultant basis. A move to Plainview had evolved from possible to probable.

Ken Fliès became the visionary on the formation of the Rural America Arts Partnership project with support from his wife, Millie, and local banker Dean Harrington and his wife, Sally.[7] Since both families owned local businesses, they wanted Plainview to be more than a bedroom community for the Mayo Clinic in Rochester. Millie and Ken Fliès facilitated development of tourism potential by feeding senior groups at the Tavern on the Green. Dean Harrington's family, who owned First National Bank, were eager to see businesses filling in some of the empty storefronts on Broadway, including the International Harvester building. The Lyric Theater was looking for a permanent home. If we built it, would anyone come? Rochester was only twenty-three miles away.

Old Man Brunner Country was an excellent match for the audience we hoped to build in Plainview, Minnesota. We remounted the show for the newly formed Rural America Arts Partnership on January 16, 1999, a day filled with sunshine. A January thaw had water running in the streets and puddling in our small parking lot where pick-up trucks filled the spaces.

We parked in front of the newly emptied building at 412 Broadway. The parts store functioned as the lobby, and we hung a "Ladies" sign on the bathroom door. The tractor repair shop was transformed into performance space, and we hung a "Mens" sign on the primitive lavatory previously used by mechanics. Where once there were tractors, now there were actors.

Carpenters from the local hardware store had built a staging platform at one end of the room, and we improvised overhead and side lighting. The open garage door at the back end of the room gave access to several strong people who pulled/pushed in two large, empty hay wagons that were set into a V for bleacher seating. The center of the V was filled with wooden folding chairs borrowed from the Catholic Church.

The soon-to-be theater was in chaos. Millie Fliès threw her unbelievable strength into hauling straw bales from delivery trucks to the hay wagons. A golden retriever belonging to Millie's son Elliot and his partner Randy raced through the theater. Randy, an interior designer, redesigned the lobby with antique farm implements and milk cans filled with natural grasses and reeds from nearby ditches. Food arrived. People moved in every direction.

The actors and crew entered carrying a rocking chair, barrels, and props. They stopped, took stock, their heads swiveling in amazement. Actor Jason Henning started sneezing from all the straw bales, so we immediately sent out for allergy medication. Stage Manager Al Crom made a beeline into the performing space to experiment, bringing up improvised lights with a dimmer switch mounted on a pole at stage left and then plugging in a boom box for sound effects. We were finding out just how flexible we could be. We had talked about traveling with this show for a long time. It wasn't as easy as we had projected. Two original cast members were not available—our Minstrel, David Carlson, and Chris Samuelson, our only woman. Kristen Mathisen substituted and captured the spirit and blocking of Chris' performance but added her own sensibility. We found a guitar player and made do with a single instrument, a far cry from our one-man band.

The matinee and evening performances were packed. One old farmer leaving the 2:00 show said to Dean Harrington in the lobby, "I've never been to live theater before, but if this is what it's like, I'm coming back!"

The production was financially successful as well. RAAP sold 503 out of 600 seats and charged $12 for evening shows and $10 for the matinee bringing in between $5,000 and $6,000. They also generated $2,000 in donations from community businesses, leaving them about $3,000 in the black. The Lyric received a fee of $4,300, enough to cover expenses with some left over.

The space had proved usable as a theater space. On September 11, 1999, Larry and I brought *Chief* to Plainview. I vividly remember the audience seated on the wooden chairs remaining from *Old Man Brunner Country* and Paul Epton, our Lighting Director, sitting behind the audience in the harvest-time heat at a table topped by a computerized light board. A full lighting system had been installed, a huge step forward.

As I watched the show, I became very concerned that there was no local person who could replace a bulb or solve a problem before the first RAAP production in June 2000. Paul Epton, a highly qualified Twin City lighting director, was interested in teaching the basics—how to hang, focus and gel a lighting instrument to add color. We scheduled a Saturday seminar for December 11. That morning I picked up Paul in Minneapolis and drove to Plainview.

Upon arrival, I watched him get out of the car and pull his backpack from the back seat. Seeing him in this rural setting made me aware of his unusual "techie-urban" appearance—long ponytail, thin acetic face that reflected his Jewish origins, his wiry body encased in sweatshirt and blue jeans. Paul was a vegetarian, and, in the Cities, his sole mode of transportation was a well-equipped bicycle that sported a windshield, headlight, reflectors, and carriers for scripts and lunch containers. Only on the coldest or snowiest days or when he was transporting a lighting instrument would Paul jump on public transit to get to rehearsal.

Paul's favorite memory of the workshop was "Dean Harrington attending the workshop and gamely climbing a ladder to get the experience of at least focusing a light." Paul quickly became integrated into the Plainview theater family, either hitching a ride with me or riding the shuttle from the Twin Cities to Rochester, where he was met by Sally Harrington.

Callaway Directs

In the meantime, Jon felt compelled to write a play from scratch for production in Minneapolis. We followed the advice of Diana Postlethwaite of *The New York Times Book Review*, "Forget Garrison Keillor and the Coen brothers. Jon Hassler is Minnesota's most engaging cultural export." We welcomed another play into the Hassler canon. Jon borrowed several characters from previous stories and then added some new ones to complete his newest script, *The Staggerford Murders*, set in the same mythic town he used in several other works.

I was inundated with organizational restructuring and production chores, so I couldn't direct the show. I started spreading the word, and someone suggested a young director who was fairly new in town, Dwight Callaway. I invited him to meet with me at my home office. He arrived with resume in hand, all six feet plus of him, glowingly handsome, his cinnamon skin made more revealing by his receding hairline and close-cut hair and beard. He was a gentle man, soft-spoken with an easy laugh. Dwight had never heard of Jon Hassler, not surprising given Jon's very pale, Catholic audience of readers. I filled him in from my overflowing font of Jon Hassler stories and then moved on to describe the Lyric Theater's uncertain future and limited stipends for staff positions. He described his background and what led him to theater. I gave Dwight several Hassler novels to read and offered him the directing position. He said he was interested and wanted to think it over. When he got home, he left the books on the dining room table, where his wife found them when she arrived home from work. She was immediately excited. She was a Hassler fan with several of his books in her personal library— some of them were duplicates of the novels Dwight had brought home. Her reaction resolved any doubts that Dwight still had about directing a Hassler production.

The Staggerford Murders

Dwight met with Jon Hassler regularly to discuss ideas and changes to the script, which suffered from many of the same conventions that I had been dealing with in former Hassler productions. I still picked at wounds created by the *Jemmy* review. I hoped that Dwight would be wiser and figure out how to solve problems with staging more clever than mine. He had great stage presence, internal grace and external height, a presence that would command respect.

The Staggerford Murders begins when Penny Jean Nichols returns to Staggerford to start inquiring into her father's death and her mother's disappearance nine years earlier. Three residents of the rundown Morgan Hotel gather in the lobby to chew over the news and begin their own investigation. Dusty LeDou, the garbologist; Grover, the hotel manager; and Sonny LeDoux, an itinerant preacher ordained by a mail order seminary in Florida, look for help from Dusty's dead wife, Caledonia; and Imogene Kite, local librarian and snoop extraordinaire. By play's end, Penny Jean learns the truth at the cost of a third victim's life.

Dwight Callaway, script in hand, with Jon Hassler. Photo by Nancy Campbell.

Penny Jean Nichols (Camilla Little) receives bad news from Grover
(Thom Pinault). Photo by Nancy Campbell.

Grover, (Thom Pinault), Caledonia, a ghost (Laurie King), Dusty (Larry
Roupe), and Sonny (Terry Hempleman). Photo by Nancy Campbell.

Chief Morehouse (Robert Berdahl) captures George Bauer
(Jim Jorgenson). Photo by Nancy Campbell.

Sonny (Terry Hempleman) and Imogene Kite(Lola Lesheim) share a
moment in a publicity shot. Photo by Usry Alleyne.

The characters were vintage Hassler, and Staggerford was as convoluted as ever, where the ordinary became extraordinary and, at the same time, darkly comedic. The cast ranged from novices through professional non-union actors to one union actor who played several roles. We rehearsed at the Academy of Holy Angels and opened on March 5, 1999, at the Hennepin Center for the Arts.

Posing for the picture that was the basis for the caricature used in marketing are Paul Smith, Terry Hempleman, Larry Roupe and Laurie King. Photo by Usry Alleyne.

Paul Smith, a favorite actor around town, wrote a bio for the program that may have departed from truth but demonstrated his sly wit and his sense of adventure:

> Paul Smith is a transplant from sunny Southern
> California (don't ask). He spent most of his
> teenage years as a male prostitute, living mainly in
> bus depots, train stations and hotel lobbies. When
> he read his first book, he realized he had personally

met all of the characters therein… and if you
believe that, etc. etc.

Paul had been born to play Grover, but during tech week, he developed health problems that forced him out of the line-up. Another well-known character actor, Thom Pinault, grabbed the script, took a day off from work, and started memorizing. On opening night, Thom stepped onstage without a script and carried on flawlessly to the end. If you have ever been guilty of thinking that an actor has a big head, it is not due to an inflated ego—it is the result of a consistent and finely honed process and incredible muscle memory.

The show ran through April 25, 1999, and as soon as the last bit of applause ended, a contingent of men arrived from Plainview that included Ken Fliès and Don Schultz, all wearing weight belts to protect their middle-aged backs. They carefully tore apart the set and moved it to the theater-in-progress in Plainview.

When the cast and crew arrived in Plainview two days later, they found the set in place, lighting instruments hung and focused and risers filled with folding chairs. The stage manager's booth had not been constructed, so that was jerry-rigged quickly at the back of the audience. Voila! we were up and running in Plainview! The biggest difficulty facing Dwight Callaway was a bird flying about onstage in the newly assembled Morgan Hotel. With script in hand and helped by Sally Harrington's long arms, Dwight managed to herd the bird into the lobby and out the front door.

On Sunday, Paul Smith delighted us when he pulled up on his motorcycle to see the matinee. He was fairly well recovered and enjoyed a post-show reunion with the cast, however briefly. We didn't tell Thom Pinault that Paul was there until after the show.

Paul Smith remained in the caricature that became the logo for the show. It was drawn from a photograph of the four main characters at an early rehearsal. We had t-shirts printed, which came in handy as marketing tools. I still use mine as a pajama top.

Over Hill and Dale

The Lyric now had productions in two locations separated by ninety miles. Then we learned that Jon Hassler's boyhood home was going to be demolished in Plainview to make way for a clinic unless money could be raised to move it across town. The RAAP folks were working on grants, including a $10,000 matching grant from the Katherine N. Anderson Foundation. They asked me to help with a fundraising event in the Twin Cities to raise the matching funds. We organized a reading of Jon Hassler's works to be presented at the chapel on the Macalester campus in St. Paul on July 7. Jon agreed to be the star attraction, and Larry Roupe and I backed him up with additional readings. Ken Flies and Dean Harrington represented the Plainview board to answer questions. This event was well attended, and Hassler fans and supporters contributed handsomely. Shortly thereafter, the house in Plainview was up on blocks, rolling across town to its new home at the other end of the block from the Jon Hassler Theater. RAAP planned to use it as their Writers' Center.

Hassler House under renovation (before) with Alva Crom, Sally Childs, and Mary Kay Spalding taking a tour. Photo by Nancy Campbell.

(And after) Jon and Gretchen are the first to use the handicap ramp to enjoy Jon's painting above the mantel (donated by Joe Plut). Photo by Nancy Campbell.

Hassler House completed and open for tours. Photo by Nancy Campbell.

Despite the planned move to Plainview, the Lyric was still open to new board members. We didn't know how long we would be running on parallel tracks and refused to ease up for a moment. Phillip Erickson joined the board after seeing *Old Man Brunner Country* at Lakeshore Players in White Bear Lake several months earlier. We were again seven strong with a balance of old and new members.

The Lyric board was in favor of the move to Plainview with only one objection. Gordon Gendler questioned the name Rural America Arts Partnership. As an attorney, he pointed out that the word "partnership" had a legal definition that did not hold true for the new organization. Since the Lyric board would not carry over to RAAP activities, he did not make an issue of this with the RAAP board. They had an attorney on their board as well.

I hoped the Macalester event wouldn't siphon off donations needed to mount our first summer season in Plainview. The Lyric had all it could handle financially to mount *The Road to Rouen* by Anne Welsbacher, which would be our last production as The Lyric Theater. Music was integral to this show, which touched a very personal chord for me. As a child, I took piano lessons from the age of seven to seventeen. At age twenty-six, I fulfilled elective credits with piano lessons at the University of Minnesota. I studied music theory for two quarters, but dropped the 3rd quarter when it demanded an ear that I didn't have. Anne Welsbacher's play was the next best thing.

The Lyric scheduled another fundraiser—with readings and an auction at the Anodyne Coffeeshop, a funky venue located just a few blocks from St. Joan of Arc Catholic Church in Minneapolis and less than a mile from Jon Hassler's home parish. Larry had cultivated an interest in Ann Mayer, who worked at the Anodyne. Ann identified herself as an "ideator," a term I hadn't heard before. She knew lots of other creative people and put us in touch with Tom Cassidy, an actor and comedian who agreed to be our auctioneer. We chose Sunday, August 1, and hoped to attract Hassler fans who worshiped nearby. We collected many unique items to be auctioned, including a painting by Jon Hassler donated by our newest board member.

When I looked at the items where they were stored on my front porch, I was saddened that my parents could no longer fill front-row seats at Lyric events. But at ninety-one, Dad still wanted to write a book. He had bought a computer, and a friend had set it up for him right next to Mom's empty bed. I spent many hours teaching him to use a Word Perfect program. When he called every few hours to ask questions, I jumped into the car to rescue him from mounting frustration and confusion. Between calls, I loaded the auction items into the car, ready for delivery to the Anodyne.

Auctioneer Tom Cassidy asks for a bid.
Photo by Nancy Campbell.

Jon Hassler makes a pitch at the Anodyne.
Photo by Nancy Campbell.

We started the event with readings by cast members from *Road to Rouen*. Then Tom Cassidy took over wearing a t-shirt with a huge picture of Spam across his chest, his white hair glowing like a spotlight. Tom turned his role as auctioneer into stand-up comedy, thereby generating $1,679 in sales. After the auction, Jon Hassler spoke, and the RAAP folks talked about our prospective move to Plainview.

Following our successful production of *Road to Rouen*, the Lyric board closed our last chapter as The Lyric Theater, and I pointed my little silver Honda to Southeastern Minnesota. I was eager to introduce Holm's dancing boxelder bugs and Hassler's small-town characters to Plainview. Based on feedback in 1998, when we introduced Dangel's Old Man Brunner to people who sat on straw bales, we would find a new audience.

Part Three
Jon Hassler Theater

Chapter 15: Pushing the Pace

Hindsight

Ron Peluso, the Artistic Director at the History Theater in St. Paul, gave me a couple of hours to pick his brains about his earlier history as the Artistic Director of the Minnesota Festival Theatre in Albert Lea following the departure of Michael Brindisi. Ron and I sat in the sunshine on the front steps of the History Theater in St. Paul, and I came away with two strong recommendations: 1) If you're going to have a professional theater, don't try to share the space with another organization except as a rental; and 2) make it clear to the new organization that they will need to have at least $40,000 in donations from the community to cover expenses in the first summer of production.

Ron's first recommendation came from the history derived from several changes in administration at the Albert Lea Theatre since his tenure there. So many Twin City Equity actors had worked in Albert Lea that the tug of war between the community theater and the professional theater was generally known. This tug of war carried over into the community at large, which did not support the professional productions. I had heard this recommendation directly from Albert Lea people who had attended an early performance in Plainview. I chose not to dwell on how I would have felt if a small professional company from the Twin Cities had moved in on Don Bronski's program in Ely, which is where I learned the basics of theater production. I told myself, *The decision isn't really yours. You've been invited by Plainview leaders to bring your organization in. They see Hassler's connection to Plainview as an asset that will add something to Plainview's development. The Plainview folks who are in the first stages of forming a community theater have not yet earned a place at the table.* I chose to rationalize rather than empathize.

Moving Along

The shift in location was a year-long process. So far, the productions in Plainview were Lyric shows that were meant to introduce the Plainview audience to the level of performance that they could expect from the Jon Hassler Theater when it opened. These shows also brought in additional income as we completed the transition. I became a part-time employee of RAAP for several months and asked to go full-time in March, giving me April and May to prepare for our grand opening as the Jon Hassler Theater in Plainview in June 2000. Regina Barr from the Lyric Board of Directors accompanied me to Plainview to assist in salary and contract discussions. The meeting was cordial, and I was happy with the offer. No negotiation needed. But having Regina's support and business savvy shored up my confidence.

When the next round of grants at the McKnight Foundation came due, Neal Cuthbert gave me permission to apply under the name Jon Hassler Theater. The legal work had been done to complete the transition, including a Dramatic Rights Licensing Agreement among the Lyric Theater, Jon Hassler and RAAP, in which "Mr. Hassler grants to RAAP and Lyric the sole and exclusive rights to dramatize, produce, perform, and represent Mr. Hassler's Literary Works for presentation on the stage for a term of thirty years beginning on August 1, 1999, and ending on July 31, 2029."

As we neared the date of McKnight's decision, Neal Cuthbert called with several questions, the last and most important being, "Sally, what do you want personally from this move to rural Minnesota?" Apparently, this move by an urban theater to rural Minnesota was a first in McKnight's funding history. I stammered to gain time and then replied, "I'd like this to be my legacy after I am no longer able to continue working." McKnight awarded a grant of $12,000.

The Lyric Theater had about $10,000 left in its bank account after all obligations were settled. That chunk of change traveled with me to Plainview. The founders of the RAAP board were Dean and Sally Harrington, Ken and Millie Fliès, and Don DeVaughan (attorney). The Jon Hassler Theater was one of the affiliates (or partners) of RAAP. A separate management committee, often referred to as our "Theater Board," was set up. In the beginning I was not included on the RAAP board but would be part of the Theater Board.

I recognized the risks I was taking. As the leader of the Lyric Theater, I had control of my future. The commitment level varied among board members, but there were no internal politics, no factions. In Plainview, I would be giving over control to a group of people whose internal politics and ethics were unknown to me. This required the biggest leap of faith I had ever taken. Would I land on solid ground? Although I would no longer be solely responsible for the financial health of the organization, I knew better than to think I was off the hook. I had walked off a cliff and would either learn to fly or land on my feet. I expected to keep on running.

Dad Carries On

My father continued living alone in his home in South Minneapolis. I took him to lunch and/or had him over for supper at least once or twice a week. He was an intelligent man who had not been able to fulfill his potential when he was called home from Carleton College in 1924 to support his family because my grandfather had been forced into bankruptcy by the impending collapse of the building trades. This left Dad frustrated most of his life. He read only non-fiction, trying to get a grasp on reality. My father demonstrated forms of dementia. He wanted me to move in with him and help him write his book, which would lay out how the world could achieve peace and happiness based on his literal belief that "God is love," which he did not recognize as any kind of metaphor. He was convinced that his book would be published and, through word-of-mouth publicity, read by people all over the world, making the world a better place. We would live off the royalties.

Dad carried his whole belief system typed up on index cards in his shirt pocket—Biblical verses, the AA twelve-step program, and a quote from Vaclav Havel. Whenever he could corner a listener, he launched into his litany on the value of euthanasia. His old friends did not call him anymore. He denied that he was depressed. He was planning his suicide. He kept a recently purchased .38 caliber pistol in his bedside drawer.

I called my brother to share the news, and we agreed to leave the pistol in the drawer. If I removed it, I couldn't stop him from buying another. Whenever Dad came for supper, Beth and I listened to his sermonizing. He could not be diverted, and even with double hearing aids, he didn't *hear* anything we said. I kept on commuting to Plainview.

Grand Opening Revised

In *My Staggerford Journal*, Jon Hassler talks about how he tried to write like Hemingway, the narrator as "fly on the wall." But then he learned that readers—and, even more, editors—wanted to hear the narrator's view. How about theater audiences?

For the official opening of the Jon Hassler Theater, Jon revised *Grand Opening*, recreating Brendan as the narrator per my request. I scheduled a reading of the new script at The Playwrights' Center for an invited audience. Two award-winning playwrights, John Olive and Buffy Sedlachek agreed to provide us with feedback.[8]

Buffy was able to attend the reading and gave comments to the full cast. Her first statement was that ordinarily, she didn't like the use of a narrator, but she was using one in her next play and understood the need for the convention, especially for this play.

John Olive could not attend the reading, so I mailed him a script. When he sent me his comments, he said that ordinarily, he did not like the use of a narrator, but he was also using one in his next play. In an odd way, I felt I had been granted permission to use this convention.

Once Brendan became the narrator, the arc of the story became clear, and the events and characters became Brendan's vehicle for telling his story. Professional theaters in New York City have out-of-town trials in outlying areas and then move to Broadway. Ironically, the Lyric's move to Plainview turned the concept on its head. Minneapolis had been our trial venue, and now *Grand Opening* would move to Broadway... in Plainview. The move was a little like being reborn, a chance to produce

Hassler, Dangel, and Holm in a rural or small-town setting.

We proceeded with auditions for the premier performance in the Jon Hassler Theater in June. At my next dinner with Dad, he said, "If you ever write a book, you should call it *Running Uphill.*"

Before I cast the summer shows, I held a local audition on a Saturday in Plainview. I hoped for some response from actors who performed at Rochester's community theaters—the Rochester Civic Theater and Rochester Rep. Although a few actors from Plainview and Rochester read for me, no one was right for the first production. I would try again before casting the second show, a musical.

Joe Plut, Jon's best friend and former colleague at the Community College in Brainerd, recommended Marion Graham of Brainerd to play Catherine Foster (Brendan's mother). Joe was right on the money, and Marion agreed to travel to Minneapolis for rehearsals in the basement of Epiphany Lutheran Church and to Plainview for tech week and performances. Brainerd became an important piece in joining Hassler's Northern Minnesota connections to the Plainview talent and marketing pool.

Catherine Foster (Marion Elaine Graham), Brendan Foster (Ryan Smith), and Hank Foster (Erik Steen) after a fire in the grocery store. Photo by Nancy Campbell.

The rest of the cast was from the Twin Cities. Two actors returned from the original production in 1996, Larry Roupe (Grandfather) and John Stillwell (Dodger).

As a kid, when Jon showed up to get paid for mowing the lawn at the Catholic Church, Father O'Connor always asked him his name and which family he belonged to. This happened every week despite Jon's additional service as an altar boy on Sunday mornings. Similarly, in *Grand Opening*, the priest could not remember parishioners' names despite serving in Plum for seven years. Longtime Plainview residents loved matching up such pieces of each Hassler play with people they remembered, and even more, they loved sharing their discoveries with a staff member in the lobby after the show. But...

Where Would I Sleep?

With the move to Plainview, I gained a full-time paid job as the Artistic Director of a theater for the first time since the Lyric was formed. Larry lost his role as a season ticket seller and fundraiser but gladly settled for Union membership as an actor. The lobby of the Jon Hassler Theater provided him with fresh access to a new fan club.

I wondered how personal relationships would change in the next few years. I was Larry's chauffeur for rehearsals in Minneapolis, but during performance weeks in Plainview, our schedules did not mesh, and Larry rode back and forth with other actors. Larry had always kept his personal life closeted, but I missed the cribbage games, daily crosswords, and long walks with Delores, his German Shepherd.

And where was Gusztav through this long transition? He had retired from SSU on a disability in 1998 when his post-polio syndrome[9] finally got the better of him, and in 2000 he was sixty-five, able to draw on Social Security and his teacher's pension. He was consumed by family matters requiring his presence in Hungary for months at a time.

With a 180-mile round trip commute between Plainview and Minneapolis, I could not afford to rent an apartment in Plainview. But where would I sleep? And where would the actors sleep? Where would we eat?

The logistics of housing so many people were engineered by the Plainview Board, with Sally Harrington leading the way. Debbie and Tom Small were extraordinarily generous with both funding and housing. They lived in California but had renovated a beautiful old brick farmhouse and outbuildings for their family's use when visiting the Rochester area where they owned the *Rochester Post Bulletin*. The farmhouse sat empty much of the time, and Debbie's brother maintained the property in their absence. Debbie envisioned the farm outbuildings as housing for artist residencies, but her plans were only partially complete when the Hassler Theater opened. She decided to offer the farmhouse itself for housing, a decision that we learned later her brother did not fully support.

Alletta Jervey (actor) and Anna Bartley (back-stage tech) pick up black walnuts at The Farm. Photo by Childs.

I joined Sally Harrington on a bright summer day to visit the farm near the tiny hamlet of Viola, ten miles away. The Viola area was the boyhood home of Frank B. Kellogg, the only Minnesotan to win the Nobel Prize for Peace. We drove southeast towards Rochester, turning left on a dirt road where we spotted a windbreak of pine trees marching in a straight line along the edge of a cornfield. Built by the Civilian Conservation Corps during FDR's new deal, this shelter belt would stand and bend with the wind for a long time.

The farmhouse

We turned right on another dirt road and followed a double row of black walnut trees spotting flashes of red brick between the polished, silvery-gray tree trunks sculpted by the wind. We turned left into a corridor fit for an entrance into the *Architectural Digest*. As we followed a hard-packed dirt driveway, the nineteenth-century red brick farmhouse emerged from behind a large tree sporting an old-fashioned swing made from a clothesline with a wooden seat. The house sat comfortably, a large square box with six windows per side, three up and three down, all framed in white with dark green shutters. A smaller one-story box with an open front porch completed the house. As we slowed to a halt, a slender, blond woman burst out of the farmhouse door, waving us into a parking spot on worn-down grass next to a small building, which we learned later was a sauna.

Debbie was talking before we could get out of the car. She grabbed Sally Harrington in a hug as I rounded the car and offered my hand.

Debbie said, "I'm delighted you could come. Please, come in and we'll start with a tour of the house." She quickly led us to the white porch.

"Yes, we would love that," Sally Harrington said to Debbie's receding back as we hurried to keep up with her enormous energy. "I can't wait to see the AGA stove."[10]

Debbie opened the screen door that led directly into the high-ceilinged living room. We paused to wipe our feet on hand-woven rag rugs. The harvest gold of the room suggested sunshine on ripening wheat, with floor-length drapes at each long, white-framed window. A pot-bellied wood-burning stove claimed center stage on the end wall, mounted on a platform of smooth stone. I imagined actors and staff gathered after rehearsal to share a bottle of wine before bedtime. As we moved through the dining room and kitchen, I saw myself at the round wooden kitchen table with early morning sun and a cup of strong coffee. Four bedrooms on the second floor could sleep five to six. *This house has not seen any wear and tear,* I thought.

Al Crom shares a Sunday crossword with Larry Roupe while Anna Bartley and Alletta Jervey playfully observe. Photo by Childs.

During the run of *To Whom it May Concern*, (Singer, Terry Tyler) enjoys the sun at the kitchen table. Photo by Childs.

The first night I stayed at The Farm, I felt like tiptoeing lest I break something, but Debbie encouraged us to feel at home—use the herbs, cut the flowers, and stoke up the sauna.

The Farm—outbuildings and windmill, cars parked beside the sauna. Photo by Sally Childs.

The Farm took on a mythic proportion (and a capital letter) as a retreat for as many of us as could fit, especially the staff who spent at least 50 percent of their work time in Plainview. When we didn't all fit, some actors were also housed in town by the RAAP Board members—the Harringtons, Fliès and DeVaughns—but the opening weekend party was held at The Farm. It was a place of enchantment and hope that first summer. It also contributed to Plainview's reputation as a great place for actors to work.

Success Breeds Success: *To Whom It May Concern* and *On Golden Pond*

Once *Grand Opening* was running, I was back in the church basement in Minneapolis to rehearse *To Whom It May Concern*. As you may remember from the Lyric production in 1993, the story starts with a group of people gathering for a worship service. They share a common ritual. Then a stranger arrives and upsets the group dynamics, and a regrouping occurs, ending in communion. Metaphorically, that described the dynamics of the Jon Hassler Theater, arriving as a stranger in Plainview, faced with achieving some kind of communion with Plainview residents. I wondered if this would ever happen and if it did, how long it would take. In any case, this show was my love letter to the people of Plainview.

The casting ranged from professionals all the way to an extraordinary high school student, Me'Lea Mackbee, who played "The Child." She was the daughter of Jewel Rae, who played the role for the Lyric and, once in costume, appeared to be a larger version of her mother. When she opened the first number on stage, her resemblance and voice were uncanny. I was delighted to discover people who had worked for the Lyric as actors were also strong singers—Duane Koivisto and Dimitri Gerasimenko. The family feeling kept on growing.

We were ready to start rehearsals but still had not cast the role of Bob, the dog owner. Bob needed a lush baritone range to sing a romantic duet, "Ain't Love Easy." One of the other actors suggested Dieter Bierbrauer, a young actor who was new to Minneapolis and working as a singing waiter at a downtown restaurant while he looked for theater work. I tracked him down, and he auditioned at my house in Minneapolis the next day. He was tall and handsome, and his exuberance drew me in. I sat on the couch while he turned the rest of my living room into a stage and began his prepared audition piece. *If he sings as well as he acts,* I thought, *by George, he's got it."*

"Can you sing something a cappella?" I asked. "You can get a pitch from the piano in the dining room."

"Sure." He walked confidently to the spinet (which had more stage time than young Dieter) and struck a couple of chords.

I don't remember the song, but I remember how it made me feel—as if I had just made eye contact with him across a crowded room. I allowed the song to linger long enough for a little more than thirty-two bars of music. Then I told Dieter about the Jon Hassler Theater and the show and offered him the role. He said yes. Dieter became a valued member of the Hassler family and returned to play other roles. He has since starred in numerous roles at the Ordway and Theatre Latte Da in the Twin Cities.

I can say "I knew them when" about many people who performed or crewed for the Lyric or Hassler Theaters and then moved on to success at other venues. Cast members Mike Mahler and Zoe Pappas were students from Benilde St. Margaret's who later pursued work in music and/or theater. Kellie Stoltz, a Plainview high school student, ran lights for Hassler productions for about two years and then went to Mankato to pursue more training. Giving young talent a place to grow gave all of us a special sense of accomplishment.

Kellie Stoltz of Plainview works on the set prior to the first opening. Photo by Mike Nadolske.

Blake Brown, a young tenor from Rochester, was perfect to play Elliott, a single parent, whom I once again placed in a wheelchair onstage. Blake's song was in waltz time, "Who Will Dance with the Blind Dancing Bear?" I interpreted the blind dancing bear as a reference to Christ, although not everyone agreed with me. The opening lyrics:

Who will dance with the blind dancing bear?

Do you <u>care</u> to, Madam, Sir?

Who will chance with the blind dancing bear?

Do you <u>dare</u> to, Madam, Sir?

The day after typing these words, I opened the Sunday *Star Tribune* to a very large picture of a very large bear, "a brown bear named Charlie, chained to a tree prior to transport to Dancing Bear Park near Sofia, Bulgaria."

The article included a review of a new book, *Dancing Bears* by Witold Szablowski, translated from the Polish by Antonia Lloyd-Jones. In her review Laurie Hertzel writes:

"Here is how you teach a bear to dance: First, you acquire a bear cub—maybe you capture it in the wild, maybe you buy it from a bear broker. Then you smash an iron ring through the most sensitive part of its body—its nose—and attach a chain to the ring.

"You might knock out all of its teeth, to make sure it doesn't bite you. Or you might not.

"You wrap its hind feet to protect them, but not its front feet, and as you play your fiddle or your drum, you lead it to a red-hot iron surface. The bear will rise up on its back legs because the pain in its front paws is searing, and over time whenever it hears the fiddle, it will stand.

"You jerk the chain to make the bear dance."

Ms. Hertzel learned all of this from the book. It reinforced my interpretation of Carol Hall's metaphor of the blind dancing bear as a Christ image. I envisioned the crown of thorns piercing Christ's head, his blood running into his eyes, his wrists and ankles nailed to the cross. The words to the song continue:

He may look funny and awkward and wrong,

Plastered with honey and stumbling along,

But his soul is singing free,

I can't say the same for me, can you?

Embedded in the song are the ritualized words of the communion service spoken by the Priest.

To this day, I will stick with my interpretation of the song, a song that could move me to tears. I never argued with those who disagreed. I am not a regular churchgoer, but religion has much to teach us about humankind, both positive and negative.

From the Plainview audition, a local singer was offered a role, but worsening symptoms of a chronic illness prevented her from accepting. We were left with Blake as our only regional actor. It was a beginning.

Father Connelly, who was a bit of a rebel, had made it possible to stage *Dear James* in the Catholic Church in 1997 and then continued to attend our opening nights. In a small town, it is good to be friends with the ministerial association, and to that purpose, we offered to bring our singers to several churches on the Sunday morning of opening weekend. The show would run only two weeks, so we had to work fast to get some Plainview people into the seats.

It never occurred to me that many actors would not want to go this extra step because they had been up much of Saturday night "celebrating." Clark Cruikshank was the self-appointed shepherd of this flock. He was one of three AEA actors but the only one who raised an objection. He didn't push it far enough to insist that I renege on promises to the local pastors. We followed through and dropped in to sing just one song at four different churches—Lutheran, Catholic, Methodist and Church of Christ. We were careful not to replicate the divisive behavior between Lutherans and Catholics noted by Jon Hassler in *Grand Opening*, but my little skirmish with Clark planted the seed of a personal adversarial relationship that slowly grew over the years.

Our Sunday morning visits worked. The second weekend, much of the audience came from Plainview, including several ministers. The more conservative ones may have objected to internal parts of the show that posed questions/doubts about Christian observances, but the show ended with unification through the sacrament of communion. No one called the theater to complain.

Visitors from afar were amazed by the high-quality performance and uniquely creative use of a building that once housed tractors. A computer programmer arrived from Boston to visit Erica Zaffarano, an old high school classmate who had recently designed his new condo. He regularly donated to encourage worthwhile projects and artists that he admired, and after seeing the show, asked Erica what was needed most. She answered, "a sprung floor that could support dancers." This anonymous donor immediately sold $14,000 worth of stock and donated it to the Jon Hassler Theater for a new sprung floor which was installed at the end of the summer/fall season.

The third show of the inaugural season, *On Golden Pond* by Ernest Thompson, was familiar to our rural audience primarily due to the popularity of the movie version starring Henry Fonda as Norman Thayer, Jr. and Jane Fonda as his daughter, Chelsea. On stage, no one could play the curmudgeon, Norman, better than Larry Roupe. He met his match in Alletta Jervey, who had played Norman's wife Ethel in a production directed by Ron Duffy at Lakeshore Players in White Bear Lake. Larry happily bonded with Alletta, running lines with her daily and praising the tasty meals she cooked expertly on the Aga. The Farm became a family setting with Larry, Alletta, our stage manager Alva Crom, tech assistant Anna Bartley and me all under one roof. The photos from that summer painted an amazingly idyllic setting.

The show was an audience pleaser. Jennifer Connelly (Chelsea) and Terry Lynn Carlson (Bill) became regulars in Plainview. David Gaustad, a young actor from Rochester, completed the cast as the fiancé's preteen son, Billy. Larry quickly gathered David into the onstage family.

**Ethel (Alletta Jervey) challenges Norman (Larry Roupe).
Photo by Mike Nadolske.**

**Ethel (Alletta Jervey) listens to Bill (Terry Lynn Carlson), supported by
Jennifer Connelly (Chelsea). Photo by Nancy Campbell.**

Ethel's toll house cookies are in the bag held by David Gaustad (Billy), who is hiding from Norman. Photo by Nancy Campbell.

In the play, Norman is at war with himself and the world in general, but especially with his daughter Chelsea. As the story plays out, Billy becomes an important element in the resolution of this conflict—both a buffer to hostility and a link to love. Sweet, sad, funny, and orchestrated to the call of loons on the lake.

Waving Goodbye

Some friends in Minneapolis encouraged me to meet a single man about my age who was very interested in theater and had retired from his job as a cop on the Iron Range. I was curious enough to invite him to drive to Plainview, have dinner with me at the Tavern on the Green and see the show. He was familiar with the plot and kept saying, "It's all about the boy." I insisted the boy was a necessary catalyst in resolving the central conflict between Chelsea and Norman. After the curtain call, my guest looked at me and said conclusively, "It's all about the boy." In retrospect, we may have been saying the same thing. I decided to let it go and allow him to feel superior. I was female, his "date." I thanked him for the lovely dinner and waved goodbye as he pulled away to drive ninety miles back to St. Paul. I never heard from him again.

"It's all about the boy." Billy (David Gaustad) makes a point.

I returned home to regroup before remounting the show in October. I invited Dad and my daughter Beth over for supper, and it took only minutes for Dad to burst my bubble of success in Plainview.

He started preaching about the value of euthanasia and talking about his suicide plan. Arguing was useless. I buttoned my lip, but Beth told her grandfather that his constant threat of suicide was abusive to me. She soon regretted these words spoken in anger.

On Saturday of Labor Day weekend, I answered the phone just as Larry arrived to work the crossword puzzle.

"Hello? Dad?"

His sobs broke up his words. "Good-bye. Good- goo- I lllove you…"

"Dad, wait for me. I'm coming…" The phone died. I muttered, "Wait for me."

I grabbed my purse and ran for the door as Larry entered. He backed out as I locked the door. I shouted over my shoulder, explaining as I bolted up the driveway.

He limped after me. "I'm coming with you. Don't back over me, for Christ's sake!"

I drove with a foot on the gas and a hand on the horn as I spun from Bryant onto 46th and then right onto Lyndale. I don't remember stopping for red lights. At 56th, I turned left and then right on Harriet. I got a foot out of the car, Dad's key dug into my hand. "Wait here while I take a look."

Larry nodded. "Go, go."

I stepped through the unlocked door into the tiny foyer holding my breath. Dad's inert body sprawled in his favorite chair atop a carefully draped plastic sheet. His head tilted, resting on his left shoulder. His left arm dangled, his finger still caught in the trigger. Blood drizzled from his mouth and nose. Some gray matter splattered the wall behind him.

I backed out of the room and onto the front stoop to reassemble a world without Dad. Larry sat in the car, bent over the puzzle. "*Huh*," I thought.

I crossed back through the house, touching my mother's chair as I passed into the kitchen and lifted the harvest gold receiver from the wall phone. I punched in 911: "My father is dead. I'm at his house. Please send help."

"How do you know he is dead?"

"I, well, I… you don't believe me? …uh, there's a hole in the back of his head, a gun in his hand and he's drooling blood. What else do you…"

"Okay, okay. Just give me the address. Help is on the way." Before I hung up, I heard sirens from the fire station six blocks away.

Then I called my brother. "Well, Dave, he did it. Dad shot himself. The police are on their way."

"The hell you say. I didn't even know Dad had a gun."

"Yes—you did. I called you weeks ago to tell you." I thought, *What kind of stupid denial is this?*

"Really? Really! You called? I don't…"

"David, it doesn't matter. For God's sake, could you just come here? I could use some help." My voice rose in pitch and volume.

"Calm down. I'll be there as soon as I can."

I called Beth next. She hollered, "I'm on my way," and hung up. I walked to the car and handed Larry my car keys.

"But how will you get home?"

"Beth will be here soon. She'll take me home."

Larry took the keys reluctantly. "I'll talk to you later."

I nodded and turned, already heading back to a house stripped of its essence. I stepped into the living room and stared at the still form in the chair.

A fireman entered followed by two policemen. They checked Dad and asked if I had touched anything. I shook my head, no.

The cop in charge sent the fireman on his way and then stood by me quietly. Finally, he said, "You need to say goodbye now. The M.E. will take your father to the morgue to perform an autopsy. It's required by law in a violent death. Don't worry. The evidence points to suicide."

"*Goodbye, Dad. Rest in peace.*" My father truly believed that he did us a favor by taking his own life. I could not cry. His truth set me free: "Beneficial no end." Dad would have been ninety-four in another two weeks.

Back in Plainview, we remounted *On Golden Pond* in October for another three weeks. Box office numbers stayed high.

The Rural America Arts Partnership Board of Directors remained strictly a fiscal board of local people. But the Theater Committee was a mix of local and Twin City people. Meetings were often held midway at Jim Bassett's palatial home on the shores of the Lake Byllesby Reservoir, a recreational lake near Cannon Falls, which was built in 1910 to utilize the Cannon River as a source of hydro-electrical power. Jim served on the RAAP board but also sat in on theater meetings. He had retired as an attorney with West Publishing in St. Paul, but he remained a faithful "Johnnie," a graduate of St. John's University, and took pride in Hassler's teaching and writing career. Jim was an avid bicyclist, tall, slim, with a little white mixed into his reddish hair. His wife Mary was a willow, with salt and pepper hair and warm brown eyes, her oval face luminous. She grew up in Plainview where her parents owned the grocery store across the street from Leo Hassler's Red Owl (the grocery store standoff in the book had been fictional). The Bassetts took an active role in many phases of development of the RAAP organization. When Larry Roupe died in 2016, the Bassetts and I found comfort in sitting together after the funeral at St. Joan of Arc Church in Minneapolis and sharing memories of this earlier time.

The Gifts of the Magi

While the Theater Board was getting organized, the RAAP board approved going ahead with a Christmas show, *The Gifts of the Magi* by Randy Courts and Mark St. Germain. This lush, beguiling musical is based on two classics by the immortal O. Henry, "The Gift of the Magi" and "The Last Leaf." It ran from December 1 to the 17 and fit well with Plainview's annual Old Fashioned Christmas celebration. The first week in December, city employees erected a very large pine tree on the snow-covered lawn of the theater and plugged the lights inside the lobby. This became a hospitality center for people who needed to warm up and use the restrooms after a hayride or stroll along Broadway. Many townsfolk donned late nineteenth-century costumes over their warmest long underwear and swung lanterns to stop traffic on Broadway whenever a horse-drawn wagon needed the right-of-way. This celebration seemed to be plucked right out of *The Gifts of the Magi:*

> It is Christmas in New York, but for two young lovers, Jim and Della, the prospects are bleak, as both are out of work and penniless. But as those familiar with the famous story are aware, their dilemma is solved when both part with their most precious possessions (she her beautiful long hair, he his heirloom pocket watch) in order to buy presents for each other thereby creating, at least for a magical moment, an aura of warmth in the cold, impersonal winter city. In addition to their story there are glimpses of various city folk (played by the same two performers) going about their holiday business, and the hilarious plight of a cheerful bum named Soapy, who wants only to get arrested so he can spend the night in a cozy cell, all gracefully enhanced by tuneful songs and neatly tied together by a newsboy-narrator, Willy, who adds his own melodious and informative observations to the delightful proceedings.

—Catalog, Dramatists Publishing

The production had to make good on that description—"magical moment," "aura of warmth," "glimpses of city folk," "holiday business." We cast Blake Brown as the Young Husband and another well-known Rochester actor, Debbie Olson, as the New York "Her." Erica Zaffarano designed and built the set, but Paul Epton was unavailable for lighting. Was there a Lighting Director hanging loose over in Rochester? I called the Rochester Civic Theater and asked for names of local lighting directors. They gave me only one, Ben Hain, but then said he was taking some time off from theater. I crossed my fingers and dialed Ben's number. After telling Ben why I was calling, he asked for a script and timeline. "I'm free of planting and harvesting chores for the winter," he said, "but I have a dairy herd to feed and milk daily from 4 to 7 p.m. If you can work around that, I might be interested in getting back to doing some theater." Ben truly represented the "rural" in the Rural America Arts Partnership. He worked the family farm as his full-time occupation.

Ben had taken a four-year leave from theater work. Later I asked what had provoked that decision, and he said, "It was 1996, and Kelly (wife) and I were at the State Theater seeing a touring show of *Kiss of the Spiderwoman*. During intermission, I thought about the show, that it was dark, literally and figuratively. And I was looking at that head sculpture that hangs in the lobby, and I thought, 'I don't like this. Why am I doing theater?' So, I quit and bought a five-string banjo."

When I asked Ben for a commitment, he said yes. An unforeseen gift for JHT.

Our first production meeting brought us together at Erica's house in Plymouth. Ben got there first and was already seated at Erica's dining room table. When he stood, he wasn't much taller than me, a robust, beefy barrel of a man with red, tousled hair and a red head's complexion, warmly pink and blue-eyed. He smiled easily, exuding heat and warmth.

The meeting focused on Erica's sketches and ideas for the set. Ben said little. I thought he needed time to see what was going on, so I didn't direct questions to him, happy that he was attentive and seemed to be enjoying the discussion. Ben's predecessor had been a listener and had worked with Erica and me long enough to absorb ideas quickly, asking for clarification only if he didn't understand something. Otherwise, we left lighting discussions for later. I didn't realize that Ben felt he was being ignored. He had everything under control—no squeaky wheels to grease, and I was focused on many other things. Ben soon learned that the highest praise I could hand him was to leave him free to design and experiment and leave me free to react.

Ben could do anything that required a combination of creativity and mechanical expertise. He became our resident Technical Director and brought his friend and designer, Paul Skattum, from the Rochester Repertory Theatre (the Rep) to work on sets and eventually design for us. Erica loved working with both of them, and they credited her with passing along helpful tips. Ben once said, "If we were stuck about painting something, she'd say, 'Just get the paint down!' The rest didn't matter, just get the paint down, and that would usually spark something and get us out of our rut." These three people filled the shop with lightness and humor.

The Gifts of the Magi had the usual casting glitches. We hadn't found the New York "Him," and rehearsals were about to begin. Our choreographer, Beth Desotelle, suggested we bring in Billy Kimmel from the Twin Cities. He was perfect for the role, a triple threat (singer, dancer, actor), and an AEA member.

We activated our AEA contract and proceeded. And then Debbie Olson twisted her ankle and was forced to get off her feet. Beth Desotelle (also AEA) stepped in as the New York "Her" and spent the Thanksgiving holiday memorizing lines and music. Beth and Billy appeared as a matched set—physically fit, short, attractive, and both trained dancers. Beth's heart-shaped face was a foil for Billy's square jaw. As character actors, they raised the performance level through improvised comic bits. They also had powerful voices.

Billy Kimmel and Beth Desotelle. Photos by Mike Nadolske.

Blake Brown came in from Rochester, and the rest of the cast drove longer distances. Sandra Struthers played Della, the young wife, filling in the high soprano notes. Soapy, the Bum, challenged Dale Pfeilsticker to pull out his best comedic performance, and Jake Mahler, a college student in Northfield, brought youth and vitality to the role of Willy, the newsboy.

Sandra Struthers with gift for her husband with Jake Mahler.

Billy Kimmel with Dale Pfeilsticker.

The show borrowed a film technique, pulling short glimpses from various scenes into a sequence, condensing space and time, creating montages to reveal the world of O. Henry. Only six actors, but when they all sang together, they sounded like thirty-six. And they weren't miked. Such is the advantage of a small, intimate theater space.

Winter driving almost prevented some of the Twin Cities actors from arriving before curtain. We built strong relationships with a few of the Rochester technical folk, especially those associated with the Rochester Rep. I hoped actors would follow them to Plainview before next winter.

A Foray to the Commonweal

I found a rhythm to the work pattern as the Jon Hassler Theater grew roots in Plainview. I was still involved in funding and grant writing, but I was no longer responsible for paying the bills. I could spend more time thinking about the productions themselves and how we could become accepted as part of the Plainview community.

Ken and Millie Fliès managed group sales for the theater, scheduling groups at various restaurants scattered along the route to Plainview, including their own. Ken wanted to sell "The Plainview Experience" to make it a major player in the tourism industry in southeastern Minnesota. This led to a discussion of the success experienced by Lanesboro, a small town with a population of 750 located south of Rochester in the Root River Valley, home to the Commonweal Theatre Company, extensive biking trails and many quaint bed and breakfasts.

Established in 1989, the Commonweal Theatre identifies itself as "the region's premier professional theater company with a rotating repertory of comedies, dramas, musicals, classics and contemporary plays." (Web page) Their use of the word "professional" elicited a competitive streak in the founders of RAAP. The Commonweal supplemented casting with actors from the Twin Cities, but they did not have an AEA contract.

In 2001 Ken asked me to visit the Commonweal and get their story, so I scheduled an afternoon to meet with their executive director, Hal Cropp, and tour the facility.

The sixty-mile drive took me to the edge of Rochester where I turned south on 52 and then east at the Fountain City (WI) exit to follow Highway 8 a few miles into Lanesboro. The strongly curved descent into the Root River Valley revealed church steeples, lush greenery that mitigated the heat on top of the river bluff, Victorian homes crusted with gingerbread trim, and then the historic main street. I turned left and parked almost in front of the Commonweal Theatre, housed in an old brick building.

When I entered the lobby, a young woman silenced her vacuum cleaner, and I asked for Hal Cropp. She reached for a phone behind the old-fashioned ticket counter while my feet settled into floral print carpeting.

Hmmm, I thought, *quaint like the rest of the town. So, what does the concrete floor at The Hassler say about Plainview?*

Within minutes Hal Cropp stepped briskly into the room, hand extended. He was of average height with a compact body and unremarkable face that could easily adapt to the varied palette of characters that he played in Commonweal productions.

I followed Hal into the theater's house, where seats were bolted to a gently raked floor facing a proscenium stage with arched doorways on either side. A typical design left over from nineteenth-century opera houses.

Hal paused. "I can't take you backstage because it is nothing more than a cross-over space. Our sets are designed and constructed at Luther College in Decorah, Iowa, and trucked to the theatre for tech week. So, we don't need a scene shop."

As Hal led me up a stairwell, we paused at a very short door that opened to the Stage Manager's booth. My eyebrows lifted in question. Hal answered, "Our Stage Managers cannot stand up straight. They walk in bent at the waist and get seated as soon as possible."

I laughed. "Unless you hire Leprechauns!"

Hal laughed, too.

I thought back to bringing *The Staggerford Murders* to Plainview and looking for the Stage Manager's booth. I don't remember whom I asked, but I do remember the answer, "What's a Stage Manager's booth?"

Hal was climbing the last few steps. "The offices are straight ahead."

A number of workstations were crammed into a modest space. He introduced two people who waved as they talked on their telephones. Cell phones were still primitive and expensive in 2001, so any staff members needing to make calls had to be in the office. I assumed many people worked from home as much as possible. There was little room to move about, and Hal and I stood in a narrow aisle as he continued to talk.

"The company is made up of eight year-round theater artists—primarily actors who double as publicists, box office personnel, grant writers, and so on. They are paid $21,000 per year. Many company members serve as adjunct faculty at Luther College or supplement their incomes with other theater work in Rochester or Winona or small towns scattered nearby."

"So, you have sort of a symbiotic relationship with Luther?"

"Yes," Hal's face nearly glowed. "Our artistic director, Eric Bunge, grew up here and graduated from Luther College. It was just a natural fit."

"So does he select the plays for your summer season?"

Hal said, "Let's keep walking," as he turned around and headed for the stairs.

I kept talking to his back. "And how did you decide to produce Ibsen every winter?"

We entered the lobby and stopped to talk. "Eric and I select the plays with help from other company members. But our choice of Ibsen came about when we were sitting around over drinks, bemoaning the oncoming winter, the snow and cold. This led to Ibsen and the whole Scandinavian profile—dour personalities sunk in darkness and heavy drinking. And then we decided to immerse ourselves in it, to quit looking for sunshine, to see if our audience would join us in the doldrums. And they did. Our annual winter play by Ibsen is part of our trademark."

I envisaged fingers of snow crossing the highways, theatergoers braving the storm to spend a night with Ibsen. Incredible.

We left the theater to walk a few blocks to a newly built dormitory. Hal continued with his story. "The Theater was started when a group of Lanesboro businessmen decided they wanted to convert the old movie theater to live theater. They raised a chunk of money and then called Eric Bunge out in Colorado, where he was in graduate school, and made him an offer. They asked him to take a leave from his studies and come home to get the Commonweal on its feet."

How perfect, I thought. *A hometown connection.*

"Lanesboro's business community was built around tourists who came to bicycle through the Root River Valley on a highly developed system of trails.[11] Many stopped overnight in bed and breakfasts and did some antiquing before they departed. The city fathers decided a stronger arts component would draw more tourists."

Since it started, the Commonweal had attracted actors from metropolitan areas, so it had to provide housing. We arrived at the dormitory, which was financed by a pooling of funds loaned by several business owners. When the dorm was successfully completed, the loan was forgiven. We were about to enter a debt-free new building that could house both short-term actors and long-term company members.

Hal's pride in the building was evident as he showed me the communal kitchen and comfortable living room area and then headed us into a hallway of small, efficient bedrooms with built-in dressers and bed frames. The dorm could house a dozen or more people.

As we concluded the tour, Hal also noted that the costume shop would soon move from Decorah to a downstairs room in the dorm, which would be more convenient for costume fittings and maintenance. Hal's energy and pride in the Commonweal, along with the physical plant, bespoke a successful and growing business. It operated as an empire unto itself—supported by—yet independent of—local businesses.

I brought a yellow legal pad filled with information back to Ken and the RAAP Board. On the long drive back to Plainview, I compared RAAP's simple operating plan to Commonweal's many-faceted plan. Was there anything we could implement from their innovative structure?

Building a relationship with a college theater department deserved some thought. Rochester was close enough and had a two-year community college with basic courses. Winona State University was farther away but big enough to have a theater department. Both were part of the State of Minnesota college system. I cautioned myself, *you're over sixty, female, introverted, and unknown. Do you think you can join the boy's club?*

I thought more about Rochester. In our first summer season, 40 percent of our ticket sales were based in Rochester. Rochester had a reputation for being elitist, a bias that was captured perfectly by a resident who told us that Plainview was just a little rural community—it couldn't possibly compete with anything that was being done in Rochester. Another elitist citizen (from Plainview), who prided himself as a theater buff, came to Millie Fliès and told her, "You need to talk to your husband because everyone in town thinks he is a damn fool, and it is hurting your business. There is not even a professional theater in Rochester with all of its rich doctors. What makes him think it can be done here?" If we were to build rapport in Rochester, it made sense to turn to the two community theaters, the Rochester Civic Theater and the Rochester Repertory Theater.

The staff at the Rochester Civic was hard to reach by phone, and when I dropped off brochures, a clerk took them and turned away without comment or conversation. The lobby was lovely but empty, with a high ceiling typical of civic auditoriums. The lobby looked like a mini-Ordway. My footsteps echoed as I left.

The Rochester Repertory Theater, a small community organization, worked on a shirt-tail budget and loads of creativity. They were located on the second floor of an old building. Sally and Dean Harrington were well acquainted with most of the actors and directors, and the first time I attended a show, I was invited backstage. Here was a pool of expertise and friendship that would become an integral part of the Jon Hassler Theater.

Ken Fliès and Dean Harrington encouraged me to keep thinking in terms of tourism. Plainview lacked shaded bike trails, flowing water, picture book settings, a college affiliation or broad-based enthusiastic community support. Instead (take a deep breath), it could tout Jon Hassler's boyhood history, an interesting cemetery filled with monuments to Civil War soldiers, the Teft House and its colorful history that included a small zoo that in its early days was a favorite visiting spot of the young brothers, Will and Charlie Mayo (now a charming B and B renovated to recapture an earlier time sans zoo), a nine-hole golf course with a good restaurant and tavern, an innovative coffee cafe called Rebekah's on Main Street (carved out of an old building that had once served as the lodge of the Oddfellows and Rebekahs), two long-time, family-owned banks, one of which was willing to play an active role in the RAAP start-up, a future fifteen-mile sun-drenched bike trail replacing a railroad track no longer in use, and a short twenty-three-mile drive from Rochester. Twenty miles to the east, the Mississippi River and Highway 61 stretched from Winona through Kellogg, Wabasha, Lake City, and Red Wing. RAAP volunteers and board members were recruited from Plainview and several outlying areas and small towns.

Chapter 16: Feet Planted Firmly on Rural Roads

The Second Year

Out of discussions with the theater board, I laid out a season for 2001 that included spring productions of *Old Man Brunner Country* and *Boxelder Bug Variations*. Hassler's *Grand Opening* was the top seller in our first summer season, averaging eighty-six patrons per show. The second summer included another Hassler show, *Simon's Night*, and a small-cast musical, *The Fantasticks*. Fall was a good time for senior group travel, so we selected *Grace and Glorie*, a story focused on a feisty older woman and her hospice volunteer. We also remounted *Grand Opening*, which we marketed heavily to area schools and added several morning matinees on Fridays. Ironically, the local school said no. Hassler hadn't made it onto their reading lists.

Ron Duffy did not want to direct *Old Man Brunner* again, so I stepped in. New actors and new staging fertilized the seeds planted in previous productions. I edited the script, and Erica substituted straw bales and fencing materials for the country store to create the interior of a barn upstage. She saved the downstage acting area for the barnyard or other neutral space. Larry Roupe recreated his role as Old Man Brunner and Kristen Mathisen returned as the only female. Terry Lynn Carlson and J. P. Fitzgibbons, both union actors, brought fresh ideas and great energy to the two younger men, and Jack Carter picked up his accordion to become our Minstrel.

**The new cast: Standing: Kristen Mathisen, Terry Lynn Carlson, and
Jack Carter; Seated: Larry Roupe and J. P. Fitzgibbons.
Photo by Nancy Campbell.**

The Bob Moss directing style worked well for staging poetry. I told
the actors how to start the poem and how to end it and then gave them
their heads. We rehearsed in Mixed Blood's second-floor rehearsal space
on the West Bank of the university in Minneapolis, where J.P. and Terry

experimented—with wonderful results. When tech week arrived, we piled in our cars and headed to Plainview with Alva Crom as Stage Manager. It was the perfect place to do this show, even without a member of the local acting community. It became Dean Harrington's favorite show for a long time. It still remains mine.

The next show up was *Boxelder Bug Variations* by Bill Holm. Bill did not want to appear in the show again, so I went back to the drawing board. The former production had been formal, elegant, presentational, and highly experimental. We continued to experiment.

Erica Zaffarano set the show in abstractions of boxelder trees drawing the audience right into the woods. The piano was embedded in a large tree trunk where the pianist became another bug, donning hats and dark glasses as needed. A second trunk created a platform, an upstage slide borrowed from a backyard swing set gave the actor bugs a fun-filled point of entrance. Triangular sweeps of sheer cloth added depth and shadow in a wooded environment. Paul Epton's exquisitely detailed lighting provided atmosphere and dappled shade.

Worn-out tires and dappled shade: Terry Lynn Carlson, Beth Desotelle, Monica Heuser, Suzanna Winter, and J. P. Fitzgibbons.

The bugs swarm the piano for the "Boxelder Bug Blues." Monica Heuser sings *I'm just a bug in a window* seated atop the piano with Beth Desotelle, and Jeremy Poetker in dark glasses lays down lines of jazz, while Suzanna Winter sinks into the blues. Terry Lynn and J. P. complete the ensemble. Photo by Nancy Campbell.

Elizabeth (Beth) M. Desotelle, Billy Kimmel, and I collaborated with the actors to create "A Meditation on an Idea in Language and Music." Describing the result of our collaboration was as difficult as Holm's description in his book:

> The material of any work—a chair, an afghan,
> an equestrian statue, a waltz—is so amorphous
> and mysterious that probably only a psychologist,
> an executioner or a full professor would be fool
> enough to try to name it or even describe it in its
> own language. An artist, on the other hand, gives
> it a body, and a body, since it exists, is true. A
> boxelder bug is as satisfactory a body as purple, or
> a saxophone, or French, or obsidian.

None of us were psychologists, executioners or full professors, and so we barged ahead, transforming the earlier script into a new staging for six actor/dancer/singers, one keyboard artist, 225 audience members, and some leftover bugs still hanging out from last summer. Our aim simply was to entertain, using Holm's surprising off-beat images to spur our imaginations.

The three themes remained— "consider the boxelder bug," "we, too, dislike them," and "a man and a woman and a boxelder bug are one." The dances became more exaggerated, more playful. Embedded in the music was the boxelder bug motif, built from the musical pitches in "Boxelder Bug" (B, E, D, G). Holm had played with this idea much like Bach is thought to have done with his own name in The Art of Fugue.

If this sounds complicated, it really isn't. It all came clear on stage once the action started. The complicated part took place offstage when four or five artists got into a dialogue about how to do this, their voices bumping into each other. Billy Kimmel remarked, "This is the most challenging project of my career." But these challenges resulted in a cleverly staged entertainment wherein humans, who have "too many of them plug-in things," learned to live more peacefully with the bug. According to Bill Holm, the bug had only one fault— and asked that we "forgive him only for being so many."

The bugs race atop a tree stump. J. P. Fitzgibbons reports as Suzanna Winter, Terry Lynn Carlson and Beth Desotelle cheer on their personal favorites. Photo by Nancy Campbell.

Terry Lynn captivates Suzanna. Photo by Nancy Campbell.

J. P. captures Monica on an improvised microphone while Suzanna listens carefully. Photo by Nancy Campbell.

It was good to let go of the previous production and fall in love all over again with this poetry and music and movement. I didn't even mind having to gather dried-out maple seeds every week from the high school lawn to use as ammo when the bugs marched off to war.

Boxelder Bug Variations was only a little over an hour long, so we added a short piece called *Chin Music* by John Calvin Rezmerski. John had performed in it at Gustavus in St. Peter, where he taught English. Rob Gardner of the Gustavus Theater Department had staged *Chin Music* as a radio play with actors creating sound effects and music much like, "Prairie Home Companion, a Minnesota Public Radio show performed for a live audience.

Ron Duffy directed John but was preoccupied with other projects. I was surprised when Ron told me that John wanted it to be essentially a one-man show featuring him as a radio personality. The concept sounded doable, but the presentation suffered from John's inexperienced acting and too little rehearsal. On opening night, John was not securely "off-book." I was held accountable by the RAAP Board, so I continued to work with him after the show opened. I shortened the script and, since it was staged as a radio broadcast, let him read some of it. I couldn't solve all of the pacing problems, but the show tightened up and improved.

When it was time to submit our annual grant proposal to the McKnight Foundation, our contact at McKnight, Neal Cuthbert, asked for an on-site visit. We were happy to show him the full RAAP campus, which included the theater, the History Center located in the old Methodist Church, and the Hassler home at the opposite end of the block from the theater. It now needed renovation to make it usable as housing for artists (primarily actors) and as a writers' center, all of it still in the planning stages. As Neal returned to his car, he asked what else the McKnight Foundation could help with. I was surprised for a moment but recovered and brought up the renovation of the Hassler house. He, on the other hand, was not at all surprised and invited us to submit a separate proposal for that.

There was always more to do.

Poet Eugene McCarthy

During the run of *Payments Due*, Larry Roupe and I attended a poetry reading at Kieran's Pub in Minneapolis, where Carol Connolly read from Payments Due and then introduced her close friend, Gene McCarthy. He read with passion from his published book Selected Poems. He drew us in, turning us into fans.

During the first summer season at JHT, Larry and I often went exploring on Saturdays. We had heard that McCarthy had been a much-celebrated reader in Oak Center over the years. So, we set off to find the Oak Center General Store, the kind of place Ron Duffy had in mind when he staged the first production of *Old Man Brunner Country* at the Wolf Creek Country Store.

We found Oak Center at the convergence of Highway 63 with local trunk routes 75, 31, and 82, where the Oak Center General Store sat like a comfortable, well-worn shoe, a "Landmark Music Venue at the Crossroads." Built in 1913, it was resurrected in 1976 by Steve Schwen, who abandoned his medical studies at the Mayo to delve full-time into organic farming and woodworking. Schwen sponsored a series called the Folk Forum, which included educational presentations on homesteading skills or current events and lots of concerts and readings.

Larry and I entered the store, time traveling onto a creaky wooden floor, where we found glass jars filled with locally grown organic comestibles as well as posters signed by musicians dating back twenty years or more. We looked for a poster bearing McCarthy's name and perhaps his signature but found nothing. We wandered into the back room but found no one to ask. We felt like trespassers. We didn't know that the owner was out in the hot sun tending organic gardens. We read lots of labels while the air temperature continued to rise in the poorly insulated building, forcing us back to our air-conditioned car.

On May 17, 2001, before the theater opened for the summer, Carol Connolly arranged a reading/fundraiser featuring Eugene McCarthy. We thought him a strange bedfellow for Republican-flavored southeastern Minnesota, but we hoped his popularity in Oak Center would carry some of those folks to Plainview.

When McCarthy arrived, his height created an eloquent presence, more a senator than a poet in his formal, navy-blue suit. Carol arrived in time to introduce him to his small but receptive audience. I was naively a-political, but I wondered if the audience would have been bigger had McCarthy been a Republican. I learned later that the audience in Oak Center was primarily from Rochester and the Twin Cities—only 10 percent of the audience came from nearby Lake City.

McCarthy's writing was known for a great sense of irony, but poet Robert Bly loved him for his "sly and musical poems, so lively and so generous to human foolishness." My copy of the book easily falls open to "The Death of the Old Plymouth Rock Hen," who was "Taken to the woodpile in the winter of execution:"

> Decapitated, she did not act
> Like a chicken with its head cut off.
> No pirouettes, no somersaults,
> No last indignity.
> Like an English queen, she died.
> On wings that had never known flight
> She flew, straight into the woodpile
> And there beat out slow death
> While her curdled voice ran out in blood.

Even this short cutting jogs personal memories of witnessing my uncle killing chickens for supper at my grandparents' house in Mantorville. I was only four and horrified. No English queens for me. But in 2001, I appreciated McCarthy's irony, his liveliness, and his take on human foolishness, killing all that is no longer profitable.

After the reading, we gathered at the Tavern on the Green for some nosh, and I leaned back and fed my memory bank while Millie Fliès sat on one side of McCarthy and Larry Roupe, a life-long Democrat, sat on the other, enjoying conversation with a man much admired.

McCarthy read without charge, as he often did at Kieran's pub and other venues in the Twin Cities, so we did not lose money on this event. Ticket sales that day were allocated to the writer's center. Although it wasn't officially launched until 2003, discussions and planning sessions began in 2001.

Summer Season: *Simon's Night* and *The Fantasticks*

The board and I wanted to include a Hassler play every season as long as we had scripts that were new to the southeastern Minnesota audiences. We opened the second summer season on June 15, 2001, with "A Minnesota Comedy Classic," *Simon's Night* by Jon Hassler. Since I was directing again and knew the show very well, I cast myself as Barbara and eliminated an item from my bucket list along with an actor's stipend. Erica Zaffarano adapted the set to accommodate Mr. Smalleye on the roof in the low-ceilinged space, and Paul Epton conjured flashbacks, lighting small portions of the Norman Home into Irish scenes, a college art room, and Simon's and Barbara's home.

Sally Childs fulfills a dream to play Barbara, with Kathleen Hardy as Hattie Norman in *Simon's Night*. Photo by Nancy Campbell.

Actors from previous shows were happy to take on new roles to continue working in Plainview. They had learned to love the theater, the town, the people they met at local watering holes, and the proximity to Rochester, Wabasha, Kellogg, and various Wisconsin border towns. Larry Roupe continued as Simon Shea, and Kristen Mathisen and Kathy Hardy split the role of Hattie Norman, performing on alternate weeks. I was in the bosom of my family—and Jon's.

The Fantasticks, the musical that had led me to an understanding of metaphor, filled the midsummer slot. I had some unusual history with the show from years ago in Ely, when Don filled his summers producing and directing small cast musicals in the party room located in the basement of Bridgeman's restaurant in downtown Ely. When he cast *The Fantasticks,* there was no part for me. He needed two fathers but no mothers. But about a week into rehearsals, one of the fathers dropped out. It was too late to hold another audition, so Don and the music director converted the role to a mother. I set aside my summer sewing projects and stepped onstage.

The show remained for years on my bucket list of directing projects, but JHT wanted to recruit directors with stronger reputations. Peter Rothstein had garnered solid reviews for his work at his own Theatre Latte Da. His directing career had taken fire with invitations to direct musical theater out-of-town. Peter accepted the Plainview job. Of the eight roles, Peter cast three new people and five actors from previous shows, including Clark Cruikshank and Thom Pinault as the fathers.

In the play, the narrator, El Gallo, invites the audience into a world of moonlight and magic in this lush, allegorical tale. Neighboring fathers trick their children, Luisa and Matt, into falling in love by pretending to feud. With help from El Gallo and his sidekicks—the Mute, the Indian, and the Shakespearean actor—the young lovers grow apart and finally find their way back to each other after realizing the truth in El Gallo's words that "without a hurt, the heart is hollow." The show spoke directly to the human condition, whether rural or elsewhere.

The boy's father (Clark A. Cruikshank) makes a point to The Mute (Jonathan Niel). Photo by Nancy Campbell.

El Gallo (David A. Anderson) restrains Matt, The Boy (Kurt David Anderson). Photo by Nancy Campbell.

Streets and By-Ways

With Peter directing, I spent less time in Plainview and worked from home in Minneapolis, focused on generating money for the theater. Group sales in the fall often generated bigger audiences, so I devoted time to contacting group sales leaders and working with Millie Fliès and other restaurant operators located along the route from the Twin Cities to Plainview. When my head overflowed and my back ached from sitting too long, I called Nancy Gormley and asked, "Can you come out and play?" She often replied, "Sure, meet-cha on the corner in 10." I'd throw on my sneakers and power-walk down Bryant Avenue to 46th, where I turned right and reached Dupont Avenue just as Nancy bobbled into view, completing the two blocks from her home at a kick-ass pace. From there, we shifted into a lower gear on the way to Lake Harriet that allowed for patter about the verities—children, mutual friends, theater, and other gossip. We completed the 2.8-mile circumference of the lake in just under two hours. Between these walks and climbing aboard my Nordic Track machine almost daily, I kept off the pounds I had lost when diagnosed with Type 2 diabetes in 1998.

In Plainview, I had to find an equivalent walking route for extended stays. When housed at The Farm, I walked the rural dirt-packed roads, often alone but with actors if they were in residence. More often over the ensuing years, for a quick twenty-minute break, I walked the ten long blocks of Broadway, to the Catholic Church at one end and back to the Lutheran Church at the other. I enjoyed walking past the writer's center (Hassler House), the public schools, the rectory, St. Joaquin's, then crossed to the opposite sidewalk to turn around, passing a few houses, the Presbyterian Church, Haley's fireplace sales shop, an electronics repair shop, the Plainview News, the auto/tractor parts store, J. T. Variety (once Hassler's grocery store), city hall, the furniture store, the bowling alley, gas station, and the old Plainview Hotel. As I walked, I envisioned the town as it must have appeared during Hassler's boyhood, with cars parked at a slant, nosed up to the curb. At Emanuel Lutheran Church, I crossed again and turned back, passing the Teft House B&B, First National Bank, the hardware store, ABA Water Systems, the municipal liquor store, Rebekah's Cafe, the dentist's office, post office, community center and ended back at the Theater. All of this without trees or shade except along the school district property.

Longer walks took me onto shaded residential streets and side streets that brought me past Finney's quaint breakfast/lunch cafe to the city park, past the creamery and American Legion, and then circling back past Kim's Restaurant and the old Methodist Church, whose original historic stained-glass windows now colored the interior displays of the Plainview History Center, a RAAP affiliate. But the most interesting walk took me from the Hassler house to the Greenwood Cemetery, walking between columns of American flags framing rows of tombstones that were coated with lichen, their engraved names and dates barely legible. Some of them rested atop Civil War veterans, including two who were brought back to Plainview by their compatriots to be buried in their beloved Greenwood soil—two of twenty from Plainview out of 825 or so soldiers from Minnesota killed or mortally wounded in the Civil War. Behind a raised dais for patriotic speeches and events, a small hill dropped away to a walking trail that circled a field alternating annually between contoured rows of corn and soybeans. The field was owned by the school district and maintained by students belonging to the Future Farmers of America (FFA).

I loved to read the tombstones, looking for names that were familiar from theater mailing lists. The most familiar were the markers that already carried a list of Harringtons, including both Dean and Sally, their names already etched, waiting for their passage. I was startled the first time I came upon these stones, unaware of such a tradition. I asked Ken Fliès about it. He laughed and said he thought there must be a very good monument salesperson active in Plainview. At first, it seemed a little ghoulish, but then I thought how comforting it must be to know that a place was already prepared for one's demise. In the meantime, I enjoyed the quiet, underground company who were more welcoming than the circles of local coffee drinkers at Finney's. This changed as I said "good morning" repeatedly to others, both walkers and coffee drinkers, but I often felt I knew the people represented by the headstones better than the people behind all the storefronts in town.

Grace and Glorie

Grace and Glorie, an irresistible two-character comedy by Tom Ziegler, played from September 28 through October 14, 2001. Chosen for its female point of view and its inclusion of an older character to attract senior groups during the fall color season, I found much in my own experience with aging parents to support my choice.

Grace is salt to Glorie's pepper when they encounter each other in the Blue Ridge Mountains of Virginia. Grace, a feisty ninety-year-old woman, checks herself out of the cancer ward and returns to her beloved homestead cottage to spend her remaining days. Glorie, a sophisticated Harvard MBA graduate recently transplanted to the rural backwater from New York, volunteers as a hospice worker. She arrives with the medications that Grace deliberately left at the hospital.

Glorie (Jennifer Connelly) records Grace (Frances Ford) in Grace's cottage in the Blue Ridge Mountains of Virginia. Photo by Nancy Campbell.

From the first moment, these women are at loggerheads, arguing about medications, the importance of mascara, and a developer's right to take down Grace's apple orchard. As Glorie, tense, unhappy, and guilt-ridden, attempts to care for and comfort the cantankerous Grace, they discuss the difficulties of marriage, the loss of children, the lot of women, original sin, and religious faith. When Grace defends the Bible as written by holy men like Moses, Glorie counters, "You think Moses was going to blame mankind's first sin on another member of the great fraternity?"

She points out that Eve tasted the "forbidden fruit," g iving us "yearning, passion, satisfaction, and poetry." Grace replies, "She also gives us death."

Grace's value system collides throughout the play with what Glorie thinks is important. Are one woman's ideals right and the other's wrong? Is Grace enough, or do we need Glorie, too? Can one exist without the other?

Eventually, Grace finds new value in her simple life, while Glorie, the sophisticated urbanite, gains new perspective on life's highs and lows through moments of gentle comedy and poignant confession.

According to the New York *Post*, the play "offers the opportunity for good, honest, grandstanding acting from its protagonist." From the moment I read the script, I envisioned Frances (Fran) Ford[12] in the role of Grace. Fran introduced herself to me in 1998 when she first arrived in the Twin Cities after losing her non-tenured teaching job at the University of North Dakota due to decreasing enrollment. Fran's headshot portrayed a woman of about sixty, a face filled with a zest for life and enormous energy. I first cast Fran in *To Whom it May Concern* in Plainview in 2000. She was strong-willed, a liberal thinker, a Quaker, and her concerns for peace and justice and the environment matched mine.

As younger actresses auditioned for the role of Grace, I looked away and listened blindly as they read with Fran. Partnering with Fran in a two-person play would require an actress of tremendous skill and strength. I found that strength in Jennifer Connelly, who had appeared as Chelsea in *On Golden Pond* for JHT the previous year. Jennifer had a long history with the Lyric Theater, where she appeared in *The Road to Rouen, Payments Due,* and *To Whom It May Concern.*

Fran and Jennifer struck sparks from the friction between these two characters. I could almost smell electricity in the air. They carried that friction off-stage as well, sending them into separate dressing rooms to regather their wits for the next on-stage battle. Every evening Jen drove back to her home in the Twin Cities, where she worked full time as a speech therapist, so she and Fran never developed a friendship, but their stage chemistry was perfection, bringing a high standard of expertise to the roles originated on Broadway by Estelle Parsons and Luci Arnaz.

Erica Zaffarano's rustic set underscored the authenticity created by the two actresses, and I re-entered the old-fashioned world of my Grandma

Childs in Mantorville in 1941. Paul Epton's lighting was so good I never saw it happen. Jeannie Galioto's costumes were spot-on. I trusted them implicitly. The sound design for this show demanded a rural gospel radio station and all kinds of offstage sound effects as machinery took down the apple orchard outside the cabin. Jack Carter created the radio hymns by laying down track after track, singing all four vocal parts of the gospel hymns as well as providing the instrumental accompaniment. I can still see Jack at The Farm, sitting cross-legged on the mattress in the corner of the living room, surrounded by electronic equipment.

This play is a rich source for discussion topics and opportunities for targeted marketing. In our lobby, we displayed printed materials about local hospice services. We strongly encouraged senior groups to attend Thursday matinees. We also had a post-show discussion on Sunday, September 30, with Carol Connolly, author of "Payments Due, Onstage and Off," and Judge Harriet Lansing of the Minnesota Court of Appeals in a lively give and take on women's issues and the elderly. Their discussion was prompted by the following questions:

> Are we our sisters' keepers?
>
> Does anyone have the right to impose her value system on someone about to die?
>
> How do we assign value to someone's life?
>
> What legal and moral responsibilities do we have for our aging population?
>
> Does a developer have any moral or ethical obligation to the land?

These questions remain relevant and provocative as women of today assert their worth, especially regarding gender discrimination.

Chapter 17
Cracks in the Road

Change in Staffing

At the end of 2000, Ken stopped taking a salary from RAAP and moved his office from the theater to the tavern. At the end of the 2001 summer season, I talked with the RAAP board about the need to staff the theater more fully. I planned to retire at or about 2006, and a fully professional theater needed a full-time staff beyond an artistic director. I asked if we could afford a second full-time person, and the board agreed to funding a second position that would pay somewhat less than my salary. The title agreed upon was Managing Director and we wrote up a job description. I didn't realize that Clark Cruikshank had bonded strongly with the Harringtons, especially Sally, and was surprised when he applied for the position. His acting experience, combined with his tenure at U.S. Bank, made him a good candidate. I recommended him for the job, which was finally funded at two-thirds full-time hours. Clark would manage productions, advertising, and fundraising-grant writing with some assistance from me. Clark started the job with the production of *Grace and Glorie*.

JHT finished out 2001 with a remount of *Grand Opening* in November and December. The play encompassed the Christmas season, so we felt justified in using the winter slot. This provided ample opportunity to find student groups to attend special Friday morning matinees. The first production of *Grand Opening* in June 2000 had eleven performances, averaging eighty-six ticket buyers per show. The remount at the end of 2001 had twenty-one performances, averaging sixty-six ticket buyers

330

per show. I don't have a record of the breakdown between the Friday school matinees and other performances. Despite the winter weather, the remount sold fairly well. Totals from June through December:

Year	Number of shows	Attendance	Average house
2000	60	3,419	57
2001	80	4,663	59

Despite the increase in the number of performances and total attendance, our average house size only grew by two. Selling school matinees was very challenging in rural areas.

We jumped into 2002, determined to become better known, better attended—just plain better all around. The Jon Hassler Theater was gathering more bulk, more contributions from local folks from as far away as Rochester, Winona, and the Twin Cities. We scheduled two fundraisers back-to-back.

In March of 2002, Bill Holm presented a concert, and the lobby filled with people lining up for tickets. Bill pulled in a full house (about two hundred people), and we learned that just one ticket seller could not get people in their seats without a late start. Bill improvised a little to keep the early arrivals entertained and then popped into the lobby to see how much more time he needed to fill. We were finally underway a half hour late. Bill contributed his time and talent, and after the show, nearly ran to his big sedan to race off to the Twin Cities, where he had another engagement. Bill was often the biggest person in the room, he drove the biggest car in the lot, drove back roads so he could ignore speed limits, and ate steaks that would have fed three people my size.

Two weeks later, the Tavern on the Green hosted a "Country Cabaret" organized and emceed by Clark Cruikshank. Joining Clark on stage were young people from previous shows—Zoe Pappas from Minneapolis and Blake Brown from nearby Rochester. I made a pitch for donations but otherwise watched from a side table.

We were cramming too much onto the calendar, and the balance between producing and marketing wobbled along. The fundraiser at the tavern had little press coverage. Clark focused on his performance but ignored the marketing piece. At the eleventh hour, Millie and Ken Fliès got on the phone with many of their regular customers, urging them to attend. We had enough responses to end the evening in the black, but we had lots to learn about generating an audience for a fundraising event in Plainview.

A Widening Fissure

I was sixty-four years old in 2002 and wanted to continue in my position for another four years. I had known Clark for years and had hired him as an actor at the Lyric, so it felt like a natural transition for him to take the position of managing director while I continued as artistic director. But it wasn't long before he became more outspoken, dissatisfied with the Hassler scripts, pushing for more input on artistic decisions.

Ever since Tom Woldt and Chris Samuelson had left the original Lyric team, I had wanted a good, collaborative partnership. On occasion, Clark and I shared rides to and from Plainview, giving us time to toss around ideas. We understood that local financial support would not sustain a fully professional theater that required using AEA actors from the Twin Cities. We talked about collaborations with small Twin City theaters with the idea that we could share production expenses, and shows would run in both Plainview and the Twin Cities. But the newer theaters in the Twin Cities were not prepared to share any risk, and the more established theaters did not need us.

Positioning the Jon Hassler Theater in grant proposals was exceptionally difficult. The continuity with Lyric Theater history was part of our story, but that was in another time and place, and the Jon Hassler Theater and its parent organization, RAAP, were still start-ups in the eyes of funders. The McKnight Foundation was still on board, and the Southeastern Minnesota Arts Council (SEMAC) was open to proposals from any organization in its funding area, but many of the funding sources listed in the Lyric's last playbill had been shepherded in the Twin Cities by Lyric Theater board members—The Honeywell Foundation, Kopp Investment Advisors, Lowry Hill, National Checking.

The Lyric list of donors had been built over fifteen years of hard work that included the diligent telephone campaign undertaken for several summers by Larry Roupe. Most of these people would not follow the Lyric to Plainview as donors to JHT. Funding had been made more difficult by the move. And now there were buildings to maintain. The RAAP board needed many more members from southeastern Minnesota with fundraising capabilities. That board should have been built prior to opening in 2000, but the Harringtons, one of the two couples pushing the project ahead, wanted to keep it close to home, to begin with. Ken and Millie were born and raised in the area, yet after some thirty years of working and living around the country and world, they were looked at as "Outsiders." Once the theater opened, Millie stepped off the board to eliminate the potential for criticism that could be generated by two members of the same family serving on the board. The Harringtons did not feel this pressure. They were ingrained residents of Plainview. They wanted to retain power over board decisions, and they were large financial donors to the project. They were blind to the reputation for elitism generated by the RAAP project itself and the people who were on the initial board.

In the meantime, Clark's penchant for bringing the best of the Twin Cities to Plainview appealed to RAAP's competitive desire to be the best theater in southeast Minnesota. Clark loved the phrase "world-class theater" or more appropriately, "Broadway in Rural America." My currency with the Jon Hassler Theater began to erode because my focus was aimed at building closer ties to the southeast Minnesota community of writers, actors, and technicians, as well as donors. Clark and I pulled in different directions. I thought I still held the winning hand. I was wrong, but I soldiered on.

Talley's Folly

We opened our third season in April 2002 with the Pulitzer Prize-winning romantic comedy *Talley's Folly* by Lanford Wilson. Described as a "funny, sweet, touching and marvelously written love poem for an apple and an orange" by the *New York Post*, it was the story of a Jew courting a non-Jewish girl, a situation frowned upon by the girl's family.

Several years earlier I had been introduced to Rob Frankel as a playwright from Rochester when he sent a script to the Lyric Theater for consideration. Rob's script was well written, and I kept it on file. When he called to schedule his audition for *Talley's Folly,* he mentioned that—like the character in the play—he was a forty-four-year-old Jew. He was also a seasoned and skillful actor. He was joined by Chris Samuelson, aka Noalen Stampe.

Rob and Chris struck a realistic chord that exposed sensitivity and vulnerability. I participated fully in production activities, but as the director, I often just held the script and helped these intense actors get off-book while they lost themselves in the characters. The three of us delved into discussions of character, time, and place during these sessions.

Matt Friedman (Rob Frankel) ponders future possibilities with Sally Talley (Noalen Stampe). Photo by Nancy Campbell.

The play was set in a boathouse on the evening of July 4, 1944, in Lebanon, Missouri, away from disapproving eyes. Erica Zaffarano designed a dilapidated Victorian boathouse that circled a center post, with walls suggested by draped fish nets and irregular panels of open latticework. A dock angled toward the audience with a rowboat tied to one side. Cat tails, fishing gear, and wooden barrels took us back to 1944. Erica finished off with a large harvest moon hung upstage to cast the appropriate romantic light. Ben Hain threw himself into creating moonlight, and then bounced it off the downstage painted floor—the moon dancing on water. Add in the actors and it was visually stunning.

Matt (Rob Frankel) and Sally (Noalen Stampe) continue to envision a life together. Photo by Nancy Campbell.

Talley's Folly had been on my to-do list for almost twenty years. I was charmed by its theatricality, its ability to create a world that I recognized from my childhood, its glorious language. The play is an interrogation without being a courtroom drama or a war story, it is a romantic comedy without resembling a TV sitcom, and it is an old-fashioned dance exploring the nature of the male-female relationship.

Talley's Folly pushed me to think more deeply. I had to concentrate when Matt told his family history, and I had to recreate in my head an older map of Europe, one that included Prussia and predated both world wars. And then I had to acknowledge that this is a very contemporary play. Bigotry, religious wars, and misunderstandings still abound, and words, especially when leavened with humor, are the only tools we have to figure out how we are going to live together and love each other. I counted on our audience to have the same understanding.

And finally, the Jon Hassler Theater decided that the spring play would be based on historical events or social issues that are suitable for high school audiences as well as the general public. The summer would bring another Hassler show followed by a musical or other family entertainment, and the fall play would be chosen with senior groups in mind. I was happy to note that we had made inroads into the regional acting and tech community.

Taken together, *Grace and Glorie* and *Talley's Folly* represent some of our finest work during my tenure at JHT.

Playing Together

I pondered ways to avoid the cracks, to proceed as a professional theater in a town without professional actors, and how to start blending more local people into our productions. We needed to start with the kids.

Beginning with our first show in 2000, Kellie Stoltz, a tall, blonde teenager with a big smile, started working as a volunteer. She began by helping Erica with building the set and then assisted Paul Epton (light designer), pulling lighting instruments from under the seating platforms, carrying them onstage, learning the difference between an ellipsoidal and a fresnel, inserting colored gels into frames that attached to lights, climbing ladders to hang instruments, plugging them into dimmers. During tech week, Kellie sat at the tech table, soaking up every word that Paul uttered. During performances, she sat next to our stage manager, Al Crom, expertly running the light board as Al quietly called the cues. Kellie continued to be employed at JHT throughout high school and then entered the theater program at Minnesota State University-Mankato, returning during the summer to work at JHT. Later, I heard through the grapevine that she changed her major and became a teacher.

While Kellie was at JHT, she proved my theory right. Once I started directing high school shows in 2003, Kellie introduced me to her grandmother, an expert seamstress, who willingly volunteered time and materials.

A year later, another high school student, Bryan Olson, came aboard as the lead production assistant, becoming our jack-of-all-trades, able to work backstage or in the booth, an invaluable asset for JHT. After several years, he moved to the Twin Cities but then returned to Plainview, worked in a local bank, and became very active in the Plainview Community Theater.

These were success stories not to be sneezed at. As JHT became more connected to the community, there would be others.

Chapter 18: Solid Gains

A New Agatha Takes Charge

The 2002 summer season opened with my adaptation of Hassler's *Dear James*. The original actors were not available. Newcomers included poet and AEA actress Denise du Maurier as Agatha McGee, a woman as tall as Nancy Gormley was short. Denise possessed an austerity that yielded to an underlying vulnerability that challenged Sheldon Goldstein as Father James. Shel, tall and a bit professorial in appearance, took on a strong clerical aura once in costume, and he mastered a lovely Irish accent.

Father James O'Hannon (Shel Goldstein) and Agatha McGee (Denise DuMaurier). Photo by Nancy Campbell.

Imogene Kite (Julie Ann Neville) pairs up with French Lopat (Dale Pfeilsticker) while Agatha is in Ireland. Photo by Nancy Campbell.

Dale Pfeilsticker as French, created some new physical comedy, and Julie Ann Neville as Imogene, slender, red-haired, and deep-voiced, was truly the woman we loved to hate. Dale had grown up in Mankato and had relatives near Plainview, but these actors, including Dale, now lived in the Twin Cities. I was lucky that Kent Griffin, a well-known and respected actor from Rochester, was available to play Myron Kleinschmidt, the cameo role previously filled by Larry Roupe. I was determined to keep looking for local talent who could match the skills of Twin City actors. I knew they were there because I saw plays in Rochester regularly, but they rarely investigated the theater in Plainview.

Agatha (Denise DuMaurier) offers French (Dale Pfeilsticker) encouragement, turning his neediness into a comic moment. Photo by Nancy Campbell.

A standoff between Agatha (Denise DuMaurier) and Congressman Kleinschmidt (Kent Griffin). Photo by Nancy Campbell.

The set held surprises for the audience that created great fun—especially a bed that utilized wainscoting on the wall of Agatha's house. With a hard push from backstage, it sailed onstage with French securely on board to create a bedroom in the Morgan Hotel. I tightened the script, especially Father James' Irish stories, so it was a far better show than the first Minneapolis production. Our stable of actors had expanded, adding our new Agatha and James into the mix.

AND THEN... Billy Kimmel told me about a new show that he had seen on a trip home to Pennsylvania.

"It's called *Honk!*" Billy looked at me, grinning as if he had a secret.

"*Honk,*" I repeated flatly. "So? Am I supposed to guess?"

Billy laughed. "It's the story of the Ugly Duckling, and it's really fun. It takes place in a farmyard with a pond, so it's perfect for a summer musical in a rural town. And it has never been done in Minnesota." Billy paused while I digested this and then looked me right in the eye and said, "And I want to direct it." After perusing the script and music, I agreed. It was perfect.

HONK!

Honk! is based on the familiar story of an oversized duckling who cannot quack. He honks instead. He is subject to all the teasing, the hurt feelings, the lack of acceptance experienced by the guy who doesn't fit in. Billy's "Director's Notes" in the program pointed out, "The universal themes of this show are as old as time but still ring true in today's world of increasing violence—bullying, homophobia, sexism, racism, ageism, etc." When the Bullfrog, played by Clark Cruikshank, sang about being accepted, "Warts and all," the whole audience smiled as if they were one person.

Queenie, a Cat (Holly Schroeder), poses with Lowbutt, a hen (Nicole Stefonek), for Ugly (Peter David Middlecamp). Photos by Mike Nadolske.

With music by George Stiles and book and lyrics by Anthony Drewe, the ugly duckling is born into a family of mother, father, and eight ducklings and is challenged by other farmyard creatures, including a turkey, a chicken, a moorhen, the cat—Maggie Pie, Greylag who commands the military geese, a bullfrog and many frogs and froglets, and ultimately, a father and mother swan. Acting opportunities spread over a range of ages, genders, and levels of experience. And so, we went ahead with plans for the most expensive show to date, with expenses budgeted at $48,000. Billy Kimmel directed, we rehearsed adult actors in Minneapolis, had separate rehearsals in Plainview for the eight ducklings/ froglets, and then put it all together during tech week. Erica and Ben fizzed with creative staging ideas, especially for the underwater scene.

> The show was clever and entertaining—full of surprises— and attracted local families, building audience numbers to the point of sold-out shows, so we planned a second production for the next season.

Mother Swan, (Jen Burleigh-Benz), poses with the Chicks (doubled as frogs later) and her son, the "ugly duckling" (Peter David Middlecamp). Chicks: Abby Harrington, Preston Hain, John Reinke, Kelsey Petit, Cassie McHugh, Jessika Stucky, Hilary Schneider, and Anthony McClellan with Ugly.

"There's No Place Like Home"

I had seen a revival of *Morning's at Seven* by Paul Osborn on a bus tour over spring break to New York City in 1981 while still a student at Mankato State. In New York, I had been lured by Kevin Kline swashbuckling his way through *Pirates of Penzance* and stunned by Patti Lupone's rendition of "Don't Cry for me, Argentina" in *Evita*. But I fell in love with *Morning's at Seven,* which was first published in 1939. If I had stepped onstage, I would have been back in my childhood at my grandparent's house in Mantorville, bringing food scraps across the street to white-haired Mrs. Mulvaney to feed her cats, with free run of the Spurbeck house down the street to play with David and JoAnn. "Sometimes when you go to the theater, it's just like going home."

That sentence opened an article by Tom Weber in the *Rochester Post Bulletin* in September 2002.

> That's the idea, anyway, behind the Jon Hassler Theater's production of *Morning's at Seven,* which opens Saturday. "It's about home," director Sally Childs said of Paul Osborn's gentle comedy/drama. That, in turn, makes it an ideal play for the Hassler Theater. "It reflects small town feelings, people, and values," Childs said. "It feels like the right choice for the time and place."

"Over at Ida's house..." Ida (Nancy Plank), her husband Carl (Marshall Hambro), their son Homer (Craig Johnson), and his girlfriend Myrtle (Jenner Snell) all cluster around sister Esther (Diane Lyons).
Photo by Nancy Campbell.

"...and on the other side of the fence," Cora (Frances Ford) and Arry (Jeanne Kussrow-Larson) give the stage to Thor (Sheldon Goldstein). Photo by Nancy Campbell.

Morning's at Seven

The action is set in the backyards of two neighboring houses featuring cozy porches. Steps lead to a path that meets on the property line at a round table and benches. A swing is mounted in a large tree constructed by the intrepid Erica Zaffarano. Paul Epton dappled her green and white painted houses with light that ranged from full sun to evening dusk. Audience members might feel they had never left their own backyards.

**The swing frames Myrtle (Jenner Snell) and Homer (Craig Johnson).
Photo by Nancy Campbell.**

The dappled setting with Carl alone (Marshall Hambro) distancing from brother-in-law Thor (Sheldon Goldstein), backed by sisters Arry (Jeanne Kussrow-Larson) and Cora (Frances Ford). Photo by Nancy Campbell.

David (George Mueller) gets after Carl (Marshall Hambro). Photo by Nancy Campbell.

The original Broadway production, directed by Joshua Logan, opened on November 30, 1939, and ran for forty-four performances. I recognized only one actress's name—Dorothy Gish. Her surname appeared again in 1956 when Robert Wallstens adapted it for performance on television as part of *The Alcoa Hour*. Lillian Gish joined her sister Dorothy as one of her onstage sisters.

The first Broadway revival opened in April 1980, directed by Vivian Matalon, and ran for 564 performances. It won four Tony and seven Drama Desk awards.[13]

Our cast included Frances Ford, matched with Sheldon Goldstein as her husband. Nancy Plank teamed up with Marshall Hambro. The other two sisters were from the Plainview Region—Jeanne Kussrow-Larson from just across the border in Wisconsin, and Diane Lyon, a Rochester resident who came out of retirement from Actors' Equity to do the show. Clark Cruikshank named this cast The Dream Team: "At the first read-through, they had me laughing so hard I could hardly breathe, and I'm known as a pretty tough audience."

Arry (Jeanne Kussrow Larson) steals a message from her sister Cora's pocket (Frances Ford), adding fuel to the flames of jealousy.

I was still looking for ways to make inroads with the Plainview kids. Since many cast members stayed in Plainview from Thursday through Sunday during performance weeks, I asked if any of them would volunteer to meet in the theater during the school day with a class of high school students to talk about acting as a career or any related topic of their choice. Three actors responded. George Muellner's presentation focused on the demands that Shakespearean plays made on actors. He involved student volunteers in a couple of Shakespearean situations, which required them to move about and improv dialog, and then followed up with discussion. A week later, Craig Johnson and Jenner Snell met another class to talk about their characters and demonstrate acting choices. My goal was to start building a relationship with the school and community and stir up interest in the theater and its programs. I don't know if any of the students came to see the show, but I believe a door opened between the high school and the theater.

A Bug Story of a Different Stripe

Clark and I wore many different hats to cover all the production, marketing, and writing chores, but in September, we donned new hats when Nancy Plank and Marshall Hambro arrived in the lobby of the theater to tell us they could not stay at The Farm amidst a moving army of bugs. Their suitcases were in the car, and they needed shelter along with several other actors who had gone home overnight and would be back shortly.

We put Sally Harrington on booking detail, and Clark and I headed to the Small Farm armed with a large canister-style vacuum cleaner and extra bags to wage war on an invasion that infested drapes, bedding, windows, nooks and crannies throughout the house. We had seen a few of these bugs for several weeks and wondered if they were a large form of our Minnesota ladybugs. They were not; they were Asian Lady Beetles, and now they swarmed in every patch of sunlight, looking for places to spend the winter.[14] Clark and I found armies of bugs marching along electric cords, entering from light fixtures and cracks around windows and doors.

Clark worked the vacuum we brought from Plainview, and I went upstairs, where I found a smaller, older vacuum donated by my oldest friend when her mother died. I started in around the bed, and when I pulled apart folds in the draperies and shook them where they puddled on the floor, massive numbers of bugs buzzed, lifting a few feet into the air, and dropping onto the bed and other furniture, exuding a foul-smelling, defensive yellow chemical capable of spotting the bed linens. Most people are only annoyed by the odor of these chemicals. Others may have allergic reactions.

After filling bag after bag and creating a huge stink in the house, we gave up for the day and headed back to report the results. Sally had found lodging for all of the actors at the home of a RAAP board member, who offered them an unoccupied basement apartment with several bedrooms.

The Asian Lady Beetles wreaked havoc in rural Minnesota for several years until sprays were developed to bring them under control. In 2002, their only natural predator was a dog or two who would leap and snap at them in a game understood only in the canine world.

Chapter 19: Two Roads Diverged…

The Spitfire Grille

After four years in production, JHT still had time gaps when the space was empty and unproductive. We didn't have to look far for a show we wanted to bring to Plainview. Zoe Pappas, who had appeared in *To Whom It May Concern*, *The Fantasticks*, and *Honk!*, was starring in Minneapolis-based Buffalo Gal's[15] staging of *The Spitfire Grill*.

Perrin Post, the director, named her company partly for her hometown of Buffalo, Minnesota, and partly for her mission—shows about women. When the show moved to Plainview, it became a co-production, the first for JHT.

The Spitfire Grill is a musical by James Valcq and Fred Alley. Based on the book by Lee David Zlotoff, the show had an Off-Broadway run in 2001. According to Graydon Royce in his "Onstage Article" in the *Star Tribune*, "Post was won over by the show's themes of redemption and healing, its score of folksy and bluegrass tunes, and its sweet, small-town characters." Following its run at the Loring Playhouse in Minneapolis, it played at the Hassler for three weekends in January 2003. A wonderful choice for rural Minnesota, especially with Zoe in the lead and Clark playing a major role, a wonderful choice for JHT.

Funding

I was worried about money, both for the theater and myself. To be funded well enough in 2006 to retire, I planned to continue pursuing directing gigs as an independent contractor, but I also needed to pursue additional income. I had appeared in *Simon's Night* as an actor and could have become a member of AEA then. I gave it little thought at the time, assuming it was a one-time opportunity. But now, the fear that my income would not sustain even a minimal lifestyle, I talked to Dean Harrington, who was the finance officer for the theater, about becoming a member of AEA as a stage manager. I had stage-managed for a summer in 1980 at Mankato State, but the technology had changed a great deal. I would need a good assistant.

JHT had to have an AEA stage manager for *Spitfire Grille*, and Bryan Olson was the best qualified JHT technician available. Bryan and I shared the job. The show needed little rehearsal since Clark was the only replacement in the original cast. Bryan called cues from the booth, and I picked up other duties. My stage manager's pay was folded into my usual paycheck without costing the JHT additional money. Dean was agreeable and put the wheels in motion.

Funding for the theater looked good on the donor's page of the playbill, but listings were misleading. The founding donors were still listed, taking up nineteen lines in the first column. That money was spent long ago. A few of the founding donors still donated smaller amounts. The McKnight Foundation was still in our corner, but since 9/11/2001, the increase in humanitarian need would soon take precedence over arts programming.

In 2002, only four donors were listed in the $1,000 to $4,999 section. Two were private donors, one was a foundation, and the other was the Southeastern Minnesota Arts Council. In 2003, there were only two individuals listed in that category. One of them was me. I had received my first Social Security check, and I donated most of it with a grateful heart for having had the opportunity to carry on my theater career in Plainview. When I reviewed the rest of the page—donors in the smaller categories—I found many names that were tied to me that I worried would no longer contribute after my retirement.

High School Drama

In the spring of 2002, the high school drama coach resigned. When school started in Plainview the following fall, no one within the school district applied for the position, so I made a formal offer to direct a high school production of *The Miracle Worker* by William Gibson to be staged in the winter of 2003 in the Jon Hassler Theater facility. My offer included writing a SEMAC grant proposal and taking on some community fundraising. Together this covered the full cost of the production including my directing fee and a fee for renting the theater. I got the job—another chance to play with the kids.

The Miracle Worker is based on the autobiography of Helen Keller, who was left blind and mute as a baby from a case of measles. The play dramatizes the volatile relationship between the lonely teacher, Annie Sullivan, and her young charge, Helen. The play offers students a familiar story with challenging roles.

The rehearsal schedule was very demanding, with four to five rehearsals a week. The girl cast as Annie Sullivan could not meet the schedule. I closed my eyes, envisioning every other girl in the cast as Annie Sullivan, but no amount of rehearsal would have achieved the toughness, or the vocal quality required to project this character. So, I talked it through with Sally Harrington, and she was excited by my idea of bringing in a seasoned guest artist who could share some of her expertise with the cast. I rearranged the budget and hired Patty Matthews, a lively young actress from Minneapolis.

Patty enriched the student's theater experience tenfold. I asked her to take charge of the warm-ups, and the students learned a routine that was designed specifically for actors. Patty included breathing and vocal warm-ups badly needed by this group of novices. We instilled leadership along with the warm-ups. In subsequent years, students who had "studied" under Patty led the exercises.

After several weeks of rehearsal, one of the boys playing an adult role was finding it impossible to loosen up enough to be heard and to be believable. I asked Patty to lead this young man on a merry chase, up and down the aisles, backstage, anywhere she chose, while he ran his lines at full volume. I told the actor he couldn't stop until he started breathing deeply enough so I could hear every word. Patty moved at a brisk, boyish pace, picking up speed, pushing for more breath, and the actor kept pace, pink-cheeked but making some real progress. The rest of the actors looked on in astonishment. When I called a halt, everybody was laughing, including the actor. I told him to hang onto that volume while we ran his scene. The improvement was almost miraculous.

I was enormously pleased with the show. Patty set the bar high, and the kids all rose to it. They met memorization deadlines, they matched the pace demanded of them, they could be heard, and they loved what they were doing. Patty was their gift from the Jon Hassler Theater.

Erica designed the set, and Ben Hain, as tech director, became a one-man band, building the set, designing and hanging the lights, training students to run the light and sound boards. Ben and Erica invited parents to come in on a weekend to help the kids paint. Ben even installed a working pump for the iconic moment at the end of the show when Helen discovers language.

I was crestfallen later when I heard that I was harshly criticized by several Plainview citizens for bringing an outside actress in to play Annie Sullivan. Their comment went something like this: "It was a high school show. She should have used another high school student, even if they weren't as good." I wish they could have seen what happened in six weeks of rehearsal—or maybe asked the students how they felt about it.

I swallowed the criticism and continued using an outside consultant for future shows. None of them were actors, so the small-town critics never squawked.

Rewriting *The Staggerford Murders*

The Jon Hassler Theater was about to open the fourth summer season, and I felt compelled to produce a Hassler script again. We had done the most polished of the Hassler-based scripts—*Grand Opening*, *Simon's Night*, and *Dear James*. I had shelved *Jemmy* for now, so *The Staggerford Murders* was the logical choice. Clark agreed with the choice, but neither of us was fond of the script.

The first version of the script had been well received by Jon Hassler's fans, but it had not fared as well with critics and general audiences. *The Staggerford Murders* was Jon's attempt to write a play "from scratch." In 1999, when Afton Press published *Keepsakes & Other Stories*, a collection of Jon's short stories, I read "Yesterday's Garbage" for the first time. The characters and plot were a close parallel to *The Staggerford Murders*. If the short story preceded the play, I would argue that it was another adaptation and suffered from the use of narrative devices. But I have no way to be certain. But Jon was still more novelist than playwright, something to which he fully admitted.

When I scanned both collections of short stories, I also found many plot elements that had functioned as the basis for extended scenes and characters in several of Jon's novels. The short stories were like composer's etudes, exercises that prepare musicians for longer performances—intended mainly for practice in technique. Sometimes etudes are performable, but the word "etude" implies that the piece may need further development.

Since we were producing the play after a three-year hiatus, I put together a team to help rewrite the script in an attempt to overcome the disjointed narrative weaknesses of the first script. Since we would have to win Jon's approval of any changes, we kept it close to the spine of Jon's storytelling. I recruited Denise DuMaurier, who had played Agatha in the 2003 production of *Dear James*, to act as Dramaturg, and added Chris Samuelson and Nancy Plank to the writing team. As changes were proposed, discussed, and agreed upon, I typed the new script on Nancy Plank's computer using her scripting software, and then I sent it to Jon, who was wintering in Florida.

Jon made several changes. The most notable was converting the character of Sonny into French, the same French who had been discovered to be Agatha McGee's grandnephew in *Dear James*. Thereby, Jon knit *The Staggerford Murders* into the canon of characters and places to which he returned time after time in his various novels and short stories. Because we are in Staggerford again, Miss McGee's presence is felt, although we never see her. And, of course, where French appears, Imogene is sure to follow. One change led to another, and the script continued to evolve, like water following its natural path to the sea.

The cast included many Twin City faces, but we found a local mortician, Mike Johnson, to play the villain. Mike had appeared in many shows for the Rochester Repertory and the Rochester Civic Theaters, as well as melodramas at the Mantorville Opera House, where he had gained experience as a villain.

Nearing the end of his acting career, Larry Roupe as Dusty presides over Marshall Hambro as Chief Morehouse. Photo by Nancy Campbell.

Gathered at the desk, Grover (Sheldon Goldstein), Chief Morehouse (Marshall Hambro), and French (Chuck Deeter). Photo by Nancy Campbell.

When the show came down, we moved the front desk from the Morgan Hotel lobby from onstage into our own lobby, where it served as the box office for the duration of the Jon Hassler Theater.

The new script was closer to being a play, taking on stronger farcical qualities, but it still felt cluttered. I don't know if it will ever be produced again, but another pair of eyes might lead to more improvements.

I was still looking for ways to interact with the community, so I turned to my lifelong love affair with…

Words

While teaching writing classes in Babbitt in the 70s, I read Emily Dickinson's statement with a catch in my throat: "Words are my life." Those four words developed sharp elbows until they sat in my brain somewhere. They nudged me into choices, wise or unwise, as I ran or stumbled or limped uphill over the last fifty years. By the end of 2001, they pushed me to start putting together the mechanics of getting another

RAAP affiliate on its feet—The Writers' Center. The renovation of the Hassler house had moved along in fits and starts, a story unto itself as Sally Harrington found ways to push it forward with family and community help. But a physical facility demands habitation to bring it to life.

Emilio De Grazia, Founder, Planner, Teacher, and Board Member from Winona.

Ken McCullough, highly celebrated writer and teacher who served as moderator and teacher for Writers Helping Writers in 2006 and 2007.

Out of conversations with Emilio De Grazia (Winona) and John Rezmerski (St. Peter), the Writer's Center developed into a functioning RAAP affiliate. Emilio and John were published writers and college professors who "knew the territory." They had vast teaching experience with similar organizations and could suggest regional writers who might serve on the Writers' Center Committee to be responsible for developing programming. We soon added more writers to our meetings in the theater lobby—people from Austin, Red Wing, and Kasson-Mantorville.

I became the liaison between the RAAP board and the Writers' Center Committee. I took the minutes, typed them up and distributed them as e-mail. I followed through, either doing the chores myself or assigning them to other people and then following up. I generated lots of words to get it all done but never found time to write creatively, not even a journal.

We decided to launch the Writers' Center with a writer's conference that could become an annual event. Faith Sullivan, a well-known Minnesota novelist, was our first choice as keynote speaker. I had met Faith years ago, so I called her to extend our invitation. She remembered me and knew a little about RAAP and where Plainview was located. Her first question was, "What do you want me to talk about?"

I gave her a thumbnail sketch of the Plainview project so far, and then I read her the Mission Statement for the Writers' Center to her:

> The Center's mission is to provide activities and programs for writers to develop their individual and collective creative abilities and skills, and to enhance the culture of rural and small-town America. To serve as a Center for the rekindling and maintenance of the voice of change in the world perspective based on agrarian life and values.

I don't remember how that statement took form. I believe we discussed it thoroughly, and I think Emilio drafted the actual words. I know they weren't mine.

I was able to offer Faith Sullivan a small stipend, and she asked for a few days to think about it.

When I called her back, she said yes and gave me the title of her talk: "We All Started at Ground Zero." She already knew the audience she would find in Plainview. Faith was born and raised in southern Minnesota and attended Mankato State University. After living away from Minnesota for twenty-five years, she and her husband returned to Minnesota in 1989 to live in Minneapolis. She started writing novels when her youngest child was in kindergarten. Faith Sullivan was well known for seven novels, including *The Cape Ann* and *The Empress of One*, and was the winner of the Milkweed National Fiction Prize.

The Rural America Writers' Center was officially launched on April 5, 2003, with a full-day conference entitled "Writers Helping Writers." After coffee and rolls in the lobby, we gathered in the theater for Faith's keynote address, followed by questions and discussion. Faith was fifty-ish, no more than five foot two, with a little white sprinkled in her soft dark curls, a heart-shaped face, and eyes that blended delight with intellect. Lunch was served at the Tavern on the Green at noon. We regrouped at the theater for our afternoon panel discussion before inviting the writers to break into smaller groups—Creative Prose led by Emilio DeGrazia, Poetry led by John Rezmerski and Young Adult Lit led by Patricia Calvert—all published writers. We closed the meeting at 3:30, but people hung out for a while, obviously reluctant to leave a setting so conducive to talking about writing, sharing personal history with new-found friends.

A month later, Emilio offered a four-week Saturday class called "Shaping the Story: a Method for Madness," and John Rezmerski offered a poetry workshop in June. These guys were off and running—no hills in sight. The Writers' Center took shape and gathered words, important words, for future reference.

How to Talk Minnesotan

Under his new mantle of authority, Clark imported another slice of entertainment, Troupe America's long-running production of *How to Talk Minnesotan*. The original book lampooned stereotypical Minnesotan speech and mannerisms:

1. useful phrases such as "You bet," "That's different," and "whatever"
2. refusing food three times before accepting
3. the art of waving
4. hotdish
5. Lutefisk
6. the art of starting cars in the winter
7. the Minnesota long goodbye

Much of the material was originally performed as sketches on *A Prairie Home Companion*, a long-running show on public radio hosted by Garrison Keillor. Howard Mohr, a writer for the show, turned his material into a book followed by a musical script. Composer Drew Jansen created songs like "Hotdish Hallelujah," "The One That Got Away," and "Probably Love or Whatever." It was staged by Curt Wollan,[16] an expert at creating hilarious bits using a grocery cart to represent a car, and so on. Actors directly addressed the audience—asked them questions and made them feel like invited guests at the Lost Walleye Lodge.

Curt originally staged the show at the Plymouth Playhouse, where my friend, Linda Twiss, worked as the marketing director. She became actively involved in marketing the show in Plainview, which carried over to JHT shows through the oncoming years.

Linda Twiss, marketing expert. Photo by Sally Childs.

In June, Curt brought the actors to Plainview, where JHT provided the space, marketing, and box office facility for a share of the gate. *How to Talk Minnesotan* played to large, appreciative audiences in Plainview. Local folks found their neighbors and themselves represented onstage and laughed at the gentle satire.

Honk! 2

We remounted *Honk!* and had to recast some of the show. Clark remained as the Bullfrog and doubled as the Father Swan, but Tod Petersen took over the role of Drake, the Father Duck. Tod had a way of bringing joy into every room he entered, and he returned to the Plainview stage many times.

I stage managed the remount of *Honk!* to gain more qualifying weeks for the AEA pension. This time I had to take full responsibility. Clark was in the show, and I don't remember specifics, but I do remember feeling crowded by him. I had never been comfortable with technical assignments, but my need for a pension overrode my anxiety.

Adrenaline charged my system every time I entered the booth to call light cues. Despite Ben Hain's short course in the workings of the computerized light board, I remained reliant on Al Crom's expertise. During one performance, we got out of sync, and the two of us tried to figure out what had happened, where we were, and how to fix it. I had to decide whether to make the next call where it was notated in the script. I made the call, and the wrong lights popped up during a black light sequence. We quickly backed out of the cue, which got us back on track but destroyed the magic of the moment. I dreaded facing Clark after the show. He was rightly furious. No apology from me was enough, but Dean calmed him down. I would choose poverty over any more paid time in the light booth.

The Children's Theatre (CTC) in Minneapolis was contemplating *Honk!* for their next season and sent a staff member to scout it out. That performance went off without a hitch. The CTC representative loved the show, and they produced it the following year. Clark and I went to see it, and we agreed that our show in a small theater in rural Minnesota had more heart, more magic, than this larger, slicker, big-budget production. Scale and proportion make a huge difference in audience perceptions.

Driving Miss Daisy

My favorite shows were small cast, intimate productions. Directing *Driving Miss Daisy,* my last show as artistic director, sits very near the top of my list.

I had a fortuitous conversation with Mary Kay Fortier-Spalding[17] and her friend, Cynthia Hayden, at the theater door as they left after seeing *Honk!* I asked Mary Kay if she had any interest in the role of Miss Daisy. She said no, she was booked, but then pointed to Cynthia, an ideal candidate, an Equity actor and old enough to be convincing but young enough to remember lines. I looked at Cindy with new eyes and found Daisy looking back at me. When she auditioned, she handed me her resume. I was bowled over by the extent of her television credits—the psychiatrist Eileen Lyndon on *Guiding Light* and featured roles in several soaps and episodes of *Law and Order.* Her film work included *Fallen* opposite Denzel Washington. I no longer remember her audition piece, but I do remember that I cast her before she could leave the room.

Then I drove to Wisconsin to see Kathy Hardy in Neil Simon's *Proposals* at the Phipps Theater in Hudson, which also included Eric Wood. Years ago, he had performed at the Hallie Q. Brown Players in St. Paul but dropped out of acting when life got in the way. His life experience had only made him a better actor. I cast Eric as Hoke, Miss Daisy's chauffeur, which he played to perfection.

Clark Cruikshank filled the shoes of Miss Daisy's son with such believability that I often forgot that I knew the actor behind the role. He also put together a fine soundtrack, adding emotional depth to every scene.

Erica Zaffarano filled the air space rising over the sparse set with a variety of large, sepia-toned drawings—abstractions of the events and places depicted. The show took on an aura of historical facts—a fusion of fiction and documentary.

Daisy (Cynthia Hayden) shares a moment with Hoke (Eric L. Wood).
Photo by Nancy Campbell.

Erica's set showing the sepia paintings that could be lit individually or
in combination, and the three acting areas. Relaxing on stage, Cynthia
Hayden (Daisy at home), Eric L. Wood (Hoke, resting in his car), and
Clark A. Cruikshank (Boolie, in the office/nursing home).
Photo by Nancy Campbell.

Winds of Change

I left *Driving Miss Daisy* on opening night, happy with a job well done, knowledge good for my soul.

My euphoria was cut short by the decision of the RAAP Board to eliminate my position as artistic director and give artistic responsibility to Clark Cruikshank as full-time managing director. I envisioned my best friends arriving for work at the Jon Hassler Theater, where I would no longer be an active participant—Erica, Paul, Ben, Linda, Al—and all the actors I had grown to love. It was a little like contemplating death when you look at your surroundings and realize that when you are gone, it will go on as it always has. I used my bio in the program to save face and to say thank you:

> Childs is grateful for wonderful support from board members and friends and from her longtime Stage Manager, Al Crom, whose first show with the Lyric was *Simon's Night* in 1991. The next step for the Jon Hassler Theater is to build a management infrastructure, which began in 2001 with the addition of Clark Cruikshank as Managing Director. Next year, Childs will become more active in fundraising and Cruikshank will take on more artistic responsibility. We are caught up in the winds of change and hope that you, dear audience, will continue to support us. You are our best asset, and we are grateful that you are here!

Nothing was official yet, not until January 1. Would I have a role? Fundraiser (sigh), high school director? I wrote in my journal in October, "Too, too tired. I need some time for myself. I'm scared. Things keep breaking, and I fall down often. Must try to shut up again."

My next journal entry on 10/17/03 demonstrates Clark's urgency to take charge:

> I was not at the theater last weekend. On Monday, Cyndy (Daisy) called to say that she was very

unhappy because the Daisy pre-show music had been replaced with Frank Sinatra recordings. Granted, Clark was the sound designer for the show, but that only made a strong case for him to stick with his musical choices to the end of the run. Changes should be shared as well with the director (me). I called Clark and asked to have the pre-show music restored within the theater and keep Sinatra in the lobby. He was in the show himself and agreed to my request. But a full week before the end of the run, he and Sally Harrington wanted to take advantage of the nice weather and replace the Daisy sign with "My Way." I asked to keep the Daisy sign in front of the public until it was done, and they complied. But I was told I was not welcome to attend the sing-through for *My Way*. Clark and others could not wait for me to be gone. I felt bruised and hurt. I faced a succession of wounds.

Meanwhile, Clark and I were both looking for outside performances to bring to Plainview and fill in between longer runs. We scheduled Prudence Johnson,[18] a well-known Minnesota vocalist, for a single performance backed by Dan Chouinard on November 10, 2003. The songs were from their new CD, *Moon Country*, based on the music of Hoagy Carmichael. Clark did the marketing, and I acted as producer on the day of the performance, and I met Prudence's husband, composer/writer Gary Rue, in person for the first time. He was there to set up the stage with the necessary sound equipment. They were all well-known in the Twin Cities. Not so in southeastern Minnesota. Attendance was light.

My Way

Although I retained the title for a few months, Clark was on his way to becoming the artistic director with his production of *My Way, A Musical Tribute to Frank Sinatra* by David Grapes and Todd Olson, which played from November 28 through December 28, 2003. Set in a bar, the show celebrates the mystique of Frank Sinatra and the music he made famous— "My Way," "Fly Me to the Moon," "I've Got the World on a String," "New York, New York" and many more from the American Songbook.

Clark's vision was encapsulated in the people he hired, including Curt Wollan as the director. Curt was out of town until tech week, so Clark took over as co-director. He hired top designers, combining Erica Zaffarano and Ben Hain with others from the Twin Cities—the much-celebrated choreographer Michael Matthew Ferrell, costume designer Kathy Kohl and as music director/pianist, Michael Erickson, who had worked at the Plymouth Playhouse. He brought back two actors from *Honk!* and added two AEA men. They were accompanied by a six-piece ensemble of local musicians. The show was well done. It was also extremely expensive compared with our previous small cast musicals.

Clark proved himself to be a capable director. I silently questioned the need and the extra cost of bringing in a second director. I didn't need to be told that it was no longer any of my business. The title of Clark's first show as the director (*My Way*) was not lost on me. I had become a lame duck.

Earlier, we had initiated a fundraiser called "Sound Dollars" to raise money for improvements in our sound system. I had been doing a pre-show welcome speech before every show for a long time, practicing my begging skills. We had raised $6,000 to date by asking the audience to drop a dollar or two in the box sitting on the radio in the lobby. Clark took on the pre-show speech, and an ad appeared in the playbill. The fund continued to grow—but slowly.

Chapter 20: Covering Ground

All But the Art

Shortly after Clark was hired in 2001, Dean asked me how long I wanted to remain, and I told him until age sixty-eight (2006). I knew Clark was assumed to be my replacement, but I thought my timeline for retirement would remain open and negotiable. My understanding was incorrect. The RAAP Board apparently had expected me to scale back or retire more quickly so that Clark could broaden his role to include the artistic direction. My gender radar kicked in. I often intuited bad vibes from Clark.

In June 2003, I turned sixty-five and enrolled in Medicare. Privately, I wanted to feel I was still a player in the workings of the theater. I had hoped to retain full-time work for JHT long enough to give me a small window to save Social Security dollars towards retirement, which was always underfunded for people in the arts.

With my imminent departure, I foresaw the development of grave financial issues and the loss of community relationships. The school would be ignored. The Writers' Center, still a fledgling affiliate of RAAP, would be left out of the equation. I wanted more time.

When I brought the Lyric Theater to Plainview, I envisioned an expansion of the Lyric's connection to Minnesota writers, an expansion that included connections to the regional theater community. I had built the Lyric Theater for over twelve years before taking the plunge into a Small Professional Theater contract with Equity, knowing that I would have to juggle the budget over time to keep building a stronger organization. As yet, my experience with Equity was short-lived. The

Lyric and, subsequently, JHT walked a very precarious line between sustainability and insolvency. Clark envisioned a fully developed Equity theater on the prairie, one that would employ the best of the Twin City acting and directing community. Clark had not participated in the Lyric's earlier developmental phase and saw only an open door to the best actors and directors available at a cost that I did not believe was sustainable.

I re-applied for my job. I wasn't ready to hand over the reins, and I didn't think JHT had existed long enough to be rooted successfully in Plainview. JHT needed to overcome the perception that it was a theater by and for people who lived in the Twin Cities and Rochester. I learned that Clark and I had never pushed the same boulder up the hill.

Ken Fliès was no longer a Plainview local, and the board had replaced him as the chairman of the RAAP Board with Dean Harrington. Clark's vision matched the ambitions of Sally Harrington with support from Dean—Broadway in rural America. Clark had connections to actors and directors by way of his work in Equity theaters that I lacked, and he was more skilled with the computer. When he was hired as theater manager, funding became a major part of his bailiwick, but he was more interested in influencing artistic choices. Once in control, I was sure he would drop the yearly production of Hassler scripts. There were only four, and they had all been done in Plainview. But I was still looking at Hassler's canon of work with the idea of producing more adaptations of his novels, especially *Rookery Blues,* which Jon had just informed me was available for adaptation.

I wrote a long proposal to the RAAP Board, based on an offer to move to Plainview during the work week (Wednesday-Sunday) and try to develop JHT as a regional facility for writers, actors, directors, and the audience who lived within an hour's drive. It meant my work would be primarily administrative, hiring outside directors and artists, with little to fill my own creative needs. But I would alter my dream to fit the circumstances and work hard towards sustainability.

Clark and I interviewed for the job at a meeting in early January 2004 at Jim Bassett's in Cannon Falls. When the choice came to a vote, it was two and two, with one member abstaining. The tie was broken when the abstainer presented a proposal that offered the position of artistic director of JHT to Clark and a job as director of development of RAAP to me. It was obvious that Ken Fliès had been the abstainer and knew the value of compromise, a compromise that would be far more beneficial for the theater than for me. I'm sure that Ken wrote the new job description.

The director of development's job enveloped all chores outside of Clark's job description—chores that were required to keep RAAP affiliates funded and functioning. In addition, I would direct two shows a year—a fall show for JHT and a high school show in the winter. The compensation was about one-third of my previous salary and could be enhanced through incentives from group sales plus deferred incentives from fundraising—what is usually referred to as working on commission, an arrangement rarely successful and frowned upon in the non-profit funding community. The list of responsibilities covered two pages of single-spaced bullet points under three general categories: Community Outreach and Relations, Fund-Raising and Grant Development, and Affiliate Programming and Development. Any one of these categories was a full-time job.

When I added the guaranteed amount of compensation from RAAP to my Social Security income, I would have about $26,000 a year, approximately what I made when I left my teaching job in Babbitt in 1980. The cost of living had gone up astronomically since that time. I lost no time in investigating other directing opportunities for 2005 and beyond.

Gusztav had driven me to the meeting in Cannon Falls and was waiting in the wings to take me home. It helped immeasurably to have an old friend to absorb some of the bitterness of this day and help me regain a positive outlook.

At age sixty-six, I had a choice—look for a new job or accept a job that I knew was impossible to encompass. But I also knew that if I survived in the position for a year, I could accomplish several bullet points in each category and add value to the RAAP Programming. Ken Fliès assured me I wasn't expected to do it all at once. And I would direct two more shows. I was invited to serve as an ex officio member of the board of directors for RAAP, which I viewed as my Emeritus position. Like a best friend, my hill was right where it had always been.

Shortly after this meeting, Jim Bassett resigned from the board of directors. I joined the board for only six months. I could not support the management decisions that the board supported.

The Rememberer

In February of 2004, I produced and directed another high school play, *The Rememberer*, written by Steven Dietz for the Seattle Children's Theater. The main character was Joyce Simmons, who lived on the Squaxin Indian Reservation in southern Puget Sound, Washington. She was born on January 31, 1901, at Mud Bay near Olympia, Washington, the third of seven children. Lacking a written language, knowledge among these Indian peoples was passed on from one generation to the next through the stories and recollections of a chosen member of the tribe—the "Rememberer."

Adult Joyce (Breanna Johnson) and Young Joyce (Emily Eggenberger) pose with Cochise Anderson, our consultant. Photo by Mike Nadolske.

The Rememberer is a memory play. Only the adult Joyce is real. Everything else arises out of her memory of the first year that she was forcibly taken from her family and put into the Tulip Training School in 1911, one of many boarding schools run by the Bureau of Indian Affairs that was designed to re-educate Indians for domestic service or other forms of "white" employment.

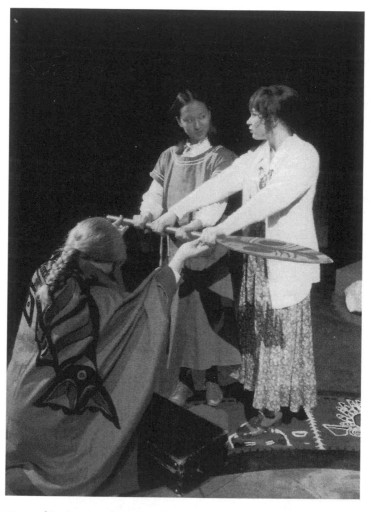

Young Joyce (Emily Eggenberger) connects to her adult image (Breanna Johnson) as they accept a paddle from Emily Sam (Erika Zarling). Photo by Mike Nadolske.

Andrew Dunbar (Mud Bay Sam) paddles Young Joyce (Emily Eggenberger) in a canoe inscribed with abstract salmon. Photo by Mike Nadolske.

Joyce Simmons Cheeka was one of the lucky ones. Early in life, she was chosen to succeed her grandfather as the Rememberer among her people, so she was allowed to return to her family every summer. She was able to take the best of both cultures and lead a happy and successful life as a wife and mother, living into her eighties, when Werdna Phillips Findley captured her stories in a manuscript, "As My Sun Now Sets." The fourth chapter was the basis for this play.

The play was first brought to my attention by Gregg Sawyer, Director of Theater at the Academy of Holy Angels in Richfield, Minnesota. He staged the play several years earlier in consultation with Cochise Anderson, a Native American from Oklahoma who studied acting at Portland State University in Oregon and the American Music and Dramatic Academy in New York City, where he founded a Native American Theatre Ensemble. After appearing in television and feature films, he became a teacher and moved to Minnesota, where he received a Jerome Fellowship for playwriting and a Bush Artist Fellowship for Performance Art and Storytelling. Cochise served as a consultant for our Plainview production, and Gregg graciously provided the use of costumes and props from his production.

Dream Event with Brittany Hassig as the Pitch Woman, Andrew Dunbar as Mudbay Sam, Emily Eggenberger as Young Joyce, and ensemble of Salmon. Photo by Mike Nadolske.

Young Joyce (Emily Eggenberger) comforts a lonely child (Sara Westholm). Photo by Mike Nadolske.

Erica researched the culture of the West Coast tribes and designed an open setting, which could suggest the shifting locale, and Ben Hain took on technical direction and lighting. Ben even stepped into a cameo role as the bad guy, Mullin. The actors doubled as musicians/set crew, and some of their parents joined a weekend painting marathon. Many of these students also participated in community theater productions, and student Mike Carter honed his skills as the lighting assistant and board operator, a role that developed into part-time paid work at the Hassler in the coming years.

To do a play about American Indians in a community made up of Scandinavians and Germans forced me into colorblind casting. Learning to fit in while retaining your own culture is a universal story, so we chose to ignore skin and hair color and limit the cultural identity to words supported by costume, music, and movement. Cochise facilitated the movement and music, and when the script asked for lines to be spoken in a Native tongue, he supplied language in his native Chickasaw.

Night Vision

Ironically, I was making inroads into the community through the school productions, simultaneously turning away onto a detour, creating distance from the theater work that had brought me to Plainview. Or was the Lyric Theater and Hassler Theater a detour from my early directing days at the high school in Babbitt?

Finding housing for me during the school plays was difficult, but several times over the years, I had been housed by two ardent supporters of JHT, Tina Thevinen and Dag Knudsen, in a lovely cottage next to their home above Lake City. The cottage was handcrafted by Tina and Dag for Tina's aging father who died shortly thereafter. The winter of *The Rememberer*, they offered me the cottage whenever I needed it, so after rehearsals, I made the long drive, often in falling snow that challenged my little Honda Civic as it carried me more than twenty miles to my solitary nest in the country. Tina was a crusader for dimming manmade lighting in favor of the night sky, so even the short walk from car to cottage was challenging.

One night I entered the house to find the interior bathed in moonlight. It was so lovely that I did not switch on the entry light as I turned to hang my coat on the landing atop the open stairway to the lower level. I missed the step down to the landing and fell headfirst into the stairwell made of highly polished wood. I rode all the way to the bottom on my right shoulder, keeping my head high enough to avoid injury. I lay at the bottom, staring up the stairs, gathering the courage to move. I started with my neck. Bent my knees. Pulled into a fetal position. Slowly I tested my arm strength and finally pushed up to my knees. I planted my palms on the steps and pushed myself upright. Nothing broken. I climbed the stairs, knowing that Dag and Tina were not at home. I had no phone connection. I soaked my shoulder with cold washcloths and finally went to bed. By morning I was stiff and very sore, but I dressed and headed back to Plainview. I had to keep moving. I knew that my osteoporosis was getting worse and that I had residual damage in my lower back from a fall on ice nearly twenty years earlier. I worried that someday I would break a hip, which was always referred to as "the beginning of the end" by my parent's generation. But apparently, I would live to see another day—and then another, etc.

Dueling Divas and a Grand Piano

I launched my new position as director of development with a fundraiser billed as "The Dueling Divas" in April 2004. One of the divas, Elizabeth Bond, grew up in Plainview and years earlier had won a Miss America talent scholarship when she represented Minnesota. She would be home for an annual visit with her mother, who lived in a local senior residence. I thought, *what a generous offer,* and envisioned a solo performance with some piano accompaniment. It turned into something much bigger. Her singing partner, Lori Isley Lynn, and their accompanist, Debra Ayers, would join her for a weekend of performances. They would expect to be paid.

The first act of the concert featured well-known opera arias with the "dueling divas" whirling in and out of each other's space. Written notes for our mostly uninitiated local audience were tucked into the program.

The second act featured more familiar songs that playfully commented on male/female relationships, starting with "Getting married today" from *Company* and ending with "Oh boy, can that boy foxtrot" from *Follies*, both by Stephen Sondheim. The show was a confection of fun, glamour, romance, and storytelling, all set to music.

Publicity went beyond the 2,500-card mailing and press release. I chauffeured Elizabeth Bond to Rochester, where she taped a song for the MPR Morning Show which aired on Thursday, April 15. At noon, the divas sang live in Rochester at the Kahler Hotel, and we handed out postcards. That afternoon they were interviewed on KNXR in Rochester. Articles appeared in the *Plainview News*, *Rochester Post Bulletin*, and *Wabasha Herald*. Clark placed ads in the local shoppers. Short of knocking on doors, we had blanketed the local region with information.

The First-Ever-15-Minute Lobby Gala

Part of my job as the newly dubbed "Director of Development" was to find a grand piano for the Plainview concerts, an instrument that we would retain for future musical theater performances. Petit Music in Eyota, a small town on the edge of Rochester, offered a used Knabe priced at $8,000. The former owners, Jim and Ruth Jacobson from Bloomington, Minnesota, donated half of the asking price. Petit Music forgave their usual sales commission, charging only $500 to move the piano to Plainview and tune it.

To raise $4,500 for our share of the cost, I proposed the "First Ever 15-Minute Lobby Gala" with a carnival atmosphere where theater patrons could test their luck. Linda Twiss and I collected goods and service certificates from over thirty businesses, primarily in Plainview, Elba/St. Charles, Greenway, and Rochester. Each prize was numbered, identified by sponsor, and displayed in the lobby. We slipped numbered tickets into balloons, blew them up, tied them, and attached a straight pin. We mixed them into big bouquets of unnumbered balloons to decorate the lobby. During intermission, Linda and Plainview students grabbed a bouquet and hawked balloons at $2 each or 3 for $5, urging everyone to try their luck. The lobby filled with noise, laughter, and much good-natured encouragement and ribbing among friends and neighbors. When Dean Harrington blew the whistle, balloons exploded and withered, white notes floating to the floor or into people's hair as winners scrambled to claim their number. The noise died down amidst a mixture of excited discoveries and groans of disappointment. Those who found numbers inside claimed their prizes and promised to collect them after the show.

I was proud of the community involvement in the Dueling Divas event. The local businesses not only gave support but also received support—in the form of publicity for their businesses. Marie's Ribbons and Roses donated the balloons and sticks. Several high school students who had appeared in *The Miracle Worker* helped prepare the balloons and sell them during intermission. A local waitress solicited prizes and shared information with diners at the restaurant where she worked. Two local women had fun assisting backstage with costume changes.

We sold $3,160 in tickets and brought in about $600 in our Lobby Gala. Although I pitched the lobby gala as a fundraiser for the piano, I recommended to the board that $500 of that money be used to help cover marketing costs. I was disappointed when I learned that only one board member outside of the Harringtons had attended. A spring gala could be a kick-off event every season if the board got behind it and started planning before the season publicity was prepared.

Debra Ayers, the accompanist, told us the piano was good but would need some work to be brought back to peak performance capability. However, it functioned beautifully for our purposes and became a standard fixture in our lobby when it wasn't onstage. During intermissions, a patron occasionally sat down and played it. I succumbed now and then as well.

Proof

David Auburn's *Proof* opened the 2004 summer season on May 8. Auburn was a screenwriter and theater director as well as a playwright. According to our director Matt Sciple, in 2001, *Proof* was nearly the most-produced play in the country and won the Drama Desk Award, the Tony Award for Best Play, and the Pulitzer Prize for Drama. Sciple, who was the literary manager for Park Square Theatre in St. Paul from 1996 to 2000, had just directed *Proof* for Park Square, where the set had been designed to be moved to Plainview by Erica Zaffarano.

According to stageagent.com, "*Proof* is a passionate, intelligent story about fathers and daughters, the nature of genius, and the power of love."

> The story unfolds on the back porch of a home in Chicago. Catherine has spent years caring for her father, Robert, once a gifted, ground-breaking math professor. Robert has died after suffering from a prolonged mental illness, but as he lost his sanity, he lost his ability to coherently work with numbers. Catherine has inherited her late father's mathematical brilliance, but she is haunted by the fear that she might also share his debilitating mental illness. Upon his death, she feels abandoned. Catherine finds both her world and her mind growing increasingly unstable when a ground-breaking proof that she wrote is found among her father's notebooks. As Catherine fights to prove her authorship, she questions her inheritance—is it her father's genius or his madness?

In his Director's Notes in the program, Matt Sciple raises the question, "What is it about this alien world (of mathematics) that playwrights and theatregoers suddenly find so fascinating? Sciple offers a personal story as part of the answer:

> My high school geometry teacher offered students a clue. For partial credit, she allowed us to fill in the missing steps of any proof with the initials T.M.O., signaling an intuitive leap across an otherwise unbridgeable gap in our knowledge to the answer on the other side. T.M.O. stands for "Then a Miracle Occurred." Eighteen years later, **anytime I know exactly where I want to be but have no**

idea how to get there, I remember Ms. Grand's generous shortcut, and ride the miracle across the unknown. As it turns out, math and science, even to those of us who don't quite understand them, make excellent metaphors.

Sciple concludes that

> *Proof* is so successful because it is less about science than the limitations of science, less about the exceptional qualities of its characters than about their essential humanity. Posing far more questions than it answers, it explores the places numbers can't reach, **opening a tantalizing window into the miraculous uncertainty at the center of it all**.

By crikey, this whole discussion—especially the phrases in bold type—could be boiled down to a description of the Bob Moss style of directing a play. Moss told his actors he knew where he wanted them to be at specific points in the dialogue but didn't know how to get them there. Then he turned them loose to find their way. An actor's intuitive leap. No math needed.

My Side of the Ledger

The program for *Proof* contained a notice from the development director (me) announcing our Knabe in the Lobby campaign. Donors could purchase one of 88 piano keys for $51.00 (when multiplied, this equals about $4,500) and sign a key in the sculptural wall hanging that Ben Hain fashioned out of a keyboard taken from a piano about to be trashed. Once all the keys were sold, purchasers were asked to join JHT staff at a party to celebrate our great good fortune.

Our list of donors for our 2004 season had grown to a full page, three columns in tiny print. The first category still consisted of "Founding Donors." Subsequent categories were based in Hassler lore: The Flock That Rocks ($500–999), Hank's Market Coupon Clippers ($100–499), Morgan Hotel Coffee Klatsch ($50–99), and Agatha's Hardscrabble Kids

($1–49). These categories were fun and worked well with our annual donor letter sent out over Agatha McGee's signature, but ghost written by Jon Hassler.

As of April 22, 2004, I had booked approximately 900 tickets for groups for the next season. Only one group booked for *Proof*—a high school group from Lourdes, a private Catholic school in Rochester. Clark tried to discourage this group because we both felt the material was for mature audiences, and we didn't want repercussions. Clark described the language to the teacher and then sent the script to her for perusal.

I continued to work on group sales, focusing on the fall play. I drafted a leave-behind piece describing RAAP—which we left behind for the first time when Ken and I interviewed someone from Rochester for board membership. I drafted the next McKnight grant proposal and prepared SEMAC grants for a July 1 submission. I met with Professor Dona Warner Freeman from St. Olaf to explore the idea of internships for St. Olaf students and surveyed Plainview High School students to determine if a theater class for area students might be of interest in the summer. The Hassler House was ready for use, so I started working on a housewarming event that would include a visit from Jon Hassler, whose Parkinson's disease had been redefined as supra-nuclear palsy and forced him into a wheelchair. Jon was the first to roll up the wheelchair ramp and enter through the front door of his childhood home.

On June 1, 2004, I submitted a "Challenge America Fast-Track Review Grant" proposal to the National Endowment for the Arts (NEA) for $10,000 to produce my adaptation of Hassler's *Rookery Blues*. This was the most complex proposal that I had ever undertaken. My personal treasures still include the two commitment letters that were required, one from Jon Hassler and the other from pianist Dan Chouinard. Dan had participated in the first reading in January 2003, and his letter said, "I am looking forward to a continued participation in the project, including a tentatively scheduled theatrical run in the fall of 2005." In his bio, Dan said he was "known in the Twin Cities and elsewhere as a singularly versatile pianist, accordionist and accompanist." That statement still holds true. The proposal met with success: the NEA awarded us the $10,000.

Clark's Side of the Ledger

Clark quickly put his stamp on the Jon Hassler Theater with his choice of plays, directors, and actors. There was little chance of hiring local actors.

Peter Rothstein came in to direct *And the World Goes 'Round: the Songs of Kander & Ebb!*—a revue of songs from the writers of *Cabaret*, *Chicago*, and *Liza With a Z*, among others. The libretto does not attempt to fabricate a continuous storyline as in *Mamma Mia!*—a show based on songs by ABBA. Instead, each song is a scene unto itself and is linked with the next song through a common element. The show celebrates life and the fighting spirit that keeps us all going. Five individuals find themselves careening through the world of love, babies, and coffee featuring unforgettable songs, including "Mr. Cellophane," "Maybe This Time," and "Cabaret."

The Hassler was producing first-rate, sophisticated theater performed by talent from the Twin Cities. Ben Hain was the lone local designer, and a local teen from Plainview worked backstage.

Michael Healey's *The Drawer Boy* completed the 2004 summer season and featured Clark and Dale Pfeilsticker as Morgan and Angus, two middle-aged Canadian farmers. Known since childhood as "The Farmer Boy" and "The Drawer Boy," veterans of WWII, they share a mysterious secret that only Morgan can remember. Angus only knows "right now." He won't remember a new name or face. When the routine of their simple lives is disrupted by a naive, idealistic young actor seeking material upon which to base a play about farming, their secret is revealed. Perhaps.

This play mixes hilarity and heartbreak as it celebrates the human spirit and the power of theatre to provoke change, encourage healing, and seek out the truth. The play is based on the actual events leading up to the creation of Theatre Passe Muraille's groundbreaking 1972 play, *The Farm Show*, and was voted one of the ten best plays of 2001 by *Time* magazine.

Clark hired Zach Curtis to direct. He was well known in the Twin Cities theater community as an actor, director, and founder of the Fifty Foot Penguin Theater. Since Zach was only partially free to attend rehearsals, Clark assisted with direction. I had a comment about pacing that I wanted to pass on to Zach, but when I tried to initiate a conversation with him, Clark walked in and cut me off immediately with fire in his eyes. Apparently, I was not permitted to enter into any artistic discussions.

Clark's priority was to fulfill his dream of world-class productions, no matter what it cost. He could always pin the problem on me as the grant writer. Maybe this was the beginning of the end and proof that this approach did not work for a rural theater that lacked sufficient local support.

Third Wednesdays

The Third Wednesday inaugural for the Writers' Center took place at 7:00 p.m. on July 21, 2004, with twelve poets and me signing in for an evening of poetry and music. We came from Austin, Rochester, Preston, Kasson, Kellogg, Red Wing, Minneapolis, and Nelson, Wisconsin. We ranged in age from sixteen to seventy-something. The next month, Third Wednesday bumped attendance up to twenty-five. I made a contact sheet and an e-mail group for sending notices. Third Wednesdays would continue monthly for years with featured authors(s) followed by an open mic session. Readers were welcome to incorporate music at their discretion. Since the event had already outgrown the Hassler House, meetings were held in the lobby of the Jon Hassler Theater.

In the beginning, featured readers came from within our own ranks, but after we ran the gamut from within, we tapped Emilio's vast list of colleagues and brought in writers from far afield who schlepped along their published books for sale and signing. When our attendance outgrew the hour allotted for open mic, readers had to sign up for one of ten available spots upon arrival, first come, first served. People came early, so coffee and cookies became *de rigueur*, with a donation cup nearby. A small portion of the money generated by the Agatha letter was assigned to the Writers' Center to pay a stipend to featured writers. Eventually, an annual membership of $25 helped defray additional costs. I became the general manager/typist by default with a lot of help from the Writers' Center Advisory Committee. I continually pushed the writers to attend the theater productions as well.

Housewarming – street side. Note the shadow cast by the pergola to turn someone into sculpture. Shadows are one of Nancy's favorite images. Photo by Nancy Campbell.

Jon Hassler's friend, Jim Secord, walks across the main street side of the house. Photo by Nancy Campbell.

Backside of Hassler House. Jon was the first to use the handicap ramp
Photo by Nancy Campbell.

The renovated Hassler House was being used for office space, and once the plumbing was complete, the plan was to schedule classes and/ or residencies for writers. On July 31, Jon and Gretchen Hassler drove to Plainview from their home in Minneapolis to celebrate a "Hassler Housewarming" with about eighty friends and Hassler fans. The mayor helped Jon officially cut the ribbon to open the house. In the shady side yard, we served ice cream with toppings and then moved to the air-conditioned theater lobby for readings and bathroom breaks. I was kept busy introducing people. As director for the fall show, *The West Side Waltz*, I ended my bio in the program by saying I was looking forward to developing more and more activity for the Rural America Writers' Center. Once again, I had become an administrator despite my best efforts to exercise the creative side of my training.

The speakers at the housewarming gather for the ribbon cutting—
Sally Childs, Ken Fliès, Sally Harrington, Mayor Steve Erwin,
Gretchen Hassler, and Jon Hassler. Photo by Nancy Campbell.

**Jon Hassler acknowledges congratulations and applause.
Photo by Nancy Campbell.**

Chapter 21: Rough Patches

The West Side Waltz

The West Side Waltz by Ernest Thompson resulted when screenwriter George Seaton offered Thompson a grant to write a new play following the success of *On Golden Pond*. *West Side Waltz* shares some of the same themes built around the physical, social, and financial deterioration caused by aging, but it lacked the family dynamic that drove *Golden Pond*.

The West Side Waltz focuses on Margaret Mary Elderdice, an aging, widowed concert pianist living in a dreary apartment on the Upper West Side, and her relationships with two other women. Her neighbor, Cara, plays the violin and has full run of the apartment, but that does not extend to actually moving in. Although these two neighbors play duets that draw them together, Margaret Mary spends her waning energy holding out against advancing age, encroaching rats, dwindling finances, and failing health. She does not want the burden of friendship. She would rather hire a young companion with no strings attached, musical or otherwise. So, she hires Robin Bird, a twenty-year-old who announces herself as an actress, newly divorced from a husband who announced himself as gay. She has no apparent qualifications as a companion for the elderly. But she does have a boyfriend who shows up now and then. The building superintendent pops in and out, sharing stories about his overweight wife and his difficult existence.

The role of Margaret Mary was written for Katherine Hepburn, resulting in a nomination for the Tony Award for Best Actress in a Play in 1981. Frank Rich, writing for *The New York Times*, titled his review, "Miss Hepburn Saves Us a 'Waltz'" but noted that Ernest Thompson

388

has written a tired play. I disagreed. So, my challenge as director was to find an actress who could "Save Us a Waltz" with the same panache as Hepburn and rescue a "tired play." Minneapolis native Nancy Marvy took on the challenge with gusto and a wonderful musical ear. Her comic timing was underscored with sarcasm, an angry defense against the world when it no longer worked in her favor. Margaret Mary may have been tired out by life, but Nancy Marvy's performance was never tired.

In an online review for *Applauze* (an online magazine featuring news, reviews, and original stories) in November 2004, Michael Lagerquist wrote, "The humor comes easily and will appeal naturally to audience members who have seen some deterioration in their own physical and spiritual worlds." An excellent description of our senior groups. I loved Lagerquist's comment that the set "works extremely well, though the reason for fragmentary rear walls is not apparent. Perhaps they are to represent the fact that many of us build our own walls between who and where we are and what lies beyond." Well said, Mike, but eliminate the word "perhaps." Set designer Erica Zaffarano was happy with this interpretation, but her reasons were as practical as they were symbolic. Since Nancy Marvy was not a concert pianist, the Knabe was angled, so we saw only her shoulders and head while she "played." A speaker was set behind an open section of the apartment wall, so the sound seemed to be coming directly from the piano.

I was fascinated when an audience member or two would leave the line of patrons exiting after the show to scuttle quickly onstage and around to the back of the piano, where they found the open wall and speaker. "I don't believe it," one said to another. "I could have sworn she was playing that piano."

Not only did I have to cast someone the equal of Katherine Hepburn (or Shirley MacLaine from the movie version), but I also had to find a second actress who played the violin well enough to keep up with the virtuoso artistry of Bob Hindel, who recorded the taped track of piano music suggested in the script. The Children's Theatre graciously provided us with access to their sound recording studio, where Bob recorded well over a half hour of music in under an hour.

Linda Twiss put me in touch with actor/violinist Karen Batdorf, who had appeared in Troupe America's *How to Talk Minnesotan* several years earlier. Karen played well enough to adjust her musical performance to her onstage character, a virginal middle-aged woman whose neediness matched that of Margaret Mary.

The building super(intendent) was played by Dimitri Gerasimenko, the St. Petersburg-trained Russian actor who had played The Stranger in *To Whom It May Concern* during our first summer season in 2000. Dimitri drew on his improv and clowning skills and delighted audiences with the clever use of his handkerchief, turning it into a bikini bottom well-placed against his groin as he talked about his fat wife. His role allowed him to rest on his Russian training if he followed his blocking and stayed in the outlines of his character. The other actors learned to hold for an unexpected laugh. They loved the fun since it provided an antidote to a health problem that landed hard on another actor in the show.

The actress playing Robin Bird was Jen Maren, a young woman who was beautiful in spirit as well as in body. At the beginning of a rehearsal about a week before we went into tech, Jen asked for a private moment. She explained that she had fallen out of remission for multiple sclerosis, a disease that she had experienced only once before. She was losing balance but was on medication and didn't have a current prognosis. It could worsen. She thought it was only fair to tell me and offered to step out of the show. She would abide by whatever decision I reached. I asked for a day to chew on it and talk it over with other staff.

When we returned to rehearsal the next day, I was still torn—worried about the final moment in the show when the actors all entered into a waltz. Actors Dimitri Gerisamenko and Joe LaForte drew me aside and assured me that they were physically strong enough to support Jen as a dance partner. And so we moved forward. Jen adapted her movement to prevent any stumbling. According to Jen, this was an "intensely terrifying moment in [her] life."

When we moved rehearsals to Plainview for tech week, Jen's balance remained undependable, and her treatment was picked up by a medical technician from Rochester. To add insult to injury, in the last week of the run, she was in a car accident and finished the show on crutches with a patch on one eye. In time, Jen's problem receded into complete remission, and she has remained free of MS to this day. I celebrated her success every time I saw her photograph on ads and rack cards for *Glensheen,* which became a summer staple at the History Theatre pre-pandemic. As theaters have gone back into production, Jen is about to leave to recreate this role first in a touring production and subsequently, in a summer production (2023).

Joe LaForte, who played Robin's boyfriend in the show, was also a caricaturist who drew a hilarious cartoon of the characters in the show. It first showed up on a dressing room wall and originated a tradition of creating a signed drawing by each subsequent cast, including not only JHT but the high school and the community theaters as well. I visited the dressing rooms on every Plainview visit.

The Super's fat wife, Dimitri Gerisemenko, Jen Maren, Joe LaForte, Karen Batdorf, and Nancy Marvy in the wheelchair. Cariacature by Joe LaForte.

The lobby gained added functions on a regular basis. The walls became display spaces for nearby artists, and our two-person love seats were formed into squares for easy conversation. Once the Writer's Group started meeting each month for readings, the love seats moved easily into a mini readers' theater. Eventually, one end of the lobby became a used bookstore that also carried copies of "The Green Blade," a publication of The Writers' Center. Dean Harrington loved selling books as much as he loved selling tickets and, on weekends, could be found comfortably settled in the lobby, his computer open to bank work. Dean was available to anyone who came in, whether to buy or just to talk.

Throughout the run of *West Side Waltz,* the lobby was filled with artwork created by Russian orphans who had participated in programs sponsored by Maria's Children International. Dimitri's wife, Jan Adams, discovered Maria and the children when she was in Moscow, clowning with Patch Adams (not related) when they both took time off from busy schedules as medical doctors. Subsequently, Jan founded Maria's Children International, a non-profit organization that funded arts programs to encourage disadvantaged children throughout the world to realize their creativity and develop talents and self-esteem that would serve them later in life. Originals, as well as note cards and framed reproductions, were on sale. To this day, an 8 x 11-inch reproduction of a Russian child's visualization of a winter night sits atop a bookshelf in my living room.

Winter Camping

As 2004 came to a close, I discovered through a harsh confrontation with Clark that we could no longer interact with each other. This changed the dynamic of my relationship with the Hassler Theater. I was dropped from the directing schedule for 2005, so I spent more time attending meetings with the RAAP board and the committee that was developing the Writer's Center. I continued to write grants and obtained permission from the NEA to extend the production dates for *Rookery Blues* to 2006. In January, I directed another high school show, *You're a Good Man, Charlie Brown,* a small-cast musical based on the Peanuts cartoons by Charles Schulz with book, music, and lyrics by Clark M. Gesner.

I had always relied on the theater to provide housing when I worked in Plainview and hadn't budgeted for this item. In 2005, I was no longer willing to drive to the Lake City cottage in white-out conditions. Like my mother learning to drive, I didn't ask for permission and risk a denial. During the week, I simply camped out on a couch in a side office and washed up in the women's bathroom, returning to my home in Minneapolis on weekends. I saw no one from the theater until opening night. My only uncomfortable moment was when I heard Dean enter the theater very early one morning to grab a shovel to clear the city sidewalk before school traffic developed. I don't know if he saw the mound of blankets through the small window connecting my contraband bedroom to the main office, but he did not acknowledge my presence then or afterward. My car was pulled into the small side lot. I made no attempt to hide what I was doing. It is not uncommon for theater technicians to nap in the theater at odd hours because they work for low pay, so I slept under the radar without challenge.

Charlie Brown

You're a Good Man, Charlie Brown was first produced in 1967 when Peanuts characters were a worldwide craze. Bomber pilots in Vietnam painted Snoopy on their planes, and college kids plastered posters on their walls. We love these characters, especially Charlie Brown and Snoopy, both born losers, because they capture our own feelings of rejection in a world that doesn't always understand us.

The show encapsulates a day made up of little moments picked from all the days of Charlie Brown, from Valentine's Day to the baseball season, from wild optimism to utter despair, all mixed in with the lives of his friends (both human and non-human). The moments are strung together into a single day, from a bright, uncertain morning to a hopeful, starlit evening.

To the six soloists, Lucy, Linus, Schroeder, Snoopy, Sally, and Charlie Brown, I added a chorus of nine and a small pit band, thereby incorporating the student actors from earlier production plus a few more. The high school band and vocal music teachers provided musical direction, and guest artist J. P. Fitzgibbons, a veteran of other JHT shows, choreographed. We scheduled his rehearsals around his appearances in *Anything Goes* at the Chanhassen Music Theater ninety miles away.

This production was a collaboration between the Plainview and Elgin-Millville schools and JHT. My press release assured the taxpayers that the whole community benefitted in several ways—the school district did not have to shoulder the costs of a theater facility, and students were provided with an extraordinary learning experience. The theater benefitted from being able to call on students as summer employees and interns. And the show was underwritten by a $2,000 grant from the Southeastern Minnesota Arts Council from funds provided by the Minnesota State Arts Board and the McKnight Foundation.

Three performances grossed $2,190 in ticket sales, with 443 people attending. In addition to the grant, local business sponsorships totaled $650. The final Income/Expense Report showed a net profit of $5.00 for the theater.

Clark hit his groove in what remained of 2005, a year free from Jon Hassler and free from me, other than the January reading of *Rookery Blues*. I believe the NEA grant reined in Clark from expressing his negative feelings for Hassler's work (and mine) publicly. He scheduled Neil Simon's *Odd Couple* with Marshall Hambro as Felix and himself as Oscar; Curt Wollan directed. Albee's *Seascape* filled the summer slot with Matt Sciple directing. This show was on my director's bucket list, so I found myself envious. The main characters were played by a married team—Stephen D'Ambrose and Barbara Kingsley. I had met them during my internship at The Cricket and then got to know Barbara better when she appeared for the Lyric in *Hunting Cockroaches*. After I saw *Seascape*, I chatted with Barbara, who built my confidence when she pointed out that I had a solid reputation as a successful woman in the arts and should parlay that into grant writing for my own projects. I was stunned at her comment after so much negativity from Clark.

Clark's selection for the fall play was *Bordertown Cafe* by Canadian playwright Kelly Rebar and directed by Richard D. Thompson from the Twin Cities. Lavina Erickson, my colleague from Lyric Theater days, played the main role. These connections kept me driving down to see shows at the Jon Hassler Theater. That and The Writers' Center activities and fundraising responsibilities. RAAP was now selling engraved bricks to replace pavement around the building and sponsorships for theater seats with engraved nameplates installed on the arms of seats.

My contract as director of development had expired. So, with no play to direct in the Hassler season in 2005, I arranged to direct *Simon's Night* for the Northern Lakes Arts Association in Ely. I was back among old neighbors and friends who shared great memories of being on stage back when Don Bronski had been in the director's chair. *Simon's Night* opened on Thanksgiving weekend with Mike Hillman, an Ely staple, onstage playing Simon Shea opposite Elizabeth McCrea as Barbara. The show took on a vibe of its own when I cast Pam Roberts, a character actor who loved to take risks, as Mr. Smalleye. With good audience response, I returned home quickly for back surgery to restore my lumbar spine. I looked forward to walking without my left foot slapping the ground.

I wasn't in any shape to continue selling Weekender clothing. I had paid off the mortgage on my house with money from the sale of my dad's house and lived on Social Security and a small annuity inherited from Dad that lasted about six months. After that, I would have to convert a small 401K account into an IRA and start drawing from it. I stopped thinking about money for a while. I had a roof over my head.

Chapter 22: Hitting My Stride

2006: My Busiest Year in Theater

I spent the first six months of 2006 recovering from surgery in my upstairs office, looking for directing work and completing my adaptation of Hassler's *Rookery Blues*. Reducing the novel to a two-hour production was like trying to fit Lake Superior into a bathtub. The show running in my head was a play with music, more of a concert but built on a story. Jon had divided the novel into five parts, each named for a well-known song from yesteryear: "These Foolish Things," "I'll Get By," "Mood Indigo," "Don't Blame Me," and "My Blue Heaven." I added nine more songs. Many were only partially performed, but a lot of music was worked into Ice Jam Quartet rehearsals and discussions.

I spent hours and hours on the phone with music publishers and ASCAP or BMI, procuring the rights to the songs and bargaining for free or low royalties. Only one song, "After You've Gone" (1918), was in the public domain. Most of the agents were New York-abrupt, but despite the title of Harold Arlen's song, "Stormy Weather," a conversation with his grandson/agent was a warm cup of soup on a cold day.

I narrowed Rookery's quirky characters to a cast of five—singer Peggy Benoit, pianist Leland Edwards, bassist Connor, drummer Victor Dash, and radio diva Lolly Edwards (Leland's mother). The script emerged as more play than concert. Playwright Jeffrey Hatcher gave me feedback during the rewriting process, which led to two major revisions.

In March 2006, I squeezed in my last high school directing job in Plainview, an adaptation of Alcott's *Little Women*. I was housed in style at the Teft House B&B, and Fran Ford joined me for a week to lead an acting workshop at the high school.

By June, the *Rookery Blues* script was complete. Ironically, I was suddenly in high demand as a director. I scheduled four shows, back-to-back, three as director and one as playwright.

Eric Wood wanted to play Hoke in his hometown of Hudson, located just off I-94 on the Wisconsin side of the St. Croix River, where, as a board member at The Phipps Theatre, he had input into play selection. The Phipps scheduled *Driving Miss Daisy* with Eric playing Hoke to open on September 8, and I was hired to direct. The timing was tight—*Rookery Blues* was scheduled to open in Plainview thirteen days later on September 21.

About this time, Clark Cruikshank left his position at JHT and returned to the Twin Cities. Carter Martin took his place as general manager. Carter's bachelor's degree was in acting/directing, and his master's degree was in arts administration from Chicago's Columbia College. As a longtime resident of Chicago, Carter had served as operations manager for the Ravinia Festival's 450-seat Bennett-Gordon Hall. His most recent position was company manager for BalletMet in Columbus, Ohio. I wondered who would make artistic choices, but it was no longer my business.

While directing in Hudson, I juggled between helping the director Jim Cada cast *Rookery Blues* and orienting Carter Martin, who would step into the staff as producer and assistant to stage manager Alva Crom. I quickly memorized the route from Hudson, Wisconsin, to Plainview and back again.

Directing *Daisy* in Hudson was a joyous experience. Since a designer's work is considered intellectual property, when asked, Clark graciously granted permission to use the soundtrack from the Plainview production. Mary Kay Fortier Spalding took over the role of Daisy. I first worked with her onstage in Ely, where she played Adelaide in *Guys and Dolls,* and here we were, twenty years later, collaborating on another great play. Eric Wood would play Hoke but finding an actor to play Boolie was difficult. The set designer, Mark Koski, a full-time employee of the Phipps Center, finally agreed to step into the role. The result was excellent, and then I was off to Plainview for two weeks.

Daisy (Mary Kay Fortier-Spalding). Photo by Bob Bergland.

Boolie (Mark Koski), Hoke (Eric L. Wood). Photo by Bob Bergland.

Rookery Blues unwinds on the campus of Rookery State College, an academic backwater, during the Vietnam War. The campus is rife with students seeking draft deferments who were being taught by a faculty of misfits. But that doesn't prevent several professors from meeting together as soulmates despite a teacher's strike on campus. The Ice Jam Quartet (a quintet in the novel) becomes a sort of support group, a place to unwind and enjoy the benefits of sharing good music. And then, the drummer takes on the role of union organizer, and harmony dissolves into disagreements.

Leland Edwards (David Saffert) and Peggy Benoit (Ann Michels) react to Victor Dash's (Beau Hayes) announcement that he has become a union organizer. Photo by Ben Hain.

To cast people who played the musical instruments required by Jon's story, I spent many additional hours calling musicians, mostly unavailable but who led me to others, building telephone trees every bit as long as those built by the union organizers at Rookery State College.

I was excited when I learned that Ann Michels was available to play vocalist, Peggy Benoit—according to the book jacket, "the most gifted and spirited of the bunch, who instills the harmony that allows the Ice Jammers to produce the kind of jazz they've all dreamed of playing." Ann had recently appeared in *The Last Five Years* by Jason Robert Brown, a musical production brought to Plainview by the Nautilus Music Theater located in St. Paul. I had also seen Ann in numerous roles, many of them at Chanhassen Dinner Theatre and one very special one—*Sunday in the Park with George*, directed by Peter Rothstein at Theatre Latte Da.

The hardest role to cast was Connor, Peggy's love interest, who had to play the string bass. I had a physical image in my mind—a dark-haired man with dark moods to match, slender and sexy. I contacted many musicians, and at the eleventh hour, someone led me to Michael Gold, a veteran New York City jazz bassist who had recently moved with his family to Minneapolis. His schedule was filling quickly, but he still had a little wiggle room. When I met him, I was gobsmacked. He was dark-haired and slender, close to my image. He had no acting experience but said he was game, and after meeting with director Jim Cada, he joined the cast.

Peggy Benoit (Ann Michels, vocalist) gets to know Connor (Michael Gold, string bass). Photo by Ben Hain.

Leland (David Saffert) is encouraged by his mother and radio diva, Lolly (Lavina Erickson). Photo by Ben Hain.

Lolly Edwards was a cross between 1940s gossip columnist/actress Hedda Hopper, who flaunted flamboyant hats and a razor-sharp tongue—and Barbara Walters, the first female network news anchor and famous interviewer of A-List celebrities. Lavina Erickson stepped into Lolly's role to report the Rookery news, seasoning it with local recipes and interviews. The show opened to decent reviews and good audiences.

The next day I scuttled off to Mankato State University to direct *Arsenic and Old Lace* by Joseph Kesselring, which would open October 18. Another tight fit. I was replacing someone who had been hired much earlier but was no longer available. They wanted a female alumnus, which narrowed the field to me. I was excited to direct in Mankato State's relatively new black box, the Andreas Theater, with Tom Bliese, my set design prof from student days, as the set designer.

While in rehearsal for *Rookery Blues,* I had also nailed down a future job for the Northern Lakes Arts Association in Ely, Minnesota, directing *On Golden Pond* by Ernest Thompson. It would open November 25, two months after the Mankato gig. I would barely have time to wash my underwear and change over to winter fleece and Ugg boots.

Much later in November in Ely, I used my days to clean up changes in the *Rookery Blues* script, while in the evening, I directed a rehearsal of *On Golden Pond*. One day I sent an e-mail to Michael Gold, asking for some language that had been incorporated into *Rookery Blues* during a rehearsal that I missed. He sent me the language and then added the following paragraph:

> Frankly, Sally, if this were produced in NYC using great jazz players—perhaps adding a few secondary roles to accommodate non actors, and the issues updated to be more relevant—like curriculum diversity—i.e., political positioning relative to the Palestinian Israeli conflict and freedom of academic expression (I'm thinking of Edward Said at Columbia and gender issues at many colleges), torrid depiction of the love affair between Connor and Peggy, a more graphic depiction of the tortures of substance abuse and family breakdown and a general message that jazz music contains a powerful set of psychosocial dynamics that bring even the most disparate people into alignment—well, you might have a real hit. Compelling subject matter and great live jazz every night. All it takes is vision.

Of course, Michael's vision would not be a Hassler adaptation. But it might be a great play. And in New York, according to Michael, "there are zillions of out-of-work actors and directors—also the best musicians in the world. Ya never know."

He was right. I would never know. I would stick with my Minnesota roots.

A Dark Play

In January 2007, JHT followed through on producing a play scheduled many months ago, *Pillowman* with Matt Sciple directing. Back when Clark was still proposing shows, he had called me as a courtesy and to get my buy-in. I said I didn't know the show. He said it was a comedy. I had no artistic say and saw no point in researching the play. Dean Harrington's comment published in the *Rochester Post Bulletin* was one I had heard him say: "Theater needs to be more than just entertainment." I may have said that myself from time to time, but I also understood that there were other factors involved, especially having the money to pay a budget deficit from producing a risky play. I told myself, "The Harrington's will support Clark's choice"—so I said, "If it's a comedy, it should work."

The plot was about the results of parental child abuse, a darkly twisted tale, a drama with fantastical comedic turns. I could barely sit through it, but I recognized Clark's choice as a very important personal statement. It had won many top awards. The language and violence elicited strong reactions. Some ticket buyers admired JHT for taking risks and others were offended. Clark was cast in a major role—his Last Hurrah at JHT, so to speak.

Lightness returned in the spring when the Harringtons asked me to stage *Grand Opening* for a June opening in 2007, using a local/regional cast. I was able to cast all but one of the actors in Plainview or Rochester. This cast became a "family affair," with three pairings of parent and child—two from Plainview and one from Rochester. Collin Chick was a very young Brendan, and his real mother, Mary Chick, played his stage mother. Nick Lange played the outcast, Dodger Hicks, and Nick's mother (Kim) filled the shoes of Mrs. Kimball, the town snoop who voiced lots of negative comments about Dodger. Ethan Scott Savage took on the villain, Wallace Flint, who was confronted by Stan Kimball (Ethan's father) based on hearsay evidence for starting the fire that killed Dodger.

Rochester actors filled in most of the other roles—Mark Colbenson as Grandfather, Kent Griffin as Rufus, Jeremy Salucka as Hank Foster, Dawn Rochelle Tucker as Mrs. Clay—and from Plainview, Joe Ulwelling and Anthony McClellan, proving that JHT could cast within the region. Only one role was left open. Alletta Jervey, who was based in St. Paul and had appeared in *On Golden Pond* at JHT in 2000, wanted one more taste of Plainview, so I awarded her a cameo role, primarily one scene. When Alletta fell ill for the last two performance weeks, I stepped in and thereby fulfilled my qualifying weeks for my AEA pension. An unforeseen benefit for me.

In 2007 I drove down to the theater for Jeff Hatcher's *Mercy of a Storm* and again for *Tuesday's With Morrie*, a collaboration between Jeff Hatcher and Mitch Albom. Over time, the balance shifted from shows produced by the Jon Hassler Theater to rentals whereby producers brought in outside shows.

A New Hill to Climb

I had wanted to see Hungary through Gusztav's eyes for years. In July 2007, I told him that with him or without him, I was going to Hungary in September.

He said, "I'll be there. How long are you staying?"

"A month would be about right."

"Done," he said.

Then tragedy struck my oldest daughter, Beth. Her life was going well—she was working as an occupational therapist, had bought a house, and had a boyfriend, a local drummer and teacher. In July, when Beth and Mike were fishing together, she started to vomit over the side of the boat. An excruciating headache ensued, and she was in the uncomfortable position of being at Mike's mother's house and flat on her back. When she returned home, the headache became even more debilitating, and she called her sister, Barb, who rushed to her side, arriving at the same time as the ambulance.

At St. John's Hospital, the doctors didn't know what was wrong. They gave her pain medicine and kept her overnight. Several days and many tests later, they still had no sure diagnosis and sent her home with recommendations for treating a migraine headache. When she and Barb followed up with her neurologist, Beth asked if a migraine would create

405

dizziness and blurred vision. The doctor ordered her to go back to St. John's Hospital immediately and check-in. He would call ahead. Barb asked to go home first and pick up a few things. The doctor said NO.

It took weeks of testing, looking for a diagnosis through the process of elimination. One day I arrived to find Beth singing, "I love Dilaudid, I love Dilaudid." She was taking a narcotic pain reliever, a temporary fix. When she asked why the walls were turning yellow and pink, the drug was withdrawn.

The doctors were researching rare diseases and finally proposed the possibility of central nervous system vasculitis, an auto-immune disease so rare that they lacked the experience to finalize the diagnosis. Everyone in the family went on their computers to research this ugly news. We learned that the disease could be put in remission with chemotherapy, but it could not be cured. It would have lasting effects, including serious fatigue. Beth would have a life-long disability.

So, I was left holding a round-trip airline ticket to Hungary that I didn't want to use because I thought Beth needed me. But if I canceled, she would suffer bouts of terrible guilt for denying me my first (and only) attempt to take a trip to Europe. Beth's father and two sisters would be available to help her, and I asked my oldest friend, Sandra Stanley, to be Beth's surrogate mother while I was gone.

And so, I spent a month in Hungary with a side-trip to Venice, and finally Vienna. After years of telling me about it, Gusztav showed me where he spent several months after he and his cousin walked to the Austrian border after the Hungarian Revolution failed. Throughout much of our time together, he showed me other significant points of interest in that bloody piece of Hungarian history, including the House of Terror. But that is a story for another book.

When I returned to St. Paul, the diagnosis was verified by doctors at the Mayo Clinic. Beth settled into her den for a year with three small dogs and daily doses of oral chemotherapy. She was left with a disability, no job, no income, no house, and no prospects. She had broken off her friendship with Mike, unwilling to impose her situation on anyone other than family. I moved in with her in January 2009, and when the foreclosure was complete, we moved to Roseville together in October.

Jon Hassler died in 2008 and Bill Holm in 2009. After Bill's death, I organized a reading of *Boxelder Bug Variations* in the Jon Hassler Theater as a celebration of his life.

My remaining days in Plainview became a kind of requiem. In June 2009, I directed *Dear James* with a regional cast, so we rehearsed in Plainview. Cheryl Frarck drove in from Kasson to become Agatha McGee opposite Rob Gardner (Father James), who was an emeritus professor of theater at Gustavus Adolphus College in St. Peter and was now living his dream as an actor. Eric Knutson (French) came from Lanesboro, where he had played many roles for The Commonweal, and Coralee Grebe (Imogene) hopped over from Rochester, where she was the artistic director for It's About Time Theater. Joe Ulwelling (Myron Kleinschmidt) could walk to the theater from his home in Plainview. This production fueled my hope that the Jon Hassler Theater would survive—not as Carter Martin succinctly described—as "Theatre Latte Da on the prairie,"—but as a showcase for a blend of regional and Twin Cities talent, renting space as needed to the school district and the Plainview Community Theater. Each organization would take on its fair share of the financial burden. This had been an unrealistic expectation in light of early history when the community theater wanted to have free use of the theater in the summers. Their request was denied because that was the time slotted for the professional theater to produce a summer season. All money for the start-up had been generated privately. No tax dollars had been used, so RAAP would charge rental fees. From then on, the community theater felt snubbed and, in return, had snubbed their noses at the JHT. They produced their annual musical at the Presbyterian Church where there were rooms large enough to accommodate their large casts. Years later, the community theater did use the JHT theater and arranged for the cast to use the Presbyterian Church for dressing rooms.

In 2010, I directed my last show for JHT, a remount of *Old Man Brunner Country*. Larry Roupe was no longer taking roles, but

Bill Studer, a retired Twin Cities' lawyer and re-emerging actor, took on the role of the Old Man. I rehearsed actors in Minneapolis, happy to work with Kristen Mathisen, David Roberts, Jack Carter, and Dale Pfeilsticker one more time and Josh Larson for the first time. Carter Martin left JHT in 2009. I saw no purpose in including Plainview area actors. This show ended an era of struggling to become a fully professional theater.

Downstage, Bill Studer (Old Man Brunner). Upstage, Josh Larson, Jack Carter, David Roberts, Kristen Mathisen. Set by Paul Skattum of Rochester. Photo by Ben Hain.

More shows followed at JHT, primarily rentals, but I have little knowledge other than playbills for some of them. The management of the Writers' Center had fallen to Dean Harrington and others, so I no longer went to Plainview on the third Wednesday for writer's events.

In 2013 Dean Harrington's letter from the RAAP Board of Directors to other stakeholders said that "after a careful review of the attendance records of our professional theater offerings over the past fourteen years, it was clear that attendance reached a plateau in the early years at a

level that does not financially support a professional theater program."
The necessary critical mass for professional theater was lacking. In the
immediate future, the theater would be rented to the local community
theater, the school district, and small theater companies.

Don't Hug Me, a series of shows written, directed, and produced
by Minnesota native Doug Olson, played in the fall slot from 2008
through 2014. The shows were advertised as two hours of fun and
farce, a Minnesota love story with singin' and stuff, terrifically silly, the
quintessential definition of fun, and so on. They appealed strongly to
Plainview locals. This income helped pay the bills, but it wasn't enough to
sustain the cutting-edge productions preferred by the Harringtons.

The Jon Hassler Theater was officially closed in 2014. The theater was
offered to the school district for $300,000 and was rejected. The school
board of directors then put together a bond offering for $1.6 million to
build a fully outfitted theater like several other schools in the area. The
bond issue was voted down by more than 85 percent of the voters. So,
the lights went out in this small town that, prior to 1999, hadn't had a
theater production other than high school plays in a gymnatorium for
some thirty years. The advent of the Jon Hassler Theater had brought
forth in the community not only unique professional theater but also
history-based and community theater plays—a rarity in small-town rural
America. The community theater would continue in a church and high
school plays on a stage in the basketball arena. The funky little theater
with its professional stage, its sprung floor, seating, lighting, and sound
system was but a footnote for the ages—a dream of what might have
been.

Epilogue

I want this blend of memoir and theater history to be useful, to go beyond the local color that was fun to capture on the page, to demonstrate that our personal lives are inseparable from our creative lives and work lives, and all are shaped by our changing culture and the times that frame our existence. And most importantly, I want my story to demonstrate the need for understanding among people. That is the essence of theater.

In writing this story over the last seven years, (with a year off to take classes in memoir at The Loft), I have tried to make sense of choices and events. I have learned that I like to exert influence, to feel compassion, and to seek harmony. I still don't like making decisions alone. I am analytical, intuitive, and terrible at improv. The hardest part of teaching or directing is verbalizing ideas, making them understandable to others. Often, I can't articulate my ideas until the meeting is over and everyone has left the room. I have tried hard to verbalize clearly in this book.

With the onset of the covid-19 pandemic in 2020, I have thought about how my theater career could have ended—with no closure. I have been able to look back from a hillside perspective to complete my historical memoir—closure of a kind. I am deeply grateful to the people who contributed to the story of the Lyric Theater and Jon Hassler Theater—and to my personal friendships and the love of my family.

On opening night, the cast takes the bows, and in recent years, the actors gesture to the stage manager's booth and the musicians in the pit before leaving the stage. That is the family that I leave behind.

I am eighty-five years old. Moving on. Ready to archive the theater memorabilia living under my bed. No longer running uphill.

THE END

Postscript

The Rural America Arts Partnership building, which housed the theater and writer's center, was purchased by the Foresight Bank, previously the First National Bank. The Hassler House was sold to a private party. Millie Fliès passed in 2017 and is survived by her husband, Ken. Larry Roupe passed in 2017; Nancy Gormley in 2018. Dean Harrington passed in 2019 and is survived by his wife, Sally.

Glossary of Commonly Used Theater Terms

Blocking - Shaping the movement on stage. A director may give actors their blocking or may give the actors freedom to experiment and then shape the blocking further to get the desired relationships of actors to each other or to furniture or props.

Black box - A large room with a high ceiling and black painted walls and floor. Seating may be flexible or installed on risers or on three sides of the room or be dependent on experimental ideas of the playwright or director.

Company - a small group of actors hired for a specified period of time to fill most of the leading roles. It is as close to job security as an actor may achieve.

Gel - The material (celluloid) used to add color to a lighting instrument. It comes in sheets that can be cut to fit the holder that is slid into a frame in front of the light.

Going up on lines - the act of forgetting lines, which the actor tries to mask with improvisation, often with help from fellow actors, until the correct sequence is re-established.

Common Lighting Instruments used by Lyric and Jon Hassler Theaters:

> **Fresnel** - smaller instruments with a special lens
> that breaks up the light, providing a general spread

of light onstage. (Often referred to as a wash of light.)

Ellipsoidal - a larger instrument with a long, bullet-shaped body and an adjustable lens.

Frames to hold colored gel are found on the end of the light pointed toward the stage.

A top hat, an extension that is named for its shape, may also be added to help frame or control the size of the lighted area.

Lamp - the term used for what the uninitiated might call a light bulb or simply a light.

Monday Nights - the traditional night off for actors who must work weekends. Auditions are often held on Mondays. Some theaters hold special events on Monday nights to generate more income.

In Repertory - Two or more plays are performed on alternate nights or alternate weekends, sometimes sharing cast members.

Tech Week - The last week of rehearsal, where all technical aspects of the production are added in, and the stage manager learns to run the show. The actors are expected to be line-perfect and very patient, waiting for technicians to make corrections. A tech table is set up in the middle of the seating area where the director, designers, and stage manager(s) may sit. The light board is brought from the booth to this table for easy access.

Unit Set - All scenes of the play are staged on a single set, requiring no major set changes. Furniture or props may be reset during act breaks or intermission. Parts of the set may be isolated through lighting to function temporarily as off-site locations.

Mission Statement - a statement that is required for not-for-profit organizations that governs the choices made by the staff described below.

Staff

Artistic Director - has overall responsibility for artistic choices and may also direct shows. Usually, a full-time position often held at first by a founder of the theater.

Director - has overall responsibility for staging a play. Directors are often independent contractors and may leave after opening night.

Managing Director - has responsibility for the business side of a theater. Usually a full-time position.

Producer - oversees all aspects of a production, especially the budget and funding. In small theaters, this function is often covered by the Managing Director.

Stage Manager assists the director during rehearsals and takes notes to use in production meetings. Stage Managers also notate in their script (their "bible") blocking directions, and light and sound cues. They manage everything that happens onstage or backstage during performances. They must have excellent communication skills and be able to solve problems, including ruffled feathers caused by egos, whether large or small. They must have enough technical skills to solve small problems during the production, i.e., replace a burned-out lamp.

Technical Director - oversees all technical aspects of the show and may function as the Lighting or Set Designer.

> Note: In small theaters (as defined by a limited budget and rental of space rather than ownership), the same person may fill several staff positions.

Acknowledgements

Writing has been peripheral to nearly every job I've held, starting with secretarial positions, where my responsibility for transcribing lay primarily in spelling, punctuation, and formatting. This left time for dreaming, an important part of any writer's life. Years of teaching high school English, including semester-long writing courses, demanded articulation of why I loved the written word so much. My long-time friend, Sandra Stanley, introduced me to Ken Macrories's *Writing to be Read,* which opened a path to learning how to "teach" writing, a concept that many academics claimed couldn't be taught. Those were fighting words, so with Macrorie in hand, I found my way to a method that worked for my Babbitt students, and I included myself as a student as well as a teacher.

With that in mind, when I started directing shows and then co-founded the Lyric Theater with Tom Woldt and Chris Samuelson, I knew that I would someday write about it. Sandra, Tom, and Chris deserve credit for getting me pointed in the right direction. Sandra read my manuscript several times and gave me sage editing notes. Her ability to separate her personal likes or dislikes from useful comments contributed to our life-long friendship while lending me support throughout my years of writing. Special thanks to Nancy Campbell, whose photography and other wonderful ideas brought an expanded vision of what was possible.

After about six years of applying for grants, which were denied, and coaxing friends and family to read and react, I signed up for a course in Memoir taught by Angela Foster at the Loft. It was exactly what I needed. I met other writers and learned to read from my work and accept comments from them and from Angela. They taught me to sort and apply good ideas and accept positive criticism gracefully. This experience led me to register for a second class with Angela, another class of wonderful students, including Eric Johnson, a fellow graduate of Mankato State and a delightfully comic writer whose comments were always useful. I registered for a third class taught by Nicole Helget, a published writer of a best-selling memoir and a novel, *The Turtle Catcher*. Nicole seemed to sense exactly what we needed to inspire confidence and desire. She invited experts to the class. I am particularly grateful to Nicole's introduction to Brian D. Fors, the Publisher of Minneopa Valley Press, who read my manuscript and gave me an overall critique and excellent suggestions when I was at a loss for how to proceed.

When the Covid pandemic shut down most normal activities, I continued to edit and rearrange. Angela Griffin sent e-mails regularly, providing energy and positivity. My daughters, Beth and Carol, became my staunch readers, culling out mistakes and asking for clarification when I failed to fill in all the blanks. At times I had to research my own files to achieve clarity. When that didn't work, I met with Set Designer Erica Zaffarano and Lighting Designer and Technical Director Ben Hain to pull information from their prodigious memories about Plainview productions. We laughed and had fun as we shared stories, and I saw backstage through their eyes as they revealed their perspective, showing me a little bit of myself that was new to me.

The final rewrite flowed from comments by Deborah Locke, a journalist and editor, and my close friend of many years. She also revealed my story through a different perspective, so I went back to my computer, rethinking, rewriting bits and pieces. And finally, I was ready to start sending the manuscript to publishers. I turned to Ed Block, a professor from Marquette University, who had just published a very erudite analysis of Jon Hassler's novels from his perspective as a professor who had included Hassler in his literature classes. Ed graciously shared his book proposal, which became my model as I wrote my own. Ken Fliès was generous in sharing details about his publication process, building my confidence level. I started sending out the manuscript, following the guidelines for each press that I found online. I expected rejection notices, but they didn't come. The silence was deafening.

I needed a consultant and contacted Laura Zabel, the Executive Director for Springboard for the Arts, an economic and community development agency based in Minnesota. She recommended David Unowsky, a consultant for folks like me. I knew him from the Lyric's producing days when he placed an ad in our programs for his bookstore, The Hungry Mind. He was happy to hear from me and immediately asked to read my manuscript. He suggested several Minnesota publishers and gave me ideas for expanding this list. His enthusiasm bolstered my confidence as he laid out a list of publishers to pursue. I met Ian Leask from Afton Press at a reading in Plainview of a memoir by Jon Hassler describing his childhood as the son of a Plainview grocer. Ian was interested in any written work about Jon Hassler, and so I told him about my book. He read it right away. He liked it, and we began discussions which led to publication.

Running Uphill found its way to Beth Williams, my editor at Afton Press, who has taught me what goes into preparing a book for publication. She fixed my errors and helped me over the bumps when I felt terrorized by technology. Thank you to her colleague, Gary Lindberg, for designing pages and making the pictures look their best. Thank you to all who wrote endorsements, and especially Peter Rothstein for giving me hope and writing the first blurb for the cover. Thank you to my daughter, Beth, for setting up a Go-Fund-Me page online. Thank you to daughters Carol and Beth, readers who caught my many mistakes. Thank you to my daughter, Barb, for fundraising help and to the donors who made my life-long dream come true.

About the Author

Sally Bronski Childs holds a B.S. in English Education from the University of Minnesota, Minneapolis, and an M.F.A. in Theatre from Minnesota State University, Mankato. A ten-week summer course at the Bread Loaf School of English (part of the Middlebury College language arts summer institute) in the Program for Teachers of Rural Writing fed Childs' passion for teaching, writing, and theater. She recently completed three courses in Writing Memoir at the Loft.

From 1968-80 she taught high school English with an emphasis in writing and multimedia classes in Babbitt, MN. "Mrs. B," as she was called by Babbitt students, directed three one-act plays and two class plays which whetted her appetite to direct plays professionally.

Childs completed internships at The Cricket Theater (in Stage Management) and the Guthrie Theater (as Assistant Director for *Hedda Gabler*). Upon completion of her M.F.A., she directed several plays at Southwest State University in Marshall, MN and served as a sabbatical replacement in 1985.

In 1985, Childs co-founded the Lyric Theater (Minneapolis) with two Mankato friends, Tom Woldt and Christine Samuelson and served as the Artistic Director for fifteen years. In 2000, the Lyric moved operations to Plainview, MN where it became the Jon Hassler Theater, under the aegis of the Rural America Arts Partnership. Childs served as the Artistic Director from 2000-2004. She also directed plays for the high school in Plainview.

Sally played a pivotal role in forming the Writers' Center in Plainview. Her adaptation of Jon Hassler's novel, *Dear James,* was produced by the Lyric Theater (Minneapolis), the Jon Hassler Theater (Plainview), and the

Barn Theater in Willmar, MN. Her adaptation of Hassler's novel, *Rookery Blues*, was produced by the Jon Hassler Theater with funding from the NEA.

From 2004 to 2010, Childs directed shows at the Phipps Center in Hudson, WI, and for the Northern Lakes Arts Association in Ely, MN. In 2018 Childs acted as dramaturg for Hassler's *Grand Opening* at Theatre in the Round in Minneapolis. She is a retired member of the Actors' Equity Association.

Endnotes

1   Click became the buzzword for the housewife's (or any woman's) epiphany when she recognized unfairness in her situation through something a man said or did. It was reported in 1973 in *New York Magazine* after becoming commonly used in *Ms.* magazine.

2   David Keirsey and Marilyn Bates, *Please Understand M*, 170–172.

3

Financial Activity				
	1988	1989	1990	1991
Ticket Sales	$1,232	$10,649	$10,382	$35,848
Fundraising Income	$10,205*	$5,708	$344	$1,378
Individual Donations	$3,576	$142	$675	$532
MRAC Grant Funding	0	$7,400	$450	$7,075
Corporate Donations	0	0	$250	$550
Total Income	$12,819	$34,690	$13,151	$34,102

*Profits from Metrodome sales generated most of this amount.

The first MRAC grant was for *Hunting Cockroaches*; the second was for *Simon's Night*. Our first corporate donation of only $250 put us on an ever-growing track as we got better at recruiting board members and gaining access to employee donor programs.

4   The Hutchinson Family Singers are credited with founding the town in November 1855. A post office has been in operation since 1856. Minnesota achieved statehood in 1858, and the city was incorporated in 1904. It has grown from an agricultural base to manufacturing and technology jobs. About thirteen thousand people live in this charming city on the Crow River, which can boast of having the oldest city park in the US— only New York City's Central Park is older.

5   In 2002 Resources and Counseling changed its name to Springboard for the Arts and now provides arts-related resources to independent artists and arts organizations including, professional development education and workshops, fiscal sponsorship, micro-lending, health care resources, and career consultation.

6   Jemmy:
     I am writing this memoir at the same time as I am reading Harper Lee's Go Tell a Watchman. I'm still chewing on the use of narrators in plays. It was the History Theater's staging of Lee's earlier published book, *To Kill a Mockingbird*, that convinced Chris Samuelson that she did not want to fall into the trap of using a narrator when she started drafting the stage version of *Grand Opening*. But ultimately, I have had to accept the use of a narrator to stage Hassler's novels.

     I listened to Public Radio's Kerri Miller's discussing *Go Tell a Watchman* with black playwright Syl Jones and two white guests, writer Jonathan Odell and Roosevelt high school teacher Molly Sheahen. An hour later, I shrugged off my nervous feelings about the white artist teaching the Native girl to paint. Syl Jones had pointed out that Harper Lee's newly published book (written prior to *To Kill a Mockingbird*) was about the way white people want to see themselves, so—" unless you have a clear white savior, the story will be shelved as ethnic." That's just the way it was. Hassler never exhibited any awareness of this. He was writing a story from his stance as a high school teacher who was upset at seeing a young life cut short by a hopeless situation. As Jean Louise points out in "Watchman," everyone needs to have hope. I reasoned that Jemmy escaped being a story about a white savior in favor of a story about not losing hope.

7   Ken Flies was not only the "visionary" on the formation of the Rural America Arts Partnership project but also its Managing Director and Chairman of the Board in its formative years. Ken and his wife, Millie, both grew up locally and attended high school in Plainview. In 1995, after almost a thirty-year absence, they purchased the local country club, which had been closed and sat idle. Millie was an accomplished chef and businesswoman and pined to own her own business in her home-town, where her dad had been eminently successful as a business owner. Ken was one of the original Peace Corps Volunteers at its inception in 1961–62 and had fashioned a successful twenty-five-year career as an

entrepreneur involved in the startup and turnaround of several companies throughout the US. Millie's effort, with her current three-hundred-seat redeveloped dining facility, would become a major factor in developing the tourism aspect of the theater by providing guided areas tours and feeding senior and tour groups, filling afternoon matinee performances—an essential ingredient in the theater's success. Ken has recently published a book about his Peace Corps experiences in Brazil called Into the Outback.

Dean and Sally Harrington's family were third-generation owners of one of two independently owned banks in Plainview—a rarity for small towns. Dean, working with Sally, had the goal of finding possible venues to make the town more than the bedroom community, principally of staff for the nearby Mayo Clinic, and also to fill vacating small business sites on Broadway (main street), including the International Harvester building. Recognizing Ken's background and talents, Dean encouraged a local business development group, PADCO, to retain Ken's services on a part-time basis to explore new growth opportunities in the town.

8   John Olive is a widely produced, award-winning playwright and the author of *Minnesota Moon, Standing On My Knees, The Voice of the Prairie, Careless Love, Killers, The Summer Moon, Evelyn and the Polka King, God Fire, Into the Moonlight Valley*, and many others. Buffy Sedlachek's plays have been produced across the country, including The Jungle Theatre and Illusion Theatre locally. She has co-authored three curriculum guides for playwriting and taught extensively at colleges and universities. Both John and Buffy were closely tied to The Playwright's Center.

9   Post-polio syndrome was becoming a household word as children who had suffered polio during the epidemic in the 1940s entered middle age. Gusztav was born in 1935 and contracted polio as a baby in Hungary, a fact confirmed by the doctors at the Sister Kenny Institute in Minneapolis.

10   The AGA stove (an acronym of the company name Aktiebolaget Gas Accumulator) was invented in 1922 by the Nobel Prize-winning Swedish physicist Gustaf Dalen who was blinded by an explosion while developing an earlier invention for storing gases. Forced to stay at home, he discovered his wife was exhausted from cooking, so he developed a stove that was capable of a range of culinary techniques and easy to use, even by a blind cook. Adopting the principle of heat storage, he combined a

heat source, two large hotplates and two or more ovens into one unit: the AGA Cooker.

The AGA works on the principle that a heavy frame made of cast iron can absorb heat from a relatively low intensity but continuously burning source, and the accumulated heat can then be used for cooking. One stove-top burner is set at simmer, the second at boil. Each oven is set to different temperatures that can be modified a few degrees by moving the internal racks up or down. The finish of glossy enamel must be treated with great care. The cooker was introduced to England in 1929, and its popularity in certain parts of English society (owners of medium to large country houses) led to a genre of fiction set amongst stereotypical upper-middle-class society. Sally Harrington became our AGA teacher, explaining and demonstrating the cooker to each new family of cast and crew. A microwave oven provided backup for reluctant cooks.

11   Bike trails were an interesting facet of the tourist business that supported theater in Lanesboro. In Plainview, Ken had seen the potential for Plainview. About the same time, he launched the idea of RAAP and the theater, he also championed saving an abandoned railroad spur that ran from near Rochester to Plainview before it could be cut up into farmland. His original vision was to develop it into a dinner train link to bring patrons from the Rochester area to the theater—a unique but bold idea indeed. This was a little too grandiose for the locals, so Ken, who was also on the Minnesota Park and Trails Council Board, initiated the effort and funding to have it established as the Great River Ridge State Bike Trail—an adjunct to contribute to RAAP's need for increased tourism that could build the theater audience.

12   Fran Ford and I spent time together at the Farm where Fran went for walks so she could sing to the corn, an action that spoke volumes about Fran's creative and independent spirit. Fran told me about her years in New York, married to a Jewish director and raising their son, Nathaniel. When Fran took her son to visit her family in Wisconsin, she encountered antisemitism directed at her child by her family. She severed her family relationship. Her marriage ended, Nathaniel earned a degree at MIT, and Fran turned to the Society of Quakers for family, spirituality, and friendship.

Fran earned a graduate degree in theater from the University of Miami and got her first (and last) teaching job at the University of North Dakota in Grand Forks in 1997. That year spring flooding of the Red River devastated the city and its residents, affecting Fran deeply. She responded by writing a one-woman show called "A Flood of Memories" based on interviews with Grand Forks flood victims. Fran staged it in one of the galleries at the Grand Forks Museum of Art with directing/coaching help from Mary Cutler, a colleague at the university. Fran played all of the parts, changing hats, boots, and jackets. Mary Cutler called it a "heroic production." When reduced student population left Fran without a teaching job, she headed to the Arts Mecca in Minneapolis-St. Paul, where a phone call to the Quakers' Society provided sanctuary and groceries until she got back on her feet. When Fran worked for Jon Hassler Theater, she asked if we would be interested in staging her play on a weekend when the theater was dark. I took her up on it. It cost almost nothing since most of the clothing and props were readily available in our storage room, and she didn't require royalty payment. We agreed to split the ticket sales, a win-win situation for both of us.

Fran's commitment to peace and justice led her to a play about Rachel Corrie, a young woman from Olympia, Washington, who went to Israel as a worker for peace and was killed when she faced down an Israeli tank that was about to demolish some Palestinian housing. The story became well-known, and when Fran could not get the rights to stage the published play, she contacted Rachel Corrie's parents and obtained the right to draft her own version. Fran asked me to help with some direction before she staged it in various churches and the Friends Meeting House. My life was made richer by my exposure to the various supporters, many of them Quakers or actors I worked with in Plainview—and one Catholic nun.

Fran was so versatile and generous with her time that several years later, she spent a week-long residency in Plainview, working with high school students who were interested in acting. Our friendship lasted until her death from bladder cancer in 2008.

13   In its second Broadway revival, which played concurrently with the JHT production in 2002, Morning's at Seven was nominated for nine Tony awards. Three of the four sisters, Estelle Parsons, Elizabeth Franz, and Frances Sternhagen, were nominated in the featured actress category. The fourth sister, played by Piper Laurie, was left out. According to an

article in the *Leader-Telegram*, Eau Claire's (WI) daily newspaper, the three nominated sisters were worried about the exclusion of Laurie, "whom they considered as essential as a fourth leg holding up a table." Sternhagen, Franz, and Parsons had foreseen the problem and lobbied the Tony organization with a solution: "We were hoping we'd get an ensemble award because we knew this kind of thing was bound to happen." Franz was quoted as saying, "You don't act by yourself. You can sing by yourself, you can dance by yourself, play the piano by yourself. But you cannot act by yourself. And if you are, it's not working."

Despite the appeals, the nominating committee didn't go for it. It became a moot point when Katie Finneran won the Tony for her role in *Noises Off.* Estelle Parsons saved face when quoted at the end of the news article: "We're just so grateful for the experience, for all of us to be at our ages and be all together and actually have a play to do." I say, Amen to that.

14   These orange-red bugs were Multi-colored Asian Lady Beetles, slightly larger than most of our native lady beetles, with adults measuring 3/8" long and 3/8" wide. They were oval or convex in shape, red to yellow in color, with as many as nineteen black spots, many more than our little ladybugs. They were aggressive and would bite, as Nancy and Marshall reported, holding out arms and hands that sported several bites.

The bugs were originally released as a biological control agent in the late 1970s and early 1980s in Pennsylvania for certain crops, including cotton. An infestation was also reported in 1988 in Louisiana from bugs thought to have escaped from an Asian ship offloading freight in New Orleans.

From those two sources, the beetles spread throughout the Midwestern and Eastern United States. This beetle fed on aphids and other soft-bodied insects that dwell on crops and trees. Soybean crops hosted a lot of important food sources for Asian Lady beetles. When the soybeans were harvested in late summer/early fall, Asian beetles migrated away from those fields in the millions. When one beetle alighted, others followed quickly. Tens of thousands could invade a single house, taking shelter in attics and walls. When the heat was turned on, they would move into the interior living areas.

15   Buffalo Gal Productions was founded in Minneapolis by performer, di-

rector, and producer Perrin Post in the spring of 1996 and was incorporated in 2001. Buffalo Gal's mission was "to produce and create original and rarely seen Broadway and Off-Broadway works that were by, for and about women, creating opportunities for artists and audience members to participate in new theatre experiences." (https://www.buffalogalproductions.com/about). In the fall of 2000, Buffalo Gal Productions negotiated the reopening of the Loring Theater space, bringing in Theater Latte Da and others as a shared venue for these various companies.

16   Since 1979, Wollan had been the president and producer/director of Troupe America, which grew from a small theatrical production company operating the Plymouth Playhouse in Minneapolis to a nationally recognized company producing shows for the national touring circuit. As part of Troupe America's slate of entertainment, Wollan eventually produced and directed all seven shows in the Church Basement Ladies series.

17   Mary Kay Fortier Spalding and I had been good friends in Ely and performed and tap-danced together. She had joined the Plainview Theater board and later moved on to acting in plays, commercials and a 2012 film entitled *Memorial Day*, a WWII story featuring James Cromwell and directed by Samuel Fischer.

18   Prudence Johnson, a well-known Minnesota-based performer with a long and happy career as a singer, writer, and teacher, had appeared on the musical theatre stage and concert stages across North America and was known for appearances with Garrison Keillor on *A Prairie Home Companion*. She had taken some time off to recover from vocal problems and was ready to get back onstage, paired with pianist Dan Chouinard in "Moon Country" based on the music of Hoagy Carmichael.

Made in the USA
Middletown, DE
08 July 2023

34534813R00262